Hungary 1956

"The historian who labours to reduce the mountain of the revolution to a few contingencies, stands as helpless before it as once stood the political leaders who sought to prevent its rise."

Isaac Deutscher

HUNGARY 1956

BILL LOMAX

Allison & Busby, London, 1976

First published by Allison & Busby Limited
6a Noel Street, London W1V 3RB

ISBN 0 85031 188 8 (hardback)
ISBN 0 85031 189 6 (paperback)

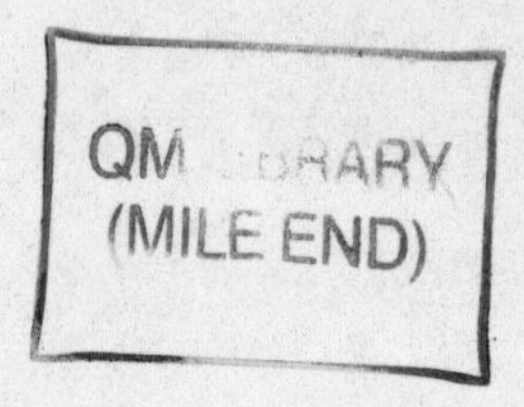

Set in 10/11 Times and printed in Great Britain by
Villiers Publications Limited,
Ingestre Road, London NW5 1UL

Contents

List of maps 6
Acknowledgements 7
Chronology 9
Introduction 17
1 The Opposition on the Road to the Revolution 19
2 The Ideology of the Opposition and the Government of Imry Nagy 51
3 The Provincial Towns: the Revolution Takes Shape 79
4 Budapest: between Revolution and Counter-Revolution 105
5 The Workers' Councils of Greater Budapest 147
6 The Hungarian Socialists against the Kadar Régime 170
7 Conclusions 193
Notes 204
Bibliography 212
Index 215

List of Maps

Hungary, showing Budapest and major provincial towns 78
Budapest City Centre, 1956 104
Greater Budapest, showing city districts and major industrial and residential areas 146

Acknowledgements

The inspiration for this book was first provided by a considerable quantity of red wine in a continental express train, after which I awoke to find myself speeding towards Budapest.

The welcome assistance of the Social Science Research Council enabled me to develop my interest in Hungary and Hungarians further, while the supervision and encouragement of two Rumanian professors, Zevedei Barbu and Ghita Ionescu, led to this book taking its first form in a doctoral thesis presented to the University of Sussex on May Day 1974.

Innumerable people have helped me in the process of completing this work. My thanks go in particular to Dr Cushing and his staff at the London School of Slavonic and East European Studies, who valiantly struggled to teach me Hungarian, and to Professor Deak and Mrs Aranov of the Institute for the Study of East-Central Europe at Columbia, who not only provided me with convenient facilities to study the material collected by the Columbia University Research Project on Hungary but also made me feel most at home in the Institute at which I had arrived unexpected and unintroduced. I am indebted to the librarians and research workers of the Bem Library, St Antony's College, Oxford; the Reading Room of the British Museum, London; the BBC Written Archives Centre, Reading; the Research Departments of Radio Free Europe in Munich and New York; the Swiss Institute for East European Studies at Bern; the Institute for Research into Central Europe of the Catholic University of Louvain in Belgium, and the libraries of the London School of Economics. the Llandaff College of Technology, and the Universities of Sussex and Nottingham. My thanks go also to Mrs Ruth Robinson and Mrs Valerie Wallace for patiently typing this study into its final form. I am also indebted to the University of Nottingham for providing a grant towards the cost of publishing this book, and to Allison and Busby for undertaking to publish it at a time when I had just about given up hope that it would ever see the light of day.

I received a great deal of help and advice from a large number of Hungarian émigrés, and from others with particular knowledge of Eastern Europe, who were good enough to meet and talk with me, often on several occasions. I am grateful to them all, but I would like to express a particular debt of gratitude to the late George Paloczi-Horvath, who not only assisted me with his considerable knowledge of Hungarian political life but also extended to me a friendship which I greatly valued.

I would like to express my appreciation to all the friends and colleagues from many countries of the world, and particularly those I have met in Eastern Europe, whom I have come to know in the course of my studies, as well as to my friends and colleagues among the staff and students of the Llandaff College of Technology in Cardiff and the Sociology Department at the University of Nottingham. Finally, thanks even to those kind friends who, when I first became interested in the Hungarian revolution, told me it was too contemporary an event to be the subject of serious study and who, now that I have completed this book, inform me that it should now be classed as ancient history.

Bill Lomax
Nottingham, May 1976.

Hungary: 1918-1958

A CHRONOLOGY OF KEY EVENTS

1918

October Defeat of Germany in first world war results in collapse of Hapsburg Empire.

November Hungary declared a republic, and government formed under premiership of MIHALY KAROLY. Communist Party of Hungary founded under leadership of Bela Kun.

1919

March Karoly government falls, and Hungarian Soviet Republic established. Coalition government of social democrats and communists set up under BELA KUN.

August Hungarian Soviet Republic falls. ADMIRAL MIKLOS HORTHY comes to power as leader of counter-revolutionary forces, and heads right-wing régime which rules Hungary until end of second world war.

1941

Hungary enters second world war on the side of Germany and Italy.

1943

Hungarian government enters into secret negotiations with the Allies for an armistice and Hungarian withdrawal from the war.

1944

March German army occupies Hungary.

October Hungarian regent, Admiral Horthy, arrested by Germans. Hungarian "nazi" party, the Arrow Cross, forms a government under Ferenc Szalasi.

December — Soviet army advances into Eastern Hungary. Provisional government set up at Debrecen.

1945

January — Hungarian Provisional Government signs armistice in Moscow with Allies.

February — Soviet army liberates Budapest.

March — Provisional government decrees major land reform. Minister of Agriculture is Imre Nagy.

April — Whole territory of Hungary liberated from Germans. Provisional government moves to Budapest.

November — General Elections. Results: Smallholders' Party 57 per cent, Social Democrats 17.4 per cent, Communists 17 per cent, National Peasant Party 7 per cent. Coalition government formed from representatives of these four parties.

1946

Hungary proclaimed a republic, inflation halted, and first measures of nationalisation implemented.

1947

Leading members of Smallholders' Party forced out of government, a three-year economic plan announced, and the banks nationalised.

1948

Further nationalisations, fusion of the Communist and Social Democratic parties, and formation of new government in which Communist Party holds all key posts. First measures of agricultural collectivisation. Cardinal Jozsef Mindszenty arrested.

1949

"Single slate" elections. Consolidation of one-party state. LASZLO RAJK and other leading "native" communists arrested as "Titoists", tried and executed. Nationalisation extended to all establishments with more than ten employees. State security police, AVH, established as an inpendent force responsible only to the cabinet.

1950

First five-year plan. Further growth of police terror. Many former members of Social Democratic and Smallholders' parties arrested.

1951

Several prominent "native" communists including Janos Kadar, Gyula Kallai, Geza Losonczy and Ferenc Donath arrested. Mass deportations and internments in forced labour camps, increasing persecution of the churches, and stepping-up of agricultural collectivisation.

1952

High point of stalinist dictatorship. General Secretary of the Communist Party, MATYAS RAKOSI — "Stalin's best Hungarian disciple" — becomes Prime Minister.

1953

March STALIN dies.

June Hungarian Communist Party leaders including Matyas Rakosi, Erno Gero and Mihaly Farkas, together with Imre Nagy, summoned to Moscow for a meeting with the Soviet leaders. On return to Budapest, Communist Party leadership reorganised in spirit of "collective leadership", and Central Committee passes *June Resolutions* criticising the party's former policies.

July IMRE NAGY replaces Rakosi as Prime Minister and announces his government programme — *The New Course* — to the Hungarian parliament. Nagy's programme includes amnesty for political prisoners and abolition of internment camps, as well as economic and social reforms. RAKOSI remains First Party Secretary.

1954

Release of several communist and social democrat political prisoners. Resistance to Nagy's reforms within party and state bureaucracy sparks off first stirrings of revolt amongst *Szabad Nep* journalists.

1955

March	Central Committee denounces Imre Nagy and the policies of the New Course as a "rightist deviation".
April	IMRE NAGY removed from all party posts, including positions in Politburo and Central Committee, and replaced as Prime Minister by ANDRAS HEGEDUS.
May	Warsaw Pact set up with Hungary a founder member. Khrushchev and Bulganin visit Yugoslavia and declare Stalin's allegations against Tito to have been false. In Hungary, Miklos Gimes criticises Rakosi and is expelled from the Communist Party.
October	WRITERS' ASSOCIATION presidium resigns *en bloc* and writers draw up memorandum to Central Committee opposing censorship and demanding greater freedom of expression.
December	Imre Nagy expelled from Communist Party. Central Committee condemns and disciplines the writers. Petofi Circle plans series of public debates.

1956

February	TWENTIETH CONGRESS of Communist Party of Soviet Union. Nikita Khrushchev delivers his "secret speech" denouncing Stalin. In Hungary Bela Kun, executed in stalinist purges in Moscow in 1939, is rehabilitated.
March	First public meeting of Petofi Circle. Rakosi declares Laszlo Rajk innocent of crimes for which he was executed, but places all blame on state security leaders. Calls for Rakosi's resignation made at Writers' Association.
April	Many of remaining political prisoners released.
May	PETOFI CIRCLE holds series of debates on application to Hungary of decisions of Soviet Twentieth Party Congress.
June	At Petofi Circle meeting Rajk's widow, Julia Rajk, demands clearing of her husband's name and bringing of his murderers to justice. At a further meeting, Tibor Dery and Geza Losonczy call for change in party leadership and return

	to power of Imre Nagy. Central Committee condemns (and later bans) Petofi Circle and expels Tibor Dery from Communist Party. Workers' demonstrations in Polish town of Poznan, put down by Polish army, find echo in wave of strikes and disturbances in Hungary.
July	RAKOSI resigns as Party Secretary and is replaced by ERNO GERO. Janos Kadar and other "centrists" brought into Politburo.
September	Annual Congress of Writers' Association elects new presidium, throwing out party-slate and electing several non-communist writers. New wave of critical and rebellious articles in press and literary journals.
6 October	Ceremonial reburial of Laszlo Rajk brings 200,000 people onto streets of Budapest.
14 October	Imre Nagy readmitted to Communist Party.
15 October	Party and government delegation headed by Gero and Kadar travels to Belgrade for discussions with Tito.
16 October	Meeting of students in Szeged decides to set up new student organisation, MEFESZ, and calls for support from universities throughout Hungary.
21 October	In Warsaw, despite Soviet opposition, Wladislaw Gomulka is elected as new First Secretary of Polish Communist Party.
22 October	Mass meeting of Budapest students in Technological University votes to join MEFESZ. Students formulate their demands in 16-point resolution, calling for withdrawal of Soviet troops, democratisation of Hungarian political life, and new government under Imre Nagy. Meeting calls demonstration for following day in support of their demands and in solidarity with the events in Poland.
23 October	Student demonstration in Budapest calls for reforms and return to power of Imre Nagy. Gero, First Party Secretary, speaks on radio denouncing demonstrators as enemies of the people. Nagy addresses crowd before Parliament. Stalin statue pulled down. Fighting breaks out at radio building and continues throughout

night. Government calls in Soviet troops and tanks to put down revolt.

24 October Radio announces IMRE NAGY's appointment as Prime Minister. GERO remains Party Secretary. Martial law declared. Street battles in Budapest against Soviet tanks. Demonstrations and armed conflicts spread throughout country.

25 October Demonstration involving fraternisation with Soviet troops ends in massacre at Parliament. JANOS KADAR replaces Gero as First Secretary of Communist Party. Nagy and Kadar denounce counter-revolutionary elements, but promise reforms once order is restored.

26 October Heavy fighting throughout country. General strike declared, workers' councils set up in factories, revolutionary committees in provincial towns. Colonel Pal Maleter joins revolution and takes over command of Kilian barracks.

27 October Formation of new government under Imre Nagy which includes non-communist politicians Zoltan Tildy and Bela Kovacs.

28 October Government orders ceasefire. Imre Nagy promises withdrawal of Soviet troops and disbandment of AVH.

29 October Soviet troops begin withdrawal from Budapest, but fighting continues in some places, e.g. Kilian barracks.

30 October Siege of headquarters of Budapest City Communist Party in Republic Square ends in massacre. Imre Nagy announces abolition of one-party system, and reorganisation of democratic parties of 1945 coalition. Inner cabinet set up including representatives of non-communist parties. Cardinal Mindszenty freed.

31 October Meeting in Kilian barracks to form National Guard. Pal Maleter appointed Deputy Minister of Defence. From Gyor comes news of formation of Transdanubian National Council; from Miskolc reports of new Soviet troops entering Hungary.

1 November Imre Nagy announces Hungary's withdrawal from Warsaw Pact, and appeals to United Nations to defend Hungarian neutrality. Janos

	Kadar announces formation of new communist party to be called Hungarian Socialist Workers' Party. Janos Kadar disappears.
2 November	Hungarian towns and airports surrounded by Soviet troops. Continuing reports of new Soviet troop movements into Hungary. Imre Nagy protests to Soviet ambassador and repeats appeal to United Nations.
3 November	Remaining stalinist ministers resign from government. New coalition cabinet set up which includes Pal Maleter as Minister of Defence. Cardinal Mindszenty broadcasts on radio. Hungarian-Soviet negotiations begin for withdrawal of Soviet troops.
4 November	Soviet troops launch attack on Budapest at dawn. Announcement of formation of new all-communist government under JANOS KADAR and FERENC MUNNICH. Imre Nagy and several of his colleagues seek refuge in Yugoslav Embassy. Heavy fighting rages throughout country.
5-11 November	Fighting continues in waning pockets of resistance. Working-class centres offer strongest resistance to Soviet invasion. Budapest industrial district of Csepel is one of last centres to fall. Mass flight of refugees to the West.
12 November	Revolutionary workers' council of Ujpest issues appeal for formation of a central workers' council.
14 November	CENTRAL WORKERS' COUNCIL of Greater Budapest formed at Egyesult Izzo factory in Ujpest. Delegation from Central Workers' Council meets with Kadar who declares his support for a multi-party system and free elections.
21 November	Conference called to establish a national workers' council is prevented from meeting by a force of Soviet tanks. 48-hour general strike declared in protest.
22 November	Imre Nagy and colleagues seized by Soviet troops on leaving Yugoslav Embassy after being given promise of personal safety by Hungarian government. Deported to Rumania.
23 November	Everyone keeps off the streets for an hour to commemorate the revolution.

25 November	Conference between leaders of the government and the Central Workers' Council in the parliament building.
4 December	Silent women's demonstration in Budapest to commemorate victims of Soviet intervention.
6 December	Wave of arrests of intellectuals' and workers' leaders.
8 December	Meeting to create a National Workers' Council proclaims 48-hour protest strike against the increasing repression, and calls for international strikes in solidarity.
9 December	Government bans the Central Workers' Council and arrests many of its leaders. Sandor Racz and Sandor Bali evade arrest and seek refuge with the workers in Beloiannis factory.
11 December	Racz and Bali arrested at Hungarian parliament after accepting invitation to meet Kadar. Government declares state of emergency, and bans Revolutionary Council of Intellectuals and all territorial workers' councils.
12 December	General strike against arrest of Racz and Bali.
13 December	Government decree establishes detention without trial and special courts of summary jurisdiction.

1958

17 June	Official communiqués issued in Budapest and Moscow announcing sentencing and execution of the leaders of the revolution IMRE NAGY, PAL MALETER, JOZSEF SZILAGYI and MIKLOS GIMES. GEZA LOSONCZY said to have died in prison. Long prison terms for other leaders.

Introduction

"No event in recent history has been so much lied about, distorted and besmirched as the Hungarian Revolution."[1]

So concluded Leslie Bain, a writer almost unique amongst Western journalists present in Hungary during the 1956 revolution for having both a knowledge of the country and a command of its language. In his opinion, the lies produced by the propaganda machines of both sides in the Cold War were remarkably similar in the way they smothered the basic issues of the Hungarian revolution. In the West, the uprising was presented as a national rebellion against communist dictatorship, while in the East the communists saw it as an attempt to overthrow socialism and restore Western-style capitalism. Both these viewpoints ignored the real issue of Hungary — that it was a social revolution aimed not at restoring a previous régime but at creating a radically new social order, one that would be both more democratic than the capitalist West and more socialist than the communist East.

Consequently some fifteen years later one of the leading socialist émigrés who had left Hungary after the suppression of the revolution, George Paloczi-Horvath, could remark: "The history of this revolution was still not cleared up by 1970 . . . because the boys and girls who had died for their cause demonstrated a number of truths that were equally repugnant to liberals and communists."[2]

The basic issue of the Hungarian revolution has been smothered not only by the more crass propagandists of press and radio, but also by their more sophisticated counterparts in the universities. Academic sociologists and political scientists alike have concentrated their attention on the rebellion of intellectuals, writers and politicians, while the actions of the popular masses, of the working class and the peasantry, the soldiers, students and youth, have been left largely out of account. For example, two of the most scholarly studies of the Hungarian events, Paul Zinner's *Revolution in Hungary* and Paul Kecskemeti's *The Unexpected Revolution,* concur in seeing the real motivating force of the revolution as the élite rebellion of writers and intellectuals. For them the mass revolution of workers, peasants and youth, however significant in other respects, remains a secondary development and not an activating force.[3]

What I shall argue in this book, in opposition to this orthodox interpretation of the Hungarian uprising, is that from the very start it was the masses of working people, not the élite of writers and politicians, who were responsible for the birth and development of the revolutionary movement. Their actions were always one step ahead of the élite of writers and politicians, and it was their pressure which urged the latter on to protest and revolt. Indeed, the so-called leaders of the opposition, far from advocating the ideas which inspired the revolution, had to continually revise their theories in the light of the more radical actions of the masses. Finally it was the industrial workers in particular who, organising workers' councils in their factories and districts, themselves created the revolutionary institutions which provided the basis for a new society.

The story of this struggle for a new society which sought to realise the most radical demands of both democracy and socialism — a struggle in which writers, journalists and politicians, workers, peasants and youth, all had a part to play — is what this book sets out to tell.

1 The Opposition on the Road to the Revolution

"Modern revolutions are not watched by masses as they occur within the palace of élites."

C. Wright Mills

The opening chapter of the events leading up to the Hungarian revolution of October 1956 is usually seen as the appointment of Imre Nagy as Prime Minister of Hungary in June 1953 and his inauguration of one of the first attempts at liberalisation of a communist régime in the "New Course" of 1953 to 1955. However, it has often been overlooked that Nagy's appointment was preceded by rumblings of discontent and revolt amongst the worker and peasant masses of Hungary.

Though less well documented than the dramatic rising of the workers of East Berlin which followed the death of the Soviet dictator Stalin in 1953, similar disturbances also occurred in Hungary. The beginning of June had witnessed the first really serious strike since 1946, when twenty thousand workers at the Matyas Rakosi iron and steel works in Budapest's industrial suburb of Csepel downed tools and came out on strike in protest against their low wages, the system of work norms, and the scarcity of food in the city. The strike was frantically hushed up by the authorities who succeeded in ending it within forty-eight hours by granting a considerable rise to the dissatisfied workers. Despite efforts to keep the strike a secret, similar disturbances also took place in other large industrial centres, most notably at Ozd and Diosgyor in Eastern Hungary, and were even accompanied by peasant demonstrations on the great Hungarian plains. According to Imre Nagy, it was the threat of popular revolt in these disturbances that impelled Khrushchev and the new Soviet leaders to appoint him as Prime Minister and inaugurate the New Course.[1]

The Hungarian Communist Party leaders were hastily summoned to Moscow where the Soviet leaders severely criticised the former stalinist dictator of Hungary, Matyas Rakosi, for bringing his country to the verge of catastrophe. Rakosi was instructed to hand over his government to Imre Nagy, who was told to implement a programme of reform. Although Imre Nagy's government was destined to survive for little more than eighteen months and to be followed by Rakosi's return to power in 1955, it did serve to create a climate of opinion within which the first signs of conscious opposition to the stalinist system were gradually to emerge, and in which the hopes and aspirations which eventually led to the uprising of October 1956 were awakened.

However, just as Imre Nagy had not been responsible for the social crisis which occasioned his appointment as Prime Minister, nor did he seek to instigate or create the movement of opposition which was shortly to emerge within the Communist Party. On the contrary, if any single individual could lay claim to having paved the way for the emergence of opposition to the stalinist régime, that person would ironically be none other than Nagy's bitter enemy, the stalinist dictator of Hungarian cultural life in the early fifty's, Joszef Revai. Revai, one of the few brilliant intellectuals among East European communist leaders, was that unique phenomenon, a consistently hard-line stalinist who was at the same time motivated by a passionate intellectual if not moral conviction. This had led him to courageously express his dissent within the top levels of the party leadership to the point of voting in the politburo against the execution of the "Hungarian Titoist", Laszlo Rajk, in 1949, and to demanding the rehabilitation of the victims of the purges in later years.

In 1945 Revai had been made editor of the Communist Party's daily newspaper *Szabad Nep* ("Free People"), and had helped to direct the party's propaganda campaign during its assault on power. During these years *Szabad Nep*'s editorial office had played an almost independent and originating role, virtually writing party policy and directing the entire party propaganda. In pursuit of this task Revai, who had little but contempt for the average party functionary, had recruited people of considerable talent and ability to his editorial and journalist staff. In this way there came together on the staff of *Szabad Nep* a grouping of committed young journalists far different from the usual party functionaries who tended to be found in most other party organs. Consequently, as one of their number was later to testify, "The staff which came to *Szabad Nep* under Revai remembered later something of these times and could never completely resign itself to the role of a servile executive organ."[2]

The journalists' opposition

Revai's two deputy editors in the late forties had been Marton Horvath, a competent if cautious administrator who remained with the paper right up till 1956, and Geza Losonczy, a brilliant young intellectual who had been active in the illegal communist movement before and during the war. Though a protégé of Revai, Losonczy was to be imprisoned in the early fifties and later to emerge as one of the leading members of the communist opposition to the Rakosi régime, and one of the brightest stars in the circle of reformist politicians to gather around Imre Nagy. Indeed, almost all of the young journalists recruited by Revai in the postwar years were to reappear again some seven to eight years later in the vanguard of young communist journalists who first attempted to rally support in opposition to the stalinist régime. Most prominent amongst them was Miklos Gimes, an editorial writer, as well as the journalists Miklos Vasarhelyi, Peter Kende, Tibor Meray, Miklos Molnar, Pal Locsei, and Tibor Tardos.[3]

In 1949 Revai joined the government as Minister of Culture and was replaced as editor of *Szabad Nep* by a ruthless and intolerant stalinist Oszkar Betlen, a man of little journalistic ability but a close friend of the country's "secret police" leaders Mihaly Farkas and Gabor Peter. Betlen had several of the young journalists removed from their posts, replacing them with less talented but subservient party hacks who helped to turn the party's paper into little more than a mediocre replica of the Soviet *Pravda.* Nevertheless, in the early fifties some talented individuals still found their way on to the paper's staff, amongst them Sandor Novobaczky and Sandor Fekete.

In June 1953 the journalists at *Szabad Nep* were amongst the first people in Hungary to learn of Rakosi's demotion, and to see copies of Nagy's speech to the Central Committee in which he outlined the policies of the New Course which his government was about to inaugurate. Already feeling cramped and frustrated by the régime at *Szabad Nep,* the journalists were quick to draw comparisons between Rakosi's clique condemned by the Central Committee and Betlens' dictatorial rule at *Szabad Nep*. The more liberal-minded amongst them got together and decided that no one was any longer going to tell them what to think, write and say.

The journalists were particularly affected by the release and rehabilitation of political prisoners who had been imprisoned during the stalinist purges, many of whom had been former friends and colleagues. Not only had the journalists believed in their guilt; they had even written articles demanding their punishment. The news of rehabilitations was a continuing topic of conversation in the newspaper's offices, and their effect was increased when it was learned that some of the victims of the purges, including Sandor Haraszti the editor of the Communist Party's underground paper during the resistance, had been imprisoned for some three years in the underground cells of the Conti Street jail, just a few steps from the offices of *Szabad Nep.*

When Imre Nagy announced the policies of his New Course to the Hungarian Parliament on 4 July 1953 it looked at first as though real changes would be brought about. Rakosi, however, retained his post as First Party Secretary and, regarding his demotion as purely temporary, soon began to openly attack the policies of Nagy's government. The majority of party functionaries also remained loyal to Rakosi, and deliberately sabotaged and undermined Nagy's attempts at reform. Particular resistance was put up to the release and rehabilitation of the victims of the stalinist purges and trials, the responsibility for which fell clearly on Rakosi and his associates.

Aware of his lack of support amongst the Party functionaries, Imre Nagy tried to reorganise the non-party *People's Patriotic Front* as a means of establishing mass support for his régime on a broad national basis. He also set up a special Government Information Office to help convey the policies of the New Course to the public, putting its direction in the hands of his old friend Zoltan Szanto, a leader of the Communist Party in the thirties. Szanto's deputy was the former *Szabad Nep* journalist Miklos Vasarhelyi, who used his position to encourage support for the government's policies in the press, and particularly in the daily paper of the People's Patriotic Front *Magyar Nemzet* ("The Hungarian Nation").

Nagy's policies, however, were only able to achieve a limited and half-hearted implementation, and during the summer of 1954 there were increasing manifestations of public unrest, highlighted by occasional and sporadic strikes. The cutting back of the industrialisation programme as giant industrial projects were either called off or slowed down resulted both in workers being laid off and others put on short-time working. At the same time Nagy's efforts to increase the availability of consumer goods and to raise living standards were being criticised for weakening the economy. Some of Rakosi's most committed supporters were in charge of the economic programme and were demanding severe austerity measures including both cuts in the social services and action which would lead to increased unemployment. It was on this issue that Rakosi made his first deliberate attempt to remove Nagy from the premiership and reverse the policies of the New Course. In Nagy's absence, the Politburo passed a resolution blaming the New Course for the country's economic difficulties and calling for an immediate change to deflationary and austerity measures.

It was at this point that the journalists at *Szabad Nep*, getting wind of the manoeuvre against Nagy, realised that he was fighting a battle alone and almost without friends in the top levels of power, and decided to band together in his support. They used what influence they could on a number of important, if second-rank members of the Central Committee, amongst them their own acting editor Marton Horvath, the Budapest Party secretary Istvan Kovacs, and the county secretary from Miskolc, Rudolf Foldvari, and also approached some of the "native" communists known to have connections with Janos Kadar. This action was the first conscious and determined opposition effort within the party machinery, and served to set in motion the reformist opposition movement which was to fight over the next three years for the creation of a humane and liberalised communist régime.

This occasion was also the only time during the entire course of his premiership that Imre Nagy himself launched a determined offensive against the Rakosi clique's attempts at a comeback. Speaking to the Central Committee, which met in the first days of October, he vigorously asserted that the economic difficulties were the result not of his policies but of deliberate resistance to them. The resolution prepared by the Politburo was then withdrawn; a new resolution was passed, restating the policies of the New Course and calling for an end to resistance to them. Over the following two weeks this resolution was discussed at meetings of lower party organs throughout the country, where supporters of Imre Nagy took up his call to crush the resistance to his policies.

Rakosi and his supporters, however, still refused to accept defeat, hoping to be able to reverse the Central Committee's decisions in the near future. Moreover, they had succeeded in voting down Nagy's request to have his speech printed in the party paper. Nagy, in an obstinate if not desperate move, rewrote his speech as an article which was published in *Szabad Nep* on 20 October, causing a tremendous sensation throughout the intellectual community of Budapest. (Even then he had had to be persuaded to tone down the spirit of his article by some of his journalist friends.) A junior reporter working on the city's evening paper *Esti Budapest* recalls how that day "everyone in the corridors was waving Nagy's article".* Three days later, Imre Nagy reached the height of his precarious victory at the opening

*This is one of many quotations and details in this section taken from material collected in the archives of the Columbia University Research Project on Hungary (CURPH) which includes a number of reports

congress of the People's Patriotic Front, where he was enthusiastically and rapturously acclaimed amid scenes reminiscent of Lajos Kossuth's reception by the Hungarian Parliament in July 1848.

At this point the communist journalists decided to step up their efforts in support of Imre Nagy. A general meeting of the party group at *Szabad Nep* spent three days debating the October resolution of the Central Committee. During the debate, calls were made for an end to the opposition to the New Course and for genuine democracy within the party. The journalists planned to mimeograph the minutes of their meeting and send copies to all members of the Central Committee and to party groups in other editorial offices, to try and stir them into action. The Politburo fumed with rage at this "inaugurating rally of the intra-party opposition" and forbade the circulation of the meeting's minutes. Even Imre Nagy now disowned the journalists who had come unasked to his defence, declaring that he could have nothing to do with such "factionalism".

Nevertheless *Szabad Nep*'s initiative was followed up by similar meetings in other pewspaper offices, at *Nepszava* ("The People's Voice") the trade union paper, at the Hungarian News Agency (the MTI), at the Budapest radio, in the universities and even at the Party Academy. Everywhere stalinist departmental heads were under attack, and calls were made for changes in the spirit of the New Course. While the movement developed a considerable spontaneous momentum, it was undoubtedly inspired and co-ordinated by the hard core of journalists at *Szabad Nep*. All the city's journalists had frequent occasions to meet one another at the Journalists' Club, where the minutes of *Szabad Nep*'s meeting were passed around, and where future tactics could be planned and discussed. The result, as one young journalist explained, was that "we knew what was coming at each newspaper".

The circumstance that the journalists' action was achieved through a wide constellation of personal contacts, rather than by a central organisation, made it difficult for the authorities to repress. Despite this, action was not long in coming against the main leaders of the journalists. In December Peter Kende, the secretary of the party group at *Szabad Nep*, and two other journalists who

---

and memoranda and some 250 in-depth interviews made between 1956 and 1958 with Hungarian refugees. I have not thought it necessary in every instance where I have drawn on such material to give specific source references (but if required they can be found in my D.Phil. thesis, in the library of the University of Sussex, which contains some 2,000 references and footnotes).

had been particularly outspoken at the October general meeting, were transferred to provincial newspapers, while Tibor Meray was sent off as a foreign correspondent to East Berlin. In like manner, Miklos Gimes who had spent the previous few months as a foreign correspondent in Geneva and Paris, was forced to leave the paper on his return to Budapest.

When Imre Nagy suffered a mild heart attack in January 1955, Rakosi seized the opportunity to mount his final attack. Taking advantage of Nagy's illness and enforced absence from public life, Rakosi called a meeting of the Central Committee at which the policies of the New Course were denounced as a rightist anti-marxist deviation and Imre Nagy was expelled from both the Politburo and the Central Committee. A few days later he was also dismissed as head of the government, in which post he was replaced by the former Deputy Prime Minister, a supporter and protégé of Rakosi, Andras Hegedus.

Rakosi's return to power was followed by a final purge of the rebellious journalists. The remaining oppositionists at *Szabad Nep* were all dismissed in the first week of May, and the former stalinist editor, Oszkar Betlen, returned to take over firm control of the paper and to staff it overwhelmingly with mediocre journalists and party functionaries.

But just as Nagy's hold on power had always been far from secure, so now Rakosi's apparent victory was to be suddenly and unexpectedly undermined. In May 1955 the Soviet leaders Khrushchev and Bulganin flew to Belgrade to seek a rapprochement with Marshal Tito, and declared that the charges levelled by Stalin when he had expelled Yugoslavia from the Cominform in 1950 had all been false. Ominously for Rakosi and the Hungarian stalinists, they had been second to none in their denunciation of Tito, and they had been responsible for the show trial and execution of the "Hungarian Titoist", Laszlo Rajk, in 1949.

On the very same day that Khrushchev issued his declaration in Belgrade rehabilitating Tito, a general meeting was being held in Budapest of the Communist Party groups in the Hungarian press. Here Miklos Gimes, former editorial writer on *Szabad Nep*, now a deputy editor of *Magyar Nemzet*, stood up and called for an immediate change in Hungary's attitude to Yugoslavia, and for a revision of the Rajk trial. But just as the real target of the Rajk trial had been not Rajk but Tito, so the real significance of this first public call for the rehabilitation of Rajk was to point out the responsibility of Rakosi for Rajk's faked trial and official murder.

Rakosi, however, was far from ready to make any admission of his guilt, and within a few days Gimes was expelled from the Communist Party and his supporters at the meeting were severely reprimanded. With this action the first phase of the opposition to the stalinist régime was drawn to a close. With Imre Nagy out of power and the journalists scattered and repressed, the stalinist leadership of the party appeared to have reconsolidated its power.

The opposition spreads to the writers

While the first phase of the opposition was characterised by the almost exclusive participation of journalists, the years of 1953 and 1954 had also seen the first stirrings of discontent amongst broader layers of writers and intellectuals. Indeed, a few of the younger writers may well have become disillusioned with the régime, individually, at least as early as the journalists. For the majority, however, it was the first actions of the journalists that opened their eyes, while it was only some time later that they came to act in any concerted and organised way. When they did begin to act, it was those who had formerly been the most committed communist intellectuals who were to become the most passionate and determined opponents of the régime.

Significantly enough it was one of the former *Szabad Nep* journalists, Miklos Molnar, who, on assuming the editorship of the Writers' Association journal *Irodalmi Ujsag* ("Literary Gazette") in early 1953, was responsible for the emergence of the first mouthpiece of the writers' opposition. From the very start of the New Course *Irodalmi Ujsag* gave open expression to the increasing disillusion of the writers, to their rebellious feelings against the stalinist régime, and their support for the policies of Imre Nagy.[4]

Over the summer of 1953 *Irodalmi Ujsag* published a succession of poems and short stories expressing the mood of guilt and remorse experienced by many young writers who had risen from the people and been able to develop their talents under the stalinist régime. This mood was voiced by the young peasant poet Sandor Csoori, declaring in August 1953:

> I have lived on high, far from the people,
> In the company of the illustrious,
> And my happy fortune hid from me,
> The heavy and bitter reality.

A further feeling of complicity or at least acquiescence in the crimes of the régime was soon to be echoed by other writers like Lajos Konya, who in October 1953 wrote: "Now we know that we could have done more, and the heavy weight of responsibility lies on our shoulders."

As with the journalists, it was the release of the communist intellectuals who had been tried and imprisoned in the early fifties, and in whose guilt many of the younger writers had believed, that was the cause of their deepest crises of conscience. Their shame and regret was expressed most poignantly by a young communist writer Laszlo Benjamin, formerly one of the most loyal disciples of the school of socialist realism, who declared in a moving poem written to his old friend Sandor Haraszti who had just been released from prison: "It is my crime — to have believed in yours!"

The whole literary world was most dramatically shaken in November 1953 when *Irodalmi Ujsag* carried a poem by another of the former practitioners of socialist realism, Peter Kuczka, entitled "Nyirseg Diary" in which he described the hatred felt by the simple Hungarian peasant for the communist régime. The Communist Party had just sent writers into the countryside to explain its new policies to the people and win them for the régime; instead it had been the people themselves who brought to the awareness of the writers the misery experienced by the majority of workers and peasants. Throughout 1954 *Irodalmi Ujsag* carried poem after poem in this new mood of self-criticism as the writers resolved never to lie again. "Rather walk naked in the streets than don falsehood ever again," as one of them was later to declare.[5]

Throughout Nagy's government, *Irodalmi Ujsag* continued to act as the mouthpiece which gave voice to the disillusion and alienation of the writers and intellectuals. However, shortly before Rakosi finally succeeded in ousting Imre Nagy from the premiership in March 1955, *Irodalmi Ujsag*'s crusading editor was sacked, ostensibly for publishing a poem by Laszlo Benjamin entitled "The Magic of Everyday Things", and replaced by one expected to be more conformist and loyal to the régime, Gyorgy Hamos. Less than five months later, the new editor too was sacked, and an issue of the paper which was already being sold on the streets was confiscated by the police.

This action spurred the writers to move from expressions of individual dissent to actions of a more organised and concerted nature. Members of the Writers' Association immediately protested about the confiscation of *Irodalmi Ujsag* and called for a meeting of their party group to discuss the matter. When their request was denied by the party's cultural department, all the Communist Party members of the Presidium of the Writers' Association resigned en bloc. Sandor Haraszti, Geza Losonczy, Miklos Vasarhelyi and Tamas Aczel then drew up a memorandum criticising the whole cultural policy of the party and calling for greater freedom for the writers to pursue their creative work. It is again significant that the first three of these writers had all been journalists formerly associated with *Szabad Nep*. It was Tamas Aczel, nevertheless, who was to ensure the success of the memorandum by obtaining signatures to it from some fifty-nine of the most prominent figures of Hungary's cultural life. One of the first to sign it was none other than Endre Enczi, just appointed to replace Gyorgy Hamos as editor of *Irodalmi Ujsag*. When a meeting of the Communist Party group of the Writers' Association was finally held at the beginning of November 1955, the memorandum was read out to it by the poet Zoltan Zelk, overwhelmingly approved by the meeting, and sent on to the Central Committee.[6]

While the writers had little hope of winning the day, they were determined to make their protest known, to speak out against the restoration of the Rakosi régime, and to resist the loss of those freedoms they had just won under the New Course of Imre Nagy. As one of them later explained: "We wanted . . . to show the people how many of us there were in opposition to the régime. . . . We wanted to kick up a shindig. . . . We wanted this to be a slap in the face for Rakosi, and we succeeded."[7]

But Rakosi, who had already silenced the journalists and expelled Imre Nagy from the Communist Party, was not slow in hitting back at the rebellious writers. They were first summoned to a meeting of party functionaries in the headquarters of the Iron and Steel Workers' trade union, where they were publicly castigated in a stormy meeting which had much of the atmosphere of a lynch trial. When the only writer to attempt to defend their actions, one of the founding members of the Hungarian Communist Party Gyula Hay, tried to speak, he was angrily shouted down.

In December 1955, the Central Committee condemned the writers for creating "an anti-party platform", and considerable pressure was brought to bear to persuade them to withdraw their signatures from the memorandum. Those who did not comply with the party's demands were severely reprimanded, almost the entire staff of *Irodalmi Ujsag* was replaced, and Sandor Haraszti and Miklos Vasarhelyi joined the company of those who had already been expelled from the party. An atmosphere of fear and isolation now surrounded the writers, and it seemed as though this second wave of opposition had been silenced and repressed just as decisively as that of the journalists several months before.

The group around Imre Nagy

The various outbreaks of opposition amongst the journalists, writers and intellectuals had always had one thing in common: their support for Imre Nagy. Nagy himself, however, throughout his premiership, had been acting almost completely alone and had few connections with his willing and enthusiastic supporters. They, rather, had had to force themselves on him, and when it came to the crunch he had more than once disowned them. However, in the months following his fall from power, a small group of reformist politicians was to slowly coalesce around Imre Nagy, forming the nucleus of a potential alternative administration to that of Rakosi.[8]

Up to 1954 Nagy's closest personal friends had been men like his son-in-law Ferenc Janosi, who was made secretary of the People's Patriotic Front, and the president of the Budapest city council, Kalman Pongracz, as well as a few of his colleagues at the Agricultural University. Towards the end of 1954, a number of prewar communists who had been imprisoned during the stalinist period and were now released, became amongst his closest friends. They included former activists in the wartime underground party like Sandor Haraszti, who now walked the city's streets denouncing to everyone he met "that old rascal — Rakosi", and his son-in-law Geza Losonczy. Other former communist militants who now entered Nagy's circle of friends included Ferenc Donath, Szilard Ujhely and Gyorgy Heltai, as well as the veteran communist Zoltan Szanto.

Another person to become one of Nagy's close colleagues at this time was Miklos Vasarhelyi, whom Nagy appointed as his press chief. It was largely through him that, in the spring of 1955, a number of the journalists who were shortly to constitute the hard core of the opposition first entered the circle of "friends of Imre Nagy". Amongst them were Miklos Gimes, Gyorgy Fazekas, Pal Locsei and Sandor Fekete. In 1955 the writers too came into this circle, people like Tibor Dery and Gyula Hay, Zoltan Zelk and Laszlo Benjamin, Tamas Aczel and Tibor Meray. Another communist to now become an active supporter of Nagy was Jozsef Szilagyi, and later on even a number of rehabilitated social democrats were to join the group, such as Zoltan Horvath and Sandor Szalai.

Far from being any form of organised opposition grouping, Nagy's circle was a chain of friendly contacts, different groups of which would from time to time visit Nagy to pay their respects and discuss questions of common interest. One observer has described the situation as he saw it:

> "His followers tried to make Imre Nagy into a political centre, a focus, and also tried to break out of the narrower

party circle . . . (but the) Imre Nagy circle spent much of its time in long and fruitless debates. . . . Nagy liked to philosophise, and these people liked to talk and talk."[9]

Those of his supporters who sought more determined action came to be increasingly frustrated by Nagy's continuing constitutionalist mentality, by his stubborn loyalty to the official procedures of the party, and his uncompromising rejection of all forms of "factional activity". After *Szabad Nep*'s rebellious general meeting in October 1954 had declared its support for him, Nagy had reprimanded the journalists for their intention of circulating the meeting's minutes. So confident in the rightness of his cause, and at the same time so faithful to the party, Imre Nagy stubbornly refused to fight back against his enemies even as they eased him out of power, even when (as one of his supporters recalls), "they were preparing the noose around his neck".

Some of his followers, however, were less easily restrained, and when he was finally ousted from power in March 1955, a group of young students sought his approval to produce an openly provocative student journal. Nagy was horrified and did his best to dampen the spirits of his young supporters. He also intervened to prevent the publication in the youth journal *Szabad Ifjusag* ("Free Youth") of a strongly worded poem by Istvan Eorsi which openly attacked the party's stalinist leaders. A few weeks later some of his more radical supporters were preparing to distribute leaflets at the May Day demonstrations with the slogan: "Rakosi=misery+servitude; Nagy=well-being+freedom." Again Nagy stepped in and insisted the action be called off.

The group of friends who continued to meet over coffee at Nagy's villa in Buda consequently functioned more as a brains trust than as a centre of opposition. Nagy himself sat down to write a statement of his views in a series of dissertations which he hoped to place before the Central Committee, and as he prepared them they provided the basis for numerous discussions with his friends.

The more radical of Nagy's supporters, however, continued to feel the need for more determined and organised action. In the spring of 1956, after the Soviet Twentieth Party Congress, Miklos Gimes with the support of younger journalists like Gyorgy Fazekas, Pal Locsei and Sandor Fekete, proposed the creation of an illegal party organisation which would not hesitate to go beyond the narrow limits of the Communist Party and launch a campaign to restore Imre Nagy to power. Members of the group prepared leaflets and posters calling for Nagy's return to power, and plans were prepared for the MP from Gyor, Attila Szigethy, to challenge the government in the National Assembly and demand a debate on the Nagy affair. Other proposals were suggested to revive the trade unions, and organise them in support of Nagy and against the existing party leadership.

Other leading associates of Nagy, however, most notably Losoncy, Donath and Ujhely, declared that they would have nothing to do with any illegal organisation. Vasarhelyi was lukewarm towards the enterprise, while Nagy himself refused even to discuss the matter and insisted that the whole attempt be called off.

Nevertheless, despite the lack of organisation and the absence of any central direction or leadership, the Imre Nagy group's influence was to grow steadily amongst the political and intellectual élite of Budapest. The leading members of Imre Nagy's inner "brains trust" would meet in their offices, as well as in the bars and cafés of Budapest, with their own circles of friends and associates who were most interested in hearing what "the old man" was currently thinking. In this way the ideas of the Imre Nagy group filtered down through society.

In the spring and summer of 1956 Imre Nagy would often stroll through the busy shopping streets of the city centre where ordinary people would stop to greet him and ask when he was coming back to power. His sixtieth birthday in June was turned into an open political demonstration when leading Hungarians from all walks of public life, including the composer Zoltan Kodaly and even one government minister, attended a party at his home. A few weeks later when the Soviet minister Mikoyan paid a short visit to Budapest, even he made a point of meeting with Imre Nagy.

Meanwhile, though they had given up their plans for an actual clandestine organisation, Nagy's supporters did now become more active in bringing pressure to bear on the decision-making bodies of the party. One of them tells the story as follows:

> "We wanted to wriggle out of the mess, to get the Rakosi gang out and Imre Nagy in. There were fantastic schemes about and the possibility of a mass movement. . . . We had a regular 'adult education' campaign. In the evening the council of war would meet somewhere, exchange information gathered since we had last seen each other, and then divide the tasks. . . . Through contacts and threats we exerted influence on the party and received excellent information."[10]

The co-ordination of this campaign was overseen by Miklos Vasarhelyi, and while the opposition had few contacts in the top party apparatus who were wholehearted supporters of Nagy, there were many others who could be cajoled or threatened into speaking and voting against the stalinist leaders, in favour of the rehabilitations, and for Nagy's readmission to the party.

The forum of the opposition

If there was a certain continuing momentum to the growth of the inner circle of the opposition around Imre Nagy, this was far from true of the wider opposition movement which developed through a series of advances and retreats, in the course of which different individuals and different groupings played the crucial roles. Between the autumn of 1954 and the spring of 1955, the journalists had been suppressed and their forces dispersed. Then at the end of 1955 the writers too were isolated and repressed. With Rakosi firmly back in the saddle, the hopes of the last two years seemed finally extinguished. This was the low point of the opposition both in its activities and its spirit, and many of its members felt oppressed by an atmosphere full of fear and anxiety.

Then, just when all seemed lost, the Twentieth Congress of the Soviet Communist Party and Khrushchev's secret speech denouncing Stalin exploded upon the communist world. Once again Rakosi's position in Hungary was undermined by the actions of the Soviet leaders, and once again a new wave of opposition was set in motion. Only a few days earlier living in fear of arrest and imprisonment, the members of the opposition could now step out boldly in the confidence that they could cite Khrushchev's speech in their support and justification. Indeed, this new surge of opposition saw its role as being to promote the spirit of the Twentieth Congress in Hungary itself, and to this end it was to establish for itself a public forum in the shape of a debating club called the Petofi Circle.

The Petofi Circle (named after Sandor Petofi, the young poet of Hungary's 1848 revolution) had been formed in 1954 as a small discussion group within DISZ, the Communist Youth League. Many of its members were "graduates" of the People's College Movement, NEKOSZ, which had been set up during the war years to help worker and peasant youngsters receive a university education, and then promoted by the communists as a means of recruiting party cadres and of campaigning against religion and other reactionary cultural attitudes. The People's Colleges were disbanded at the time of the Rajk trial, but they had already served as a natural breeding ground for national communist tendencies, and the personal friendships and loyalties created there were to survive the years of stalinist oppression.

It was former members of the People's Colleges who came together once again in 1956 to inspire and direct the activities of the Petofi Circle. The leaders of the Petofi Circle were the former People's College directors and prewar communists Laszlo Kardos and Antal Gyenes; its secretary was a wartime member of the illegal Communist Party and People's College student Gabor Tancsos, his assistant another former People's College student, the young historian Balazs Nagy. Under their leadership the Petofi Circle was to develop into "the movement of young Hungarian intellectuals, including all the professions, teachers, economists, physicians, engineers etc." By early 1956, while the Circle's small meetings on literary and professional subjects had attained little mass significance, they had established a network of reliable personal contacts between party members in many organisations engaged in intellectual activities.[11]

Wholeheartedly embracing the decisions of the Twentieth Congress, the Petofi Circle was to lead the movement calling for the implementation of the Congress's spirit in Hungary itself, for the "destalinisation" of the Hungarian Communist Party. While its leaders kept in touch with the journalists and writers and with the Imre Nagy group, whose members also participated in its meetings, the Petofi Circle was undoubtedly a separate and independent organ of the opposition. By the summer of 1956 it had become the chief platform of the opposition, and was even described by the party's stalinist leaders as the "second political centre" of the country.

It was on 18 June, at a meeting held specially for former underground communist militants, that the debates of the Petofi Circle first really fired the public imagination. Mrs Julia Rajk, the widow of Laszlo Rajk who had led the underground party in Hungary before and during the war and who had been executed in the stalinist purges, rose to demand justice for her dead husband and punishment for his murderers, declaring: "I shall never rest until those who have ruined the country, corrupted the party, destroyed thousands, and driven millions into despair receive their just punishment. Comrades, help me in this struggle."[12]

When the Petofi Circle met again some ten days later, every seat had been taken three hours before the debate was due to commence, even though the meeting had been transferred to one of the largest public halls in Budapest and entrance was supposedly by ticket only. Loudspeakers were set up to carry the debate into overflow meetings and even out into the street, and it has been estimated that some five to six thousand people attended.

The debate was on the topic of the Hungarian press, and one of the first speakers was the communist novelist Tibor Dery who outspokenly attacked the party's cultural policy and called for the freedom of literature and the press. Then, turning to more directly political affairs, he argued that it was no longer sufficient to demand mere personal changes in the party leadership, but that structural changes were needed in the system itself. Finally he called upon the nation's youth to step forward in the manner of their forebears of 1848. Then one of the former *Szabad Nep* journalists, Tibor Tardos, rose to assert his belief in the freedom of the press. Moreover, he declared, the opposition were the only true representatives of the ideals and principles of the party.

The most rapturous applause of the night was reserved for Geza Losonczy who, closing the debate in the early hours of the morning, called upon the forces of the opposition to step out decisively at the head of the party and the people, and raised the slogan of the return to power of Imre Nagy. At this the whole meeting rose from their seats and for minutes on end cheered the name of their former Prime Minister.[13]

This daring and bold raising of the banner of the opposition before the Hungarian public was too much for Rakosi. Within days the Petofi Circle was banned, and Dery and Tardos were expelled from the Communist Party. Once again a campaign was set in motion throughout the Party to purge it of the forces of the opposition. This time, however, the opposition refused to lie down, and the very meetings called to denounce them were turned into forums for further attacks on Rakosi and the party leadership. At one of these meetings in the working-class district of Angyalfold, a young history teacher, Gyorgy Litvan, stood up and told Rakosi to his face, "You are guilty! You should resign!"[14]

Resigning, though, was not something Rakosi had in mind. If the opposition were not prepared to submit, he would just have to use stronger measures against them. To this end he now prepared plans for the mass arrest of his opponents, drawing up a list of four hundred names headed by that of Imre Nagy. But such measures, in the year of the Twentieth Congress, were no longer acceptable either to his colleagues in the Hungarian Politburo, or to the Soviet leaders in the Kremlin. In the middle of July the Soviet minister Mikoyan arrived unexpectedly in Budapest, went straight along to a meeting of the Central Committee which was already in session, and demanded Rakosi's resignation. A few hours later it was announced that Rakosi had been relieved of his post and replaced by Erno Gero.

The appointment of Gero as First Party Secretary could hardly be seen as a victory for the opposition. He too was an old stalinist and muscovite who, as Tito was later to declare, "differed in no way from Rakosi".[15] Gero, however, would no longer be able to use the same methods of dictatorial rule as Rakosi had employed. He would increasingly be forced into making concessions in line with Khrushchev's rapprochement with Tito, and would finally find himself unable to control the growing swell of opposition and revolt.

The beginnings of social ferment

With Rakosi's removal from power, the first and most central objective of the opposition had been achieved, and many of its members became hesitant and unsure about the next steps they should take. Several of those who had sided with the opposition out of personal dislike for Rakosi felt that Gero should now be given a chance. Even Imre Nagy contemplated seeking an honourable compromise and joining forces with the new leadership. Some writers and intellectuals too felt they need no longer fear restrictions on their freedom of expression.

However if writers and intellectuals felt their interests could be safeguarded by the leadership changes, the mass of Hungarian working people saw little occasion to rejoice. Indeed, while many commentators have contended that it was the action of the intellectual élite that stirred the masses to revolt, the actual facts suggest that it was the constant discontent amongst the masses that kept the intellectuals on their toes, and prodded them time and again into pushing ahead with the struggle which finally led to the revolution. After all, the writers' first open criticisms of the régime had come when they were sent to the people in 1953 and 1954 to explain the party's new policies to them, and when it had been the people who had shown them the depths of social misery and the bitterness against the party which existed throughout the country.

A feeling of deep and bitter opposition to the régime had become widespread by the early fifties, not least amongst the younger generation. According to one seventeen-year-old schoolboy's description: "We spoke less about political subjects, but if we did, we were cursing the Russians, that was most of the time what it amounted to."[16]

This generation's disillusionment had taken place in the secondary schools in the early fifties. As another of their number recalls: "The members of my class distrusted each other at first, but by our second year there was a wild anti-communist spirit rampant. . . . We were the first generation which was not scared. After all we had nothing to lose and we also had the feeling that we couldn't bear this for an entire life."[17]

Even before 1953 and Stalin's death (which several of these youngsters claim to have met with wholehearted enthusiasm) a number of small debating circles had arisen in the schools where discussions were held on various topics of art, literature and politics. "It was logical", one member of this age-group tells us, "that when we got to the university there would be trouble." When they did get there, the atmosphere in the university was certainly unique. As one student relates:

> "All the students at the university were very interested in politics. After the first two years, we had become so bold that we discussed politics in the halls. By 1955 we talked only politics.
>
> The marxist-leninist seminars were awaited eagerly because at these we could ask embarrassing questions about Tito and about the responsibility of the party leaders, etc."[18]

Groups of students took particular interest in Western writers such as Aldous Huxley and George Orwell, young artists experimented with modern painting and music, small groups studied existentialist philosophers like Karl Jaspers and Martin Heidegger, modern psychology became fashionable and young psychologists experimented with mescaline and other drugs. In their social and personal relations too, these students felt the need for greater freedom and experimentation. We are told that "a freer sex life was a form of opposition, a way of rejecting the given régime. Young people could not travel, and not buy things for themselves so they . . . drank, made love, went on excursions on the Danube."[19]

Not only was this new generation in the process of finding itself, but it was reaching out for the widest possible sources of inspiration. A young student explains: "A counter-scale of values developed among us and in the entire country against the scale of values of the régime."[20]

The more literary inclined of the students were active in a Young Writers' Group set up in the Arts Faculty of Budapest University in March 1955. Here works of the young writers themselves like Istvan Eorsi and Sandor Csoori were often read, as were poems and articles refused by the official journals including a translation of the Pole Adam Wazyk's "Poem for Adults" and Laszlo Benjamin's famous poem to Sandor Haraszti. By 1956 the students also participated in the meetings of the Petofi Circle, and a number of similar debating circles were set up in the separate faculties of the university.

At the same time these early student rebels, just like the communist writers, were a small élite viewed with considerable suspicion by the mass of young students of worker and peasant origin, who were tempted to see their moves as constituting yet another communist tactic. Moreover, while the younger intellectual leftists elaborately construed teasing questions on abstruse points of marxist ideology, the peasant and worker students more simply and clearly expressed the direct grievances of their class. As one student remarks:

> "The peasants' and workers' sons were the most outspoken. They were more insolent than those of middle-class origin. They could ask questions like, 'Isn't the delivery quota too high?' . . . It was perhaps the peasant kids, who went home regularly and saw the misery in the village, who were most outspoken in their criticism."[21]

These students from poorer working-class and peasant families were reflecting the general mood of dissatisfaction that was becoming ever more openly expressed by the working people themselves. Both the peasantry and the working class had benefited from the communist régime in the first years after 1945, but from 1949 on the screws were tightened by increasing the workers' norms and raising the forced deliveries from the peasants, until the whole country became filled with a seething discontent. A fifty-year-old cutter in a Budapest shoe factory recounts:

> "There was a general discontent among the workers and it came out whenever two people began to talk. The workers did not believe in anything the communists promised them, because the communists had cheated their promises so often."[22]

Similarly, a factory worker from Csepel explains:

> "The communists nationalised all the factories and similar enterprises, proclaiming the slogan, 'The factory is yours — you work for yourself'. Exactly the opposite of this was true. They promised us everything, at the same time subjugating us and pulling us down to the greatest misery conceivable."[23]

This intense and bitter opposition to the political régime was to be found at its strongest in the very proletarian centres of the communist industrial system. The following experiences are those of a young student and communist sympathiser in 1952:

> "Then I went to Csepel and built socialism there too, as an iron worker in the Matyas Rakosi works. It was there that I realised how much the workers hated the régime. . . . The workers hated the régime to such an extent that by 1953 they were ready to destroy it and everything that went with it."[24]

This accumulated tension was to burst out like sudden darts of lightning in the years immediately following Stalin's death. In the wake of the disturbances in East Berlin and Czechoslovakia in June 1953, the first really serious strikes to occur in Hungary since 1946 took place at Csepel and in industrial centres in northern and eastern Hungary. A number of similar, though sporadic and isolated strikes followed in the spring of 1954. The workers' dissatisfaction was also expressed in the high frequency with which they changed jobs. In the Ganz shipyards, for example, a third of the labour force was turned over in one year alone. Many factories were also plagued by epidemics of petty pilfering, by which means the workers tried to keep up their falling standards of living. The extent of this is best illustrated by the story of a rehabilitated intellectual who was hired as a truck driver's mate, and then fired — because he refused to take part in the stealing. Employees also gave vent to their feelings by deliberately damaging machinery and committing acts of what one shipyard foreman describes as "spontaneous sabotage".

The extent of these actions is also attested to by the rise in the number of workers to be found in Hungary's jails. One estimate suggests that in 1953 there was hardly a single Hungarian family without a member or close relation imprisoned for political or economic crimes, the majority of these being workers convicted of stealing. This situation is confirmed by Imre Nagy, writing at the beginning of 1956 in a final section of his dissertations:

> "The number of persons imprisoned is greater than ever before. . . . But the most alarming fact is that the majority of those convicted come from the ranks of the working class, the industrial workers."[25]

The summer of 1954 also saw a number of riotous outbreaks on sporting occasions. When a Russian basketball team beat the Hungarians, the predominantly student crowd booed the referee and shouted abuse at the Soviet team. Several arrests were made, and subsequently two students were jailed and six expelled from the university. Similar happenings at football matches, particularly when the crowd felt the Hungarian players had deliberately muffed their chances to let the Russians win, led on more than one occasion to irate crowds smashing shop windows in the city centre. When the Hungarian football team lost the World Cup championship to the West Germans, people rioted on the streets for three days, and the police were almost helpless to drive them from the city centre. A similar scene occurred when police tried to evict a "semi-underworld family" from the disused store in which they were living. When the family resisted, a large crowd gathered and prevented their removal. A police riot detachment was sent to the scene, whereupon the crowd grew and fought directly with the police. The police, lacking either training or experience in dealing with unarmed demonstrations, eventually withdrew to leave the victory to the crowd.

Though such occasions served to let off steam, the workers' discontent increasingly took on a more concrete and radical nature. More and more frequent were the occasions when ordinary workers, often long-standing Communist Party members, got up at meetings and spoke out against the waste and economic bungling of the régime, and the misery it created. When news reached Hungary of the Poznan disturbances in Poland in June 1956, a new wave of workers' protests and strikes swept the country. Even accounts published under the Kadar régime admit that, in the Ajka mining districts, voices were to be heard suggesting that "the communists' game is already up", that the miners too should be prepared to do something, and that even armed action might not be very far away. Once again the huge Matyas Rakosi iron and steel works in Csepel was brought to a halt as the workers demanded improvements in their standard of living. Similar protest strikes were held in other large factories throughout Budapest.[26]

This new upsurge of mass rebellion also spurred on the intellectuals themselves to more outspoken behaviour. In April 1956 Sandor Lukacsy, a young literary critic, had stood up at a general meeting of the Writers' Association and expressed his feelings in much the same way as the workers had long been talking, describing Rakosi as "a Judas whose hands are stained with blood". It was also the mood of almost open rebellion amongst the masses that provided the ground in which the debates of the Petofi Circle were to take root and flourish.

By midsummer, the party functionaries "were scared stiff . . . people spat on their cars, etc. By August and September they didn't dare walk in the street". However, in this atmosphere of bitterness and hatred openly expressed against the régime, even the loyalty of many of the functionaries began to waver. In the past they had borne the brunt of public dissatisfaction with the régime; now they found the party's new leaders trying to pass off all responsibility for the past on to the lower functionaries themselves. Many now felt they had carried the can for the leadership for long enough, and began to range themselves on the side of the people and the opposition.

The role of the ordinary police in trying to act as neutrals in any conflict between the party leadership and the people had been obvious for some time. Now, however, even officers of the "secret police" — the hated *AVH** — were to be found standing up at party meetings in the Ministry of the Interior to criticise the leadership, and demand greater independence for their country from the Soviets.

With these latest developments it became clear not only that the mood of opposition had spread throughout the broadest layers of the population, but that it was being accompanied by the growing disintegration of the whole apparatus of party and state control. The situation within the party has been perhaps best described by Dora Scarlett, an English communist who had been living and working in Hungary for the previous three years. She writes:

> "It would be wrong to think that there was any such organisation as 'The Party' any longer, with a unified control. It was breaking up into its component parts — the tiny, rigid core surrounding Erno Gero, and the mass of members who were in varying degrees drawn into the tide of opposition, criticism and independent action."[27]

The continuing campaign against stalinism

While the summer months of 1956 had seen the activities of the earlier opposition groups largely overtaken by the growing ferment of the masses, the journalists, writers and reformist politicians could still be found continuing to play their own important roles within this larger mass movement.

A number of prominent left-wing political prisoners, including the writers Paul Ignotus and George Paloczi-Horvath, were released from prison around this time and added their voices to the movement of dissent. The literary journals now overflowed with critical poems and stories, many written earlier but only now appearing in print, and in the words of Tamas Aczel and Tibor Meray, "this was the summer of thought freely expressed".[28]

The supporters of Imre Nagy now seem to have quite deliberately set about placing their own people in leading positions in the administration, and to have met with their first and earliest successes in the field of the press. At the end of 1955 Geza Losonczy had been appointed to the editorship of *Magyar Nemzet* which was

---

*The initials *AVH* stand for *Allamvedelmi Hatosag* ("state security force"). This force has generally been referred to in the West as the "secret police" but this expression is considerably misleading, as the AVH were a uniformed force of order, a state or political police similar to the Soviet KGB.

to become, under his direction, one of the leading champions of the opposition's campaign for change. A short time later the editors of *Esti Budapest,* the evening paper of the Budapest city Communist Party which had previously been considered even more stalinist than *Szabad Nep,* were replaced by supporters of Imre Nagy. Within days the new editors were being seen to "kill stalinist copy on technical grounds" and "introduce a reign of terror at *Esti Budapest*" — a reign of terror that for once favoured the opposition and was directed against the stalinists.

The writers also began to act more independently. A meeting of the Writers' Association in March had called for the dismissal of Rakosi, and another in May demanded the rehabilitation of Imre Nagy. Finally at their annual congress in September, the writers rejected outright the party slate for their Presidium elections. In an unprecedented assertion of autonomy they elected a number of their country's most respected non-communist writers to their leadership, several of whom had only recently been banned or even imprisoned by the régime. The congress also passed a resolution calling upon the writers to go out to the factories and take their message to the industrial workers.

In the following weeks the Writers' Association journal *Irodalmi Ujsag* was to publish a number of critical articles far more daring than any that had so far seen the light of day. It was here that appeared Judit Mariassy's article "Unpleasant Questions", in which the truth was told for the first time about the privileged life of the party's leaders, and about the special shops, private villas and holiday resorts reserved for their use. Other articles launched even more provocative attacks on the party functionaries and bureaucrats, amongst them "Special People" by Sandor Novobaczky and Gyula Hay's even more scathing "Why do I dislike Comrade Kucsera?" which ended with the lines:

> "Lies are not lies for Kucsera, murder is not murder, justice is not justice, and man is not man. Kucsera preaches socialism and means a system which . . . keeps him going. He preaches unity and means himself and a handful of others who are up to the same game. . . . He preaches democracy and means his own hegemony. . . . That is why I dislike Comrade Kucsera."[29]

Carrying articles such as these, *Irodalmi Ujsag* soon became so popular that crowds of people would assemble before the newsstands waiting for it to appear. People paid two or three forints although the price was only one, and when the issue had sold out copies would change hands at even higher prices.

Also in September, a new weekly paper, *Hetfoi Hirlap* ("Monday News"), was started up and called for the opening of a clean page in the party's conduct of the nation's affairs. Most prominent amongst its contributors was Miklos Gimes who wrote several particularly radical articles demanding a clean sweep of the party leadership, and the public trial and punishment of Matyas Rakosi and his secret police chief Mihaly Farkas. The paper was to raise tremendous interest, indeed near riots, when it was sold on the city's streets where scenes arose which were little short of spectacular. Here are just a few of the eye-witness accounts:

> "The first number of *Hetfoi Hirlap* was such a sensation that the people were tearing each other to pieces in order to get one, and the happy owners had literally to climb up the lampposts in order to keep their copies."[30]
>
> "One Sunday evening, one of the newsmen had been simply pushed against a shop window. The window smashed — the poor newspaper seller found himself in the shop window, bleeding from his wounds. . . . He dropped in terror his bundle of *Hetfoi Hirlap,* for which the crowds began such a fierce fight that the police were called out and had to bring order by using their truncheons."[31]

We are even told of one news-seller climbing up a statue from which to hand out his papers, of another doing so from the security of a ladies' toilets. Yet a further observer reports the police cruising around one such gathering — and selling the paper from the windows of their squad car. Finally, on another evening in the city centre:

> "In front of the offices of the paper the street was full of people, and the police were unable to keep order. The police took out their truncheons but did not dare to use them because they were surrounded by a big crowd. The police were forced to withdraw by car . . . this was a small revolution in itself."[32]

In this atmosphere of latent mass revolt, the opposition press and the reformist politicians were able to step up their campaign against the remaining stalinists in the party leadership, and for the arrest and trial of those responsible for the faked trials, torturings and judicial murders of the stalinist years. Only by a clean sweep of the whole party leadership, declared Geza Losonczy in a particularly outspoken article, could the victory of the spirit of the Twentieth Congress be achieved.

The opposition now also stepped up their efforts to win positions of influence and power within the administration, and in the final weeks before the uprising they were gaining increasing influence within the Budapest City Party. One of their number, Bela Szabo, became the city party's press chief, while Imre Mezo, a prewar communist and longstanding friend of Imre Nagy, was appointed to the secretariat of the city party and thereby to membership of the Central Committee. It even appeared that Mezo was being groomed to take over from Istvan Kovacs as First Secretary of the city Communist Party.

An interesting illustration of the way in which the opposition went about its business has been provided by Bela Kiraly, a former Hungarian general who had fought with the Russians at the end of World War Two and was later imprisoned under the stalinists. Released from prison in September 1956, he soon received a visit from an old acquaintance who asked if he would like to meet some "friends of Imre Nagy". Kiraly agreed immediately, and the meeting was arranged for the very next day. At it he was told:

> "Several former political prisoners have already been rehabilitated. Some of them have even been reinstalled in their previous positions with the state and the party. Several of them support Imre Nagy's plans for reforms and are doing their best to get him back into the government and the party leadership. . . .
>
> Our aim is to get as many decent people who believe in Nagy's mission into state and party positions as possible in order to speed up the start of the reforms. . . .
>
> Only two institutions have refused to accept rehabilitated former political prisoners back into their old positions: the army and the secret police. . . .
>
> We have Imre Nagy's backing for an effort to have you reinstated as Commander-in-Chief of the Infantry if you are agreeable. If and when you are reinstated, you would be in a position to help more anti-stalinist officers to join the army."[33]

Kiraly agreed to the offer, indeed he came to believe that the Imre Nagy group had even had a hand in his release from prison. They now arranged for him to enter hospital and receive special treatment to help him recover from his prison ordeal.

Although still officially banned, the Petofi Circle began to hold meetings once again. It now became a real popular forum drawing large numbers of young people and students who were attracted by the notoriety occasioned by its earlier banning, and who declared themselves "intoxicated" by the atmosphere of free and lively debate. Similar debating circles were also set up in many university faculties and in the larger provincial towns, and through these the Petofi Circle began to establish a nationwide network.

Under its auspices several members of the Imre Nagy group, amongst them Geza Losonczy, Gyula Hay and Jozsef Szilagyi, went out to address meetings all over the country and to take the campaign of the opposition to the nation as a whole.

Rajk's reburial and the students' revolt

For nearly two years Laszlo Rajk's widow Julia had been conducting a persistent and at times almost solitary campaign for the rehabilitation of her dead husband. Her intervention at the Petofi Circle in June had made a particularly striking impact, and she had kept in close contact with the Petofi Circle's organisers and with several of the journalists. Moreover, it was now a good year since a special party commission had completed its report into the stalinist trials which completely exonerated Rajk and those accused with him. The report's publication however had been suppressed, first by Rakosi, now by Gero.

Finally, as the party leaders prepared for a goodwill visit to Yugoslavia, they agreed to Rajk's rehabilitation as a move to placate Marshal Tito. They hoped to do so with as little fanfare as possible, and it was only on Mrs Rajk's insistence that on 4 October *Szabad Nep* carried a very small announcement that Laszlo Rajk — "who had died a martyr's death" — and three of those executed with him would be reinterred on Sunday 6 October. But the party daily refused to publicise the reburial in any more significant way, and when certain former friends of Rajk asked for space to make a private announcement even this request was turned down.

It was these procrastinations concerning the reburial that forced the leaders of the different opposition groupings into united action. For the first time leading individuals from the Imre Nagy group, the writers, journalists and Petofi Circle organisers, as well as representatives of the university students and even of the workers of Csepel, all came together in the flat of Gyorgy Adam, a prominent former communist and university professor. They were all in contact with wider sections of the population, often through official party organisations, and they decided to use their influence to try and mobilise the people for the coming funeral procession.

Aware of these preparations, and under increasing pressure from former colleagues of Rajk within the top circles of the party itself, the party leadership was forced to retreat and agreed to a public ceremony at which top party leaders would deliver funeral orations. The journalists at *Szabad Nep*, previously denied action, now went to town with a full front-page spread carrying photographs of the executed communists under the headline: THIS MUST NEVER HAPPEN AGAIN.

On the Sunday afternoon, a march the like of which the city had rarely seen before, took to the streets of Budapest. Some put the number as high as two hundred thousand. In the Kerepesi Cemetery, where many of Hungary's most famous literary and political figures lie buried, speaker after speaker demanded to know why Laszlo Rajk had died innocent, and one of them, a fellow prisoner of Rajk, declared: "We shall not forget!"

By the end of the day, members of the opposition just as much as leaders of the party were staggered by the fact that so many people had so easily been mobilised. As one of the intellectuals remarked later:

> "It was then that we realised, that everybody realised, that this wasn't just an affair of a few communist intellectuals, but that everyone felt as strongly, the same way, against the régime."[34]

More than one person left with the opinion that "perhaps if it had not rained, there would have been a revolution that day."[35]

6 October also saw the students of Budapest first embarking boldly on political action. As the funeral orations in the cemetery drew to a close, a group of some two to three hundred students marched off behind Hungarian national flags and red party banners towards the city centre, singing revolutionary songs and raising the slogan that was soon to become their most popular rallying cry: "We won't stop halfway, stalinism must be destroyed!" Shouting slogans against the AVH and in praise of the Hungarian writers, the marchers passed through the city's streets, stopping briefly outside the Yugoslav Embassy to cheer Tito and Yugoslav socialism, and finally holding a small ceremony before the memorial to Lajos Batthany, the Hungarian Prime Minister executed after the suppression of the 1848 revolution. Throughout their march, the city's police took no action against them, never thinking for a moment that this could be anything other than an official demonstration by the communist youth organisation.

In the following days the leadership of the movement of opposition, which had so far passed from the journalists to the writers and on to the organisers of the Petofi Circle, was to fall firmly into the hands of the students. Already at the end of September, a panel of Central Committee members had come to the university to find themselves showered with questions about the Sovietisation of Hungarian culture, the Soviet troops in Hungary, the norms system in the factories, and the privileges of the party élite. At a meeting of high-school students, the Minister of Education himself had been shouted down and walked out. As one student recalls: "In the weeks before the revolution, there was meeting after meeting at the universities, which demanded the introduction of a freer atmosphere, as well as university autonomy."[36]

By early October political slogans began to appear in the toilets at the university — a phenomenon which hadn't been seen since 1947 — while the students' journal and the communist youth paper appeared to be battling with each other to print the most radical criticisms of the régime.[37]

The first moves towards independent action by the students, however, came from the provincial towns. At a meeting in Szeged University on 16 October, students demanded an end to the compulsory study of Russian and called for a strike in support of their demand. Before the meeting was over they had even decided to set up a new student organisation independent of the Communist Party (to be called the MEFESZ), and to send representatives to all the other universities in Hungary to win support for this new national organisation. The movement begun in Szeged quickly won support throughout the country, even within the official communist youth movement itself, and on 19 October the communist youth paper declared in an editorial: "We are engaged in a struggle for independence exactly like the one our forebears waged in 1848." In these same days, meetings at the Technological University in Budapest demanded better conditions for the students and threatened public demonstrations if their demands were not met within two weeks.

By Monday 22 October, student meetings could be found in permanent session in nearly every faculty of Budapest University, and at most other universities throughout the country. The largest meeting of them all went on throughout the night at the Technological University where a programme of demands, rapidly growing from ten to sixteen points, was prepared and argued out. This meeting also decided to call a mass demonstration for the following day to express solidarity with the events in Poland where Gomulka had just been restored to power. But as yet there was little central direction, and the different faculties had different plans as to where they were to assemble, where to march, and whether or not they should carry posters or shout slogans. Indeed, far from planning for an armed uprising on 23 October as some people later suggested, the students were preparing to convene a national student conference on 27 October to launch a national debate around their demands.

The opposition on the eve of the uprising

While most members of the various opposition groupings took part in the demonstration called by the students, it would be wrong to assume that they had directly inspired or organised it. Indeed, in many cases they appeared hesitant and alarmed by the new turn of events.

The Petofi Circle's leaders, for instance, only met late on the evening of 22 October to consider appeals from the students for support. They passed a resolution echoing some though by no means all of the students' demands, and decided a little reluctantly to participate in the demonstration. When the demonstration was officially banned the next morning, the Petofi Circle sent a delegation to the Politburo where they found total confusion and disarray. While the party's hardliners declared their determination to shoot on anyone defying the ban, the more moderate members of the Politburo desperately appealed to the Petofi Circle's leaders to place themselves at the head of the demonstration and try to control it. In the event, as one of the Circle's secretaries has testified, "The Petofi Circle curbed rather than encouraged the movement, considering that the hastening of events could lead to a catastrophe."[38]

Although it was perhaps the most radical of the opposition groups, even the Petofi Circle had not planned for more than an orderly reform of the system to be achieved by changes in the political leadership. The changes they sought were ones that would have to be controlled, and even the Communist Party's leaders could appeal to them to help with this very task.

As for the writers, far from leading events they were literally running in vain to keep up with them. Before the students' plans were known, the Writers' Association had decided to hold a silent demonstration outside the Polish Embassy a good way from the city centre. Forming up here they agreed to join in the students' march, but by the time they got to the Petofi statue where the students had at first assembled, the crowd had already left and was marching across the Danube to the statue of General Bem. It was only running and out of breath that Peter Veres, President of the Writers' Association, arrived in time to read out the manifesto of the writers. As Miklos Molnar concludes: "The movement of the writers had been passed by. It had accomplished its task, but was now finding itself lost in the revolution which had developed a life of its own."[39]

A dramatic turn was given to the events as the élite of writers and intellectuals — the earlier core of the opposition — was being pushed offstage by the nationwide upsurge of the masses. As one of the writers themselves has clearly recognised, "It was not we (the writers) who decided that there should be a revolution."

The journalists alone continued to act radically, at least in the editorial pages of their newspapers. On the morning of 23 October *Szabad Nep* gave direct encouragement to the students, praising their meeting of the night before as "a new spring parade".

Even the students, though it had been they who had mobilised the masses, almost turned back when they realised what they were doing. Student delegates had gone to the factory gates in the early morning of 23 October where they had held impromptu meetings and been greeted enthusiastically by the workers. At many factories the workers had offered to stop work for the afternoon, to show their solidarity with the students, and so that any who wanted could march in the demonstration. The student leaders, however, demanded that the workers should not strike, nor join in the demonstration, lest this should provoke the régime. They also insisted that the demonstration should be a silent one, and that the students should march in closed ranks. Some, fearing the demonstration might get out of control, even considered calling it off.

Had it not been for the law students who turned up at assembly points with banners and duplicated lists of slogans, the attempt to tone down the demonstration might well have succeeded. As it was, the day's developments dismayed and frightened many of the students. One has expressed how he and most of his friends felt: "If we are unable to put on the brakes, the situation will get out of hand and nothing good can come of it."[40]

As for the "Imre Nagy group", the more the revolution approached, the more they became disconsolate and disunited. Remaining for the most part political reformists who refused to act outside the official channels and procedures of the Communist Party, none of them had sought to mobilise a mass demonstration, let alone an armed uprising. The events, however, soon passed them by, and within the following days the Imre Nagy group was to fall apart into its component parts, each of which went its separate way.

While the students had been preparing to act, Imre Nagy himself had been on holiday near Lake Balaton. When he returned to Budapest at midday on the twenty-third, some of the closest of his friends — Losonczy, Gimes, Vasarhelyi, Janosi and Haraszti — met him to discuss the latest developments with which he appeared both unacquainted and surprised. While Gimes appealed to him to place himself at the head of the demonstration, Nagy refused even to take part, and stayed out of town all day in his Buda villa. Only in the evening after many appeals, and not until officially requested to do so by the Politburo, did he finally agree to go and address the crowd outside the Parliament. Even then his speech was far from inspiring, and served only to lessen the crowd's earlier enthusiasm for him.

Nagy's "first lieutenant", Geza Losonczy, spent the evening of 23 October in the editorial offices of *Magyar Nemzet,* together with a number of his journalist associates. Another journalist who sought them out there reports that they were all looking depressed and felt that the situation had been hopelessly spoilt by Gero's speech and the fighting at the Radio building.* "They sat there in total impotence," he recalls. As the fighting outside reached new heights, as the Soviet tanks sped towards Budapest, this group — later to be cast by the Hungarian authorities as "counter-revolutionary conspirators against the people's power" — adjourned to the New York Café where we are told, while the fighting raged in the streets, "the waiters served us with the utmost calm". Some urged Losonczy to go to the party headquarters and demand government changes in response to the unrest. But Losonczy was very reluctant to act. He tried to telephone to Imre Nagy, but was unable to speak to him. He finally agreed to go to the party headquarters, but didn't. As this journalist concludes, "Losonczy didn't know what he should do now," and he was afraid to act lest he be held responsible for the outbreak of revolt.[41]

A similar scene was also to be witnessed at the headquarters of the Writers' Association. The writers did send delegations throughout the night to the party headquarters, but each returned in complete despair. As one eye-witness recalls: "The Writers' Association wrote four memoranda that night . . . the fourth was written in so delicate a tone as to be almost spineless, but even this was opposed by Gero and the rest."[42]

One writer describes the scene he encountered on turning up at the Association in the following words:

> "Those who are now the heroes of the revolution had very long faces. They didn't really know what was going on, but they did know that they didn't feel happy about it. Disoriented . . . lost . . . very much behind events . . . they didn't take any part in the actual revolution."[43]

---

*Gero's uncompromising speech and the first outbreaks of fighting at the Radio building on the evening of 23 October are described in more detail on p. 113.

Even several of the journalists who had previously been the most radical of the opposition's members felt far from enthused by the sudden outbreak of revolt, fearing that the gains made in the last few months might be lost because of this unruly mob behaviour. A young journalist present in the crowd outside the Parliament found it difficult to believe his ears when he overheard two men he recognised as Miklos Gimes and Gyorgy Fazekas declaring that the crowd were acting like idiots and saying in apparent despair that "this isn't what this is all about now". There was nothing wrong, however, with our observer's ears. The fact was indeed, as another journalist recalls, that, "Many of those who had opposed the communist system during the last years felt that a tragedy had happened."[44]

2 The Ideology of the Opposition and the Government of Imre Nagy

"An illusion has been created: if treacherous leaders have spoiled things the honest leaders can easily put them right."

Hungaricus, December 1956

As the previous chapter has indicated, many tendencies came together to constitute the movement of opposition to the Hungarian stalinist régime.

Some of the older generation of writers, particularly those who had spent the war and the prewar years in the West in exile from the right-wing Horthy régime, were — even when they happened to be Communist Party members — often influenced by Western social-democratic and liberal traditions. Others of this generation were idealists who had been drawn to the communist movement by the inspiration of such men as Lenin and Bela Kun far more than by Stalin and Rakosi. Of those who had stayed in Hungary throughout the prewar years, many were adherents of the school of Hungarian populism — the belief that Hungary could advance to socialism by a "third road" programme based on the peasantry and led by the intelligentsia. Even many leading members of the Communist Party were influenced by this tradition, particularly those connected with the People's Colleges and subsequently active in the Petofi Circle.

The majority of the opposition's members, however, were drawn from those younger intellectuals who had enthusiastically joined the Communist Party in the forties out of abhorrence at the deeds of Hitler and the Nazis. Soon to become the most loyal and uncritical disciples of stalinism, the members of this group included most of the Party's younger journalists as well as the more talented of the young communist writers. Once disillusioned by the revelations of the early fifties, it was these former militants who were destined to become the most passionate and determined opponents of the régime and the pacesetters of the opposition.[1]

Made up as it was of these differing and often divergent tendencies, the opposition movement as a whole never came to adopt any single or united doctrine. Its ideology, if it can be said to have had one, was rather an uneasy amalgam of varying and divergent trends, often themselves in the process of continuing change.

The views of Imre Nagy himself were neither more nor less a unified ideology than those of the opposition, but he was one of the few people to attempt to put them together in any consistent and coherent form. Moreover, as the figurehead of the opposition, his views certainly provided the focal point of their demands for change, and as leader of the government in the turbulent days of the October revolution he was to make the attempt to put their policies into practice.

Nagy had set about formulating his views following his removal from power in March 1955, when the party leadership had denounced him for "right-wing deviation" and called upon him to practise self-criticism and confess his errors. Instead of retracting his views as demanded, Nagy sat down to write a series of dissertations aimed at justifying his former actions, on the basis of which he hoped to be able to campaign for his readmission to the party. It is these dissertations, written mostly over the summer of 1955 and with a few additions completed in the following winter, which constitute the most formed version of Imre Nagy's political views, and it is on them that the present analysis of his contribution to the ideology of the opposition will be based.[2]

The communism of Imre Nagy

Imre Nagy himself cannot be seen as either an adherent to or a representative of any of the different tendencies within the opposition. Indeed, it would probably be wrong to see him as an intellectual in the same way that many of his supporters were, let alone as an ideologist. His overriding motivation was not one of ideas — neither ideals nor theories — but rather one of human feeling, of compassion for his fellow men. He was more of a social moralist than a radical politician, and it is this characteristic that makes his ideas so difficult to classify or systematise. If anywhere, the essence of Imre Nagy's "ideology" is perhaps best expressed in Marx's call to the First International, which Nagy himself quotes, for the defence of "the most simple basic laws of morals and justice, which must rule the relations between private individuals, and which must also be the chief laws governing the contact between nations."[3]

It is these basic moral and social values of justice, fairness, decency, and respect for all other men as equals, which form the foundations of Imre Nagy's views on almost all the issues of domestic and international politics. It is also Imre Nagy as a man representing in himself these basic human values, rather than as a man of either action or theory, that accounts for the warmth and sympathy felt for him by his supporters and admirers. He was for them "a communist who has chosen the people", and the representative of "a communism which has not forgotten mankind".[4]

But Nagy was not just a decent, fair and humane person, not just the congenial "Uncle Imre" as his younger followers came to know him. He was also a lifelong member of the Communist Party apparatus, who had first joined the Communist Party as a participant in the Russian Revolution and Civil War. Following the overthrow of the Hungarian Soviet Republic of 1919, he had spent over fifteen years as a Comintern functionary in exile in the Soviet Union, and after returning to Hungary in 1944, he had spent a further eight years as a fairly docile and conformist member of the communist administration. Indeed, at the height of Rakosi's stalinist régime, Nagy had behaved in thoroughly conformist fashion, and on the morning after Stalin's death it had been Imre Nagy who delivered the eulogy before the Hungarian Parliament in which he referred to Stalin as "the great leader of humanity". Moreover, in his dissertations written during 1955 in defence of the New Course of his government, he continually quotes Stalin in his support and denounces his opponents for following "anti-stalinist policies" which Nagy sees as differing little from those of the Left Opposition in the early years of Stalin's rule in Russia.

That Imre Nagy could express himself in such a way shows up his central and most tragic weakness — the lack of any clearly thought-out ideological standpoint beyond his commitment to the vague values of humanism and decency. Throughout most of his life his political actions were to be based on an almost unshakable faith and loyalty to the Communist Party, on a trust which meant in practice a strangely stubborn and self-willed subservience to the narrow interests of the existing party bureaucracy. Unlike the more extreme stalinists who clearly sought to use the bureaucracy as a means for implementing their own ends, and unlike other reformist communists who sought to moderate the role of the bureaucracy, Nagy very rarely, and perhaps never consciously, rose above the level of the functionary within the machine, albeit a very decent and reasonable functionary.

What was unique about Nagy, what separated him from the normal party functionary, was as Miklos Molnar has remarked that:

"Party work was unable to kill the human being in him, party policies did not make him forget the 'idea'. . . .

Imre Nagy had also gone to the party school, the Comintern, the Kremlin, and the Budapest Party HQ palace revolts and intrigues, which killed off in all party leaders the ideals that had once driven them to the Communist Party. Nagy is one of the rare, very rare, exceptions."[5]

But Nagy, while still believing in the ideals, refused to see any contradiction between them and the system through which he sought to achieve them. He lacked any ideological comprehension of the relationship between the ideals and the realities, any key to the interrelationship of theory and practice. Consequently when he sought to impose his ideals upon the system and when the system refused to go along with the ideals, he was to be rapidly passed over by events. When the revolution broke out he was to find himself without any means of orientation in a world which had already broken in practice the bonds within which he was still held captive by the limits of his own thought.

This is, however, to jump more than a few steps of the argument. First it is necessary to examine in a little more detail the main features of Nagy's thought.

The revisionism of Imre Nagy

From the outset, Nagy makes it clear that for him marxism is not a system of rigid and absolute dogmas, but a theory which is dynamic and continually developing, capable of enriching itself by discovering new truths and discarding old ones. Marxism is a science and as such, unlike previous idealist philosophies, lays claim to no absolute and eternal truths. For Nagy, "Marxism is a science that cannot remain static but must develop and become more perfect. . . . There are no eternal, never-changing teachings which remain applicable regardless of time or space and independently of concrete situations."[6]

Marx and Engels, Nagy declares, did not bind the hands of future generations with their theories. Rather he contends, citing Lenin in his support, that "Marx's theories must be expanded in all directions, in order to keep pace with life." Nagy frequently cites Lenin's assertion that life is always richer than any theory, and argues that "marxist-leninist theory teaches us that if in practice, in life, a theory is disproved, this theory should be reexamined." From this standpoint he accuses his opponents within the Hungarian Party of "resurrecting their theory which has been shattered by life", of drawing theoretical conclusions on the basis of preconceived notions rather than scientific analysis. The result, Nagy claims, is a contradiction between theory and practice, and the falsification of marxism itself.

As against the past dogmatic interpretation of marxism, he calls upon communists to be prepared, "to learn from past experience, to search for the roots of the errors, and to listen to Lenin"; only in this way can marxist-leninism be creatively applied to actual situations.

The rigidly dogmatic interpretation of marxist-leninism, Nagy continues, developed in the Soviet Union after Lenin's death and resulted in serious theoretical mistakes. The time has now come to "return to Lenin's teachings", and to reject the viewpoint according to which the history of the Soviet Union provides the only and exclusive model for constructing socialism. As against this, Nagy argues:

> "All nations will arrive at socialism — this is inescapable —but they will not arrive there in a completely identical fashion. . . . The concrete ways and means of achieving this change are necessarily very diverse and they must remain so."[7]

This principle, Nagy contends, had been reaffirmed by the Soviet leaders in the declaration issued on the occasion of their reconciliation with Marshal Tito in Belgrade. According to it, the exact methods of building socialism are strictly the concern of individual nations, and marxist theory must be applied flexibly according to the specific conditions of the countries concerned. In this way can peaceful co-existence be achieved and the monopoly of marxism by any one country eliminated.

Here Nagy has employed his undogmatic interpretation of marxism, backed up by quotations from Lenin and recent declarations of Soviet leaders, to assert the principles of different national roads to socialism, peaceful coexistence, and even polycentrism within the socialist camp. Essentially, and this is really the whole point of the exercise, he has established the right of Hungary to build socialism on an independent basis, on the basis of specific Hungarian conditions through, in his words, "the applications of the teachings of marxism-leninism to the concrete Hungarian situation."

Nagy's belief in an independent Hungarian road to socialism is also combined with a rejection of the mechanical application in Central Europe of the dictatorial methods of building socialism which were employed in the Soviet Union under very different historical circumstances. He argues that the dogmatic interpretation of the concept of "people's democracy", which demands identical developments irrespective of the diversity of conditions, "rigidly prevents the working-out of the characteristic forms of socialism". This has resulted in the people's democracies being deprived of any popular or democratic characteristics. In contrast, Nagy suggests that the people's democracies should have developed the widest possible co-operation:

> ". . . developing towards socialism by systematically decreasing the use of force to eliminate existing differences.
>
> . . . utilising democratic forms and methods in the interest of close co-operation on the widest possible scale with the masses of working people."[8]

The dictatorial methods of "the leftist crackpots", as Nagy calls them, have undermined the confidence of the working masses in the Communist Party and are thereby jeopardising "the power of the proletariat". Rakosi and Gero are roundly condemned for "the attempt to solve with revolutionary rules the most crucial and complex question of the transition — instead of taking the course of gradual development via progressive reforms."[9]

As against the dictatorial imposition of socialism from above, Nagy argues for "gradualism", greater flexibility in politics, and the exercise of more patience and consideration with regard to the intelligentsia, the petty bourgeoisie and the peasants. The dictatorship of the proletariat, as Nagy sees it, is to be achieved by the democratic co-operation of different classes.

The set of beliefs which Nagy has here asserted constitutes the core of what in the history of marxist thought has usually been known as "revisionism":

— the replacement of marxism as an absolute dogma by marxism as an action-guiding but flexible theory;

— the replacement of "proletarian internationalism", in the sense of mechanical conformism to the Soviet model, by the principle of different national roads to socialism;

— the replacement of revolutionary transformation by gradualism and progressive reforms;

— the replacement of class struggle and proletarian dictatorship by class collaboration and democratic co-operation.

Just how Imre Nagy envisaged these principles being realised in practice, just how he hoped to apply them to "the concrete Hungarian situation", we shall see by examining his more specific proposals concerning the economic, political, and cultural questions of building socialism in the period of transition from capitalism.

Building socialism

Large parts of Nagy's writings consist of efforts to refute the charges made against him that, as the leading spokesman of "right-wing deviationism", he was opposed to both socialist industrialisation and the socialisation of agriculture.

Nagy is adamant that at no point in his career has he ever rejected the aim of socialist industrialisation and the constant development and expansion of production. Indeed, the constant expansion of the means of production is, for him, a basic economic law of socialism. During his premiership, he asserts, "the development of the means of production, including industry, heavy industry . . . was the primary goal". At the same time, he has no hesitation in attacking what he describes as "ultra-industrialisation" — the excessive tempo of over-hasty industrialisation. To criticise this, however, is not to give up the aim of socialist industrialisation. The point is rather that the expansion of production under socialism must never lose sight of the ultimate goal of socialism — the raising of the people's standard of living. Expanding the argument, Nagy explains that the maximum satisfaction of the material and cultural requirements of society necessitates the constant raising of the standard of living of the people. This too is a basic economic law of socialism. While recognising that the raising of the standard of living itself depends on increased production, Nagy maintains:

> "Under socialist conditions it is inadmissible . . . that almost exclusively production means are produced . . . that the numerically growing people be forced to satisfy its needs at an unchanged or even declining level as in the period between 1945 and 1953."[10]

Getting right the balance between the production of industrial goods and the production of consumer goods is, for Nagy, the central problem in the construction of socialism. Through his policies, he promises to bring into harmony the further development of production forces with the further increase of the standard of living.

Such a policy, in its turn, cannot be successfully carried through without paying more serious attention to the development and expansion of agriculture, in order to satisfy the growing requirements of the industrial workers. The promotion of agricultural production is thus a key question in the development of socialism. During the years of ultra-industrialisation, however, while heavy industrial production had increased threefold, agricultural production had been left to stagnate, thus suffering a relative decline. The reconstruction of agriculture, Nagy argues, should have gone hand in hand with that of industry. In the present situation it was imperative to raise agricultural investment in order to increase agricultural production. This would in turn require the socialist reorganisation of agriculture, the development of large collective farms. Collective farming, Nagy declares, is the sole viable and effective road to increasing agricultural production and improving the lot of the peasantry.

However, having stated the principle, Nagy modifies his stand when he applies it to the actual Hungarian circumstances. It would simply not be possible, he contends, to realise both industrialisation and collectivisation at the same time. Nor would it be feasible to implement collectivisation at the same time as increasing agricultural production. Any attempt to achieve all these aims at once would, he warns, result in a drastic fall in the workers' living standards.

Consequently, Nagy rejects any prospect of immediate collectivisation in favour of a more "moderate tempo". Collectives should be encouraged, but only on the basis of free choice. Individual peasants should retain the freedom to leave the collectives if they so desire, and the collectives should be allowed to disband if a majority of their members so wish. At the same time, the independent peasant farms must also be allowed to expand and develop. For the foreseeable future two roads in agriculture — the socialised collectives and the independent peasant farms — would continue side by side. The eventual victory of socialism in the countryside would come about by the gradual and democratic transition from private farming to socialised collectives. Socialism, Nagy declares in opposition to the left-wing extremists who would establish it by force, cannot be built, "without the political co-operation, alliance and agreement of the working peasants and the peasant masses".[11]

The June road: the policies of the New Course

The general principles for the building of socialism which Imre Nagy has so far elucidated were put into practice in the policies of the New Course, the programme of his government from June 1953 to March 1955.

The basic statement of these policies was set out in the June 1953 resolutions passed by the Central Committee of the Hungarian Communist Party at the instigation of the Soviet leaders. At the time, however, Rakosi and his closest colleagues succeeded in preventing the publication of the resolutions — on account of the serious charges they laid against Rakosi and his associates for their actions and policies during the years of 1949 to 1953 — and they have never been published since. Nevertheless, Imre Nagy in his writings summarised what he considered the essential points of the New Course, while he also outlined his policies in his speech to the Hungarian Parliament on 4 July 1953.

Nagy's starting point is to locate the New Course within the transitional period from capitalism to socialism, and to relate it to the New Economic Policy (NEP) promoted by Lenin in the 1920s. During the transition period, he emphasises, the main task of the Communist Party is to lay the economic foundations of socialism. At the same time, it is the NEP which is the fundamental instrument of building socialism — "the NEP is the specific means and form of building socialism, and is absolutely necessary in every country where there is a sufficiently large number of small peasants".

The NEP represents a degree of compromise, based on the collaboration of the working class and the peasantry through the market exchange of goods between socialised industry and private agriculture. This is a compromise which prepares the ground for the eventual victory of socialism, for Nagy believes that the NEP will gradually wither away as the socialised sector of the economy expands.

Nagy argues that during the years of ultra-industrialisation from 1949 to 1953, the principles of the NEP were violated and the relations of production became unbalanced. This had brought socialism in Hungary to the verge of a catastrophe which could only be staved off by a re-evaluation of the methods of building socialism. The re-evaluation was provided by the June resolutions and the New Course which constituted a turning point of historic significance — "the first step towards the application of marxist-leninist tenets to fit specific Hungarian conditions".

At the same time, Nagy is quick to point out, the New Course did not involve any change in the overall strategy or the main goal of building socialism. It gave expression to new tactics within a constant strategy; it was a change of course within a given period, a minor transition within the wider transitional period. As a result of the policies of ultra-industrialisation pursued by the previous party leadership, the ratios of development had become unbalanced. While the production of heavy industry was much too high, agricultural production had come to a standstill, and the standard of living was deteriorating, leading to increasing dissatisfaction in the working class. The New Course was needed to bring the ratios of production back into balance, by slowing down the rate of increase in production of capital goods for heavy industry, and channelling investment released from this field into the increased production of consumer goods and the development of agriculture.

More specifically, the basic policies of the New Course were outlined in Nagy's parliamentary speech of 4 July 1953, in which he declared his government's aims as being:

> "to slow down substantially the pace of progress in heavy industry, which manufactures instruments of production . . .
>
> to place much greater stress than before on light industry, which produces consumer goods and food . . .
>
> to increase substantially agricultural investments and the development of agriculture . . .
>
> to enable the continuous improvement of the living standard and the social and cultural position of the working people and above all the labouring class. . . ."[12]

To achieve these aims, Nagy proposed that the collectivisation of agriculture be slowed down, that individual farmers should be allowed to leave the collectives if they so desired, even to disband them if a majority so wished, and that the kulak list be abolished. To promote the supply of consumer goods, Nagy proposed not only to encourage light industry, but to permit private enterprise in the field of retail trade and small business.

These changes were to be carried out within an overall context of democratisation of public life. This meant an increase in the role of Parliament and in the authority of the Council of Ministers, and the enforcement of collective leadership, as well as the creation of opportunities for greater popular participation in public affairs through a reinvigoration of the People's Patriotic Front and the local councils. At the same time "socialist legality" was to be strengthened, all unjustly condemned political prisoners and deportees were to be released, and the forced labour camps were to be closed down.

That this reform programme was never carried out, that the determined resistance of the Communist Party bureaucracy prevented the thoroughgoing implementation of any single measure, is now a historical fact. The programme nevertheless stands as one of the most sincere and far-reaching sets of reforms ever to be put forward by a communist government in Eastern Europe. It also served to awaken the hopes and aspirations of both intellectuals and working people, to bring to their awareness the possibility of both change and progress. As Imre Nagy himself recognised, one of the major consequences of the New Course was to be "the unfolding political activity of the masses . . . the freeing of the spirit of criticism and self-criticism . . . (with) the inevitable consequence that . . . the party membership and the working masses began to criticise the leadership".[13]

The New Course and democratisation

Throughout his writings Imre Nagy's most constant charge against his opponents, and the one to which he returns over and over again, is that their reckless and scatterbrained policies are serving to alienate the people and shatter their faith in the Communist Party. In this process the dictatorship of the proletariat is degenerating into the dictatorship of a party clique:

> "Power is increasingly being torn away from the people and turned sharply against them. . . .
>
> The people's democracy . . . in which the power is exercised by the working class . . . is obviously being replaced by a party dictatorship . . . (in which) power is not permeated by the spirit of socialism and democratisation but by a bonapartist spirit of minority dictatorship."[14]

As against the autocratic views of the leadership clique within the party, Nagy declares his faith in the creative power of the masses. He argues that public opinion has become a powerful force which the party must recognise and respect, and that it is incumbent upon the party to win the support of the people for its everyday tasks. "There is no question," he asserts, "that we cannot calmly take to the people for their judgement." Indeed, the battle within the party is a battle to keep power within the hands of the people, and he throws down a challenge to the party leaders: "In the interests of the people, the country and socialism, let them depend not on bayonets but on the people."[15]

Nagy roundly condemns the situation in which force has come to be employed in so many aspects of social, economic, political and cultural life. While recognising the necessity for censorship in the arts, he objects to the proportions to which party intervention has grown, and demands a freer atmosphere for cultural work. Indeed, referring to the revolt of the writers, he declares, "I agree with their views and their standpoint on principles", and he praises their "united struggle for the freedom of literature".

The bonapartist dictatorship, however, is not seen just as an aspect of party rule over the non-party masses. The spirit of personal dictatorship had also come to rule within the party itself, destroying both collective leadership and democratic centralism. The result was that, "Instead of being led by elected party organs, the party was actually led by a clique". Bonapartism, führerism, clique dictatorship and the personality cult were destroying internal party democracy with the result that "party life, debate, the exchange of ideas, and the cleansing of ideological deviations through the free battle of opinions . . . are dying out".[16]

The result was on the one hand "administrative directives, terrorisation, vilification", on the other hand, "corruption . . . opportunism . . . servility". Nagy calls for the reinvigoration of internal party democracy, for the participation and debate which is laid down in the party's own rules as the fundamental right of party members. Exchange of views, conflict of opinions, and theoretical debate, is the basis of democratic centralism, and always necessary to prevent the degeneration of the party into führerism and bonapartism.

A democratised party should also be prepared to democratise its relations with the state. According to Nagy, the party has been guilty of expropriating the functions of state organs, of violating their independence, and discrediting their reputation. In this way, the entire constitutional system of the people's democracy had been distorted to serve the interests of the leadership clique rather than the interests of society. The result had been to undermine the belief in socialist legality.

Nagy calls for the restoration of their proper powers to the Council of Ministers, Parliament, and the courts, all of which had become "mere devices for personal dictatorship . . . in the hands of the bonapartist power". Socialist legality and the elimination of bureaucratism could only be restored by placing the judicial and state security systems "under the democratic control of the masses". To this end, local councils should be revived and the constitutional rights of citizens restored.

During the New Course, Nagy had sought to place the party's and the government's power on a broader and more democratic base by reviving the People's Patriotic Front as a mass organisation which would organise support for the party and the government's policies among the non-party masses. Nagy saw the function of the PPF as being to create "a federation that is supported by the masses . . . , a mass base wider and more extensive than the worker-peasant federation". It would also seek to unite the spirit of Hungarian patriotism with the ideals of democracy and socialism: "The idea of independence and freedom and our centuries-old traditions, which are a powerful force for moving the masses, must be fused with the concept of democracy and socialism."[17]

The PPF would work to mobilise in support of socialism those major sections of the intelligentsia and the peasantry which were not prepared to commit themselves wholeheartedly to the ideas of communism. In this way Nagy believed he could bring about the reconciliation of communism with the Hungarian people. Moreover, it was Nagy's intention that the PPF should be made up of individual members free to set up their own independent local branches and thereby to exert a powerful influence in the political life of the nation.

With his views on the role of the PPF, Nagy clearly envisages political activity being freely undertaken even outside the limits of the Communist Party. Although this is yet by no means to deny the leading role of the party — his commitment to which Nagy constantly reaffirms — it certainly implies the possible emergence of political forces which would have a certain independence of the party. That Nagy saw socialist democracy as involving such independent political activity also becomes clear from his analysis of the rise of bonapartism, where he argues that "the degeneration of power . . . dates back to those times when the clique headed by Rakosi . . . crushed the basis of Hungary's young democracy and liquidated our people's democratic forces and the democratic partnerships of socialism".[18]

And Nagy does not fail to point out that the bonapartist clique to which he refers came to power only after destroying democracy on two levels:

> "To bring about the triumph of bonapartism, the allies of socialist democracy had to be destroyed.
>
> To bring about individual dictatorship, the party's leading cadres had to be exterminated."[19]

These statements would seem to make it clear beyond all doubt that Nagy saw the degeneration of power not only in the elimination of internal democracy within the Communist Party, but also in the prior destruction of "Hungary's young democracy", of "the democratic allies of socialist democracy". Nagy could hardly have been referring by these phrases to anything other than the coalition system of government which had been overthrown in 1948, and the democratic parties then banned by the communists. The direct implication of these statements was surely that the ban against the democratic parties should be lifted, that a return to the coalition based upon them should not be ruled out.

In sum, Nagy's rejection of what he termed the bonapartist dictatorship of the Rakosi-Gero clique led him to demand the restoration of democratic rights both within the Communist Party itself and within the political life of the nation as a whole. While such demands implied the relinquishing of the Communist Party's monopoly of power, Nagy saw in them no threat to the future of socialism, for he believed:

> "The party membership and the Hungarian people . . . do not want a return to capitalism. . . . They want a people's democracy where the working people are masters of the country and of their own fate, where human beings are respected, and where social and political life is conducted in the spirit of humanism."[20]

Imre Nagy and Hungarian independence

Nagy's faith in the Hungarian people leads him to support not only democracy but also patriotism, which he defines as love of his country and his people, declaring: "As a son of the Hungarian people and as a man of the Hungarian nation I am proud of my Hungarian past."[21]

Such patriotism, he asserts, is in no way contrary to the internationalist principles of socialism, for: "Socialism should not deprive the people of their national character, nor of their national sentiments and qualities; on the contrary, it is with these that people enrich and universalise the moral-ethical values of socialism."[22]

Nagy violently condemns the viewpoint according to which socialism supersedes nationalism, and the internationalist extremists who have turned against the national feelings of the Hungarian people. For Nagy, "true patriotism, together with a love and respect for other peoples and nations, is the basis and essence of proletarian internationalism".

Indeed, Nagy believes that patriotism will be enriched and strengthened under socialism which, in abolishing class society, makes national unity and independence really possible for the first time. Capitalism had failed to realise national independence because the bourgeoisie had subordinated the universal interest of the nation to its own class interest. The working class, however, has no interests apart from those of the nation, and can only liberate itself by liberating the whole of society. The working class is consequently a more consistent fighter for the ideals of independence and freedom than was the bourgeoisie, and in this struggle it will win over to its side the powerful petty-bourgeois strata of the population, including the majority of the peasantry, thus creating "a popular unity wider than the worker-peasant federation".

Nagy also bases his claim for national independence on the five principles of international relations — independence, sovereignty, equality, non-interference in internal affairs, and self-determination — which had been laid down at the Bandung Conference of non-aligned nations in 1955. These principles were gaining increasing influence in an era marked by the anti-colonial revolutions in Africa and Asia, the growing thaw in East-West relations, and the expanding role of the United Nations. They had also been declared the basis for settling international problems by the communiqué issued in Belgrade on the occasion of Khrushchev's rapprochement with Tito.

These principles, Nagy declares, should not be limited to the capitalist system, but must also be the basis for relations between countries in the socialist world. They are necessary as guarantees that within the socialist camp, the independence, sovereignty, and equality of individual nations will be preserved. Nagy asserts that no nation can be free if it is not independent, and that the socialist camp must become an association of free and sovereign nations, respecting the principle of non-interference in each other's affairs. In this way, he believes, the socialist camp can become the rallying point for the newly emerging independent nations of the third world.

However, Hungary should recognise that it is a member not only of the socialist camp but also of "the great community of nations". If a nation is to be sovereign and independent within this wider community, it must also have the right to pursue its own independent foreign policy. Moreover, in a world dominated by big power groups, it is important for small countries such as Hungary to avoid either belonging to a power group, or becoming a pawn on their fields of battle. The best solution for such countries, Nagy concludes, is a policy of "neutrality or active co-existence". Indeed, in a sentence which Nagy's friends left out of the versions of his writings published in the West, but which Nagy himself had indignantly refused to omit at the time, he had gone so far as to recommend "the possibility of neutralising Hungary on the Austrian pattern".

Such small countries should seek to co-operate with other similar countries, whatever their social systems, in order to defend themselves against the policies of the power groups. One means of doing so, he suggests, would be by a federation of the people's democracies of the Danube Valley, similar to Lajos Kossuth's proposals for a Danubian Federation at the time of Hungary's 1848 revolution. The time has now come, concludes Nagy, to return to the Kossuth ideals on which an independent Hungarian foreign policy can be based.

As in the question of democratisation, so here too Nagy has passed considerably beyond the bounds of communist orthodoxy. He has taken all the necessary steps to pave the way for the actions of his government during the revolution in withdrawing from the Warsaw Pact, declaring Hungarian neutrality and appealing to the United Nations. This was to be the culmination of what Imre Nagy had described as "the long, stormy, centuries-old battle for the independence and sovereignty of our nation", of Hungary's struggle "to find for itself a place in the family of nations".[23]

The "ideology" of Imre Nagy

From the account of the preceding pages, it would seem that there is perhaps more than a grain of truth in his opponents' allegations that Imre Nagy's beliefs represented a comprehensive system of right-wing views deviating substantially from the marxist-leninist interpretation of socialism.

Certainly his main ideas do appear to fit together into a quite coherent and comprehensive system, the main themes of which are: the interpretation of marxism as flexible theory rather than rigid dogma; the slowing-down of the pace of industrialisation coupled with a changeover to consumer goods and the expansion of agriculture; the rejection of forced collectivisation and the toleration of private enterprise in farming and retail trade; the replacement of one-party dictatorship by a democratic coalition; the replacement of class conflict by national unity, of ideological warfare by neutralism and peaceful co-existence. In sum, the belief that the class struggle is no longer the primary factor in either domestic affairs or international relations.

However, these ideas by no means stand out so clearly in the actual writings of Imre Nagy, nor are they so systematically expressed. Rather they are smothered amid a mass of self-righteous indignation and efforts at self-justification, and couched in a communist jargon that often distorts and obscures their significance. Moreover, the vast mass of Nagy's writings consists of detailed rebuttals of the charges made against him, efforts to prove by strings of quotations exactly what he had or had not said in the past. The charges against him are described as unfounded accusations, falsifications and libels, and he insists, "I have consistently represented . . . the correct marxist-leninist ideology . . . (and) I continue to do so." Again and again he asserts the rightness of "my standpoint, my rights, the correctness of my views, my marxist-leninist faith".[24]

The more radical and novel aspects of Nagy's ideas only become clear when this enshrouding verbiage of self-righteousness, common-sense moralising and third-rate marxist-leninist theorising is cleared away. It is thus very likely that Imre Nagy himself was the last person to be aware of the underlying clarity and system of his views. It is even unlikely that he realised just how far he had gone on any single issue in revising the basic tenets of marxism. Certainly his actions immediately before and in the first days of the revolution make it abundantly clear that he had not become aware of the full implications for political action of the far-reaching views he had expressed in his writings.

The central weakness of Nagy's position derived from the fact that, despite the radical divergence between his socialist ideals and the reality of the communist state, he believed that the errors and mistakes of the stalinist era were simply the result of the usurpation and misuse of power by a group of evil and unprincipled leaders. The disease had only affected the élite; it was not a structural defect in the system itself. It could be cured by "a changing of the guard", enabling a return to the correct policies and the noble ideals of socialism.

Nagy failed to see any fundamental contradiction between his idealistic beliefs in individual freedom, democracy, national independence, and humanism, and his continuing loyalty to the leninist party, the communist system, and the Soviet Union. Once the "anti-marxist, anti-leninist, left-wing extremists" had been removed, they would be replaced by honourable and reasonable persons who could not fail to be persuaded of the correctness of his views.

Imre Nagy's constant failure to see any conflict between the ideals he professed and the power-interests of the Communist Party is nowhere better illustrated than in the orthodox and mechanical way in which he reacted to the growing signs of mass dissatisfaction in the months preceding the revolution. The policies of the left-wing extremists, he declared, were bringing the country to the brink of catastrophe, and broad masses of the people were turning ever more openly against the party and the government. However, far from meeting such a popular movement with enthusiasm, the prospect of it merely drives Nagy back into his role as the party functionary who denounces it as the spread of reaction and counter-revolution. Far from recognising such a movement as a possible basis for the realisation of his ideals, Nagy sees the first priority as safeguarding the interests of the party bureaucracy by controlling and rechannelling the dissatisfaction of the masses. As he writes:

"Today probably a return to the policy of the New Course

and the application of the June principles . . . could still check the growing crisis and avert catastrophe.

But it is doubtful whether a return to the June principles would suffice as a solution tomorrow. . . . Before long, there is a danger that the masses, having lost their faith, will reject both the June way and the Communist Party, and it will become necessary to make a much greater retreat in order to keep the situation under control."[25]

Nagy confronted by the revolution

When the revolution broke out, Imre Nagy's first reactions to it were more in line with his actions in the months and years preceding it than with the more radical ideas he had recently expressed in his writings.

During the increasingly stormy months before October, he had consistently rejected the demands of the more radical of his followers for the creation of any clandestine organisation, of any organised opposition, and of any political actions outside the official limits of the Communist Party. A typical illustration of his attitude is provided by an instance when a former social democrat suggested that the opposition should seek to revive the trade unions and mobilise them in their support. Nagy was outraged by the very idea. Under socialism, he declared, trade unions no longer acted as interest groups, let alone political pressure groups, but must serve as transmission belts to help propagate and implement the government's policies.

This naive and stubborn orthodoxy in one who had expressed such unorthodox and radical notions, and who had been so consistently rejected and persecuted by the communist leadership in both Budapest and Moscow, is one of the most puzzling features of Nagy's character. Even during his first government in 1953, he had seemed to think he could carry through his reform programme without having a single committed supporter amongst his colleagues in the government and party leadership — "not even a secretary in whom he could trust". He appeared to believe that his opponents would dutifully implement the new party line, just as obediently as he had served them when he had been in the minority. Equally calmly, Nagy seemed quite willing to accept his defeat when Rakosi finally prepared to bring his short premiership to an end. "He would not fight back," recalls one of his young supporters, "even though they were preparing the noose around his neck, because of his ideas about party unity."

His friends had been even more discountenanced when, shortly after the replacement of Rakosi by Gero, he had accepted an invitation to meet the new leadership of the party. Cautious and on his guard, he had gone to the Central Committee headquarters with a group of his supporters, who waited in a nearby café, on the understanding that they would immediately alert his family and other friends should he not return by midday:

> "Midday had already passed, and his friends were getting ready to carry out his instructions, when Nagy reappeared, beaming and relaxed. 'With people like these, one can truly discuss things . . .!' he declared to his dumbfounded friends."[26]

Later, when this same party leadership prepared to readmit him to membership of the party, Nagy is alleged to have promised to free himself from the influence of his intellectual supporters, who it was said were working behind his back to undermine the party.

This dogmatic loyalty and trust in the party, despite both his principles and its practices, seems to have stemmed from a naive dedication to democratic centralism, a belief not only in its possibility in some ideal leninist party, but its reality in the corrupted and deformed Hungarian party itself. Despite the radical nature of his ideas, despite his clear recognition of the degeneration of the Hungarian party, it was to be way beyond the eleventh hour before Nagy would even consider acting outside the official framework and beyond the strict limits of party constitutionality.

As his biographers Miklos Molnar and Laszlo Nagy point out, he had passed beyond the frontiers of all existing communist régimes, yet he still continued "to nourish certain illusions . . . and consider himself a communist loyal to his party". In their opinion the political thoughts and the ideology of Nagy were much closer to the "radical wing" of his group, while it was his character that inclined him towards the methods of moderation. He was consequently to become a revolutionary despite himself:

> "He became the founder of new ideology although he wanted nothing but to preserve the purity of the old ideology."
>
> "Destroyer of the Hungarian Communist Party, he was also its last defender."[27]

Such an interpretation certainly seems to fit best with Imre Nagy's reaction to the outbreak of the revolution on 23 October. Meeting with his leading supporters around midday, he expressed his agreement with the changes in Poland, but voiced extreme caution concerning the Hungarian situation, and strong opposition to the students' demonstration. Already a split began to develop between him and the most vocal of his friends — urged to place himself at the head of the demonstration, he flatly refused, declaring that he would not have a hand in any "coup" but would act only at the request of the party.

Later in the evening, as angry crowds gathered at different points of the town, Nagy resisted repeated appeals from his supporters to go and address the demonstrators. Finally, and then only when asked to by the Politburo, Nagy agreed to come into the city and speak to the crowds outside the Parliament. On first seeing the streets full of people, he seemed tense and stupefied, expressing both amazement and horror at the sight of national flags from which the communist emblem had been torn out. With the first words of his speech he turned the crowd's attitude towards him from wild acclamation to bitter mistrust. "Comrades!" he began. "We are no longer Comrades!" they roared back. Far from rising to the occasion and declaring his solidarity with the people, Nagy expressed once again the constitutionalist mentality of the party functionary, explaining: "The possibility of a proper outcome will be found in negotiations and the resolution of problems at the centre of the party."[28]

Invited to head the government, Nagy seemed prepared once more to provide his prestige to bolster up the discredited party leadership, and to accept his reintegration into the party and governmental system. Many of his friends, increasingly disillusioned if not yet embittered, considered his action a capitulation, and prepared instead to throw their support directly behind the people. Geza Losonczy and Ferenc Donath refused to accept their election into the Central Committee, and demonstratively left the party headquarters.

Nagy, meanwhile, was prepared to agree to the imposition of a curfew and martial law, and to call upon the insurgents to lay down their arms. In his first radio broadcast as Prime Minister on 24 October he spoke of "hostile elements (who have) turned against the people's democracy". The following day he was to assert that "a small number of counter-revolutionaries have launched an armed attack on our people's republic" and to claim that the Soviet intervention had been necessary to preserve the vital interests of the socialist order.[29]

Some writers have suggested that during these first two days Imre Nagy was held prisoner by the AVH (state security force), that his broadcasts were either forcibly pre-recorded or actually made at gunpoint. Other commentators suggest that Nagy was more a prisoner of his own former ideas. As one of his supporters seeks to explain:

"Nagy was not a prisoner of the AVH or the Rakosi-Gero

group. He was a moral prisoner of his own loyalty which did not leave him even in that extremely critical moment."[30]

The party to which he had dedicated his life needed him, and he had been waiting for its call. By answering the call of duty he was not only admitting the rightness of the party, but establishing also the rightness of his own views and actions, the only validator of which was, if belatedly, the party. Moreover not only his loyalties to the party but the whole experiences of his life as a party functionary and member of the apparat led Nagy to act instinctively as though he were faced with a counter-revolutionary uprising, as though the sole aim were to keep the situation under control.

In like manner, though the views expressed in his writings had passed by a long way the limits of his reform programme of 1953, though he had recognised that a simple return to the policies of the New Course might no longer suffice, and though the masses had overnight cast aside the bonds of party rule, at the moment of crisis Nagy fell back mechanically into the position he had left in 1955, into the role of the nation's doctor with the now old "New Course" of reform. Thus, in his first broadcast on 24 October he had thought it sufficient to announce:

> "We will realise, as soon as possible, on the basis of the June 1953 government programme as I expounded it at that time in Parliament, the systematic democratisation of our country in every field of party, state, political, and economic life."[31]

That even under the pressure of revolutionary upheaval Nagy had still failed to see clearly the implications of his own stand is well evidenced by his first meeting in those days with a group of former opposition friends. Believing that he was cut off in party headquarters from the real events taking place in the streets, they had already made several unsuccessful attempts to contact him. However when they did meet, and Miklos Gimes tried to explain to Nagy that the people were demanding the return of the multiparty system, and that its acceptance was necessary to give the revolution a political channel and bring the shooting to a halt, Imre Nagy's indignant reply was: "Never! Over my dead body!"

Nagy accepts the revolution

Following the replacement of Gero by Janos Kadar on 25 October, and the flight of the most discredited of the old leaders from Budapest in Soviet tanks and planes, Imre Nagy gradually consolidated his power and moved slowly but surely into step with the revolutionary demands of the Hungarian people.

At first it looked as though Nagy was making greater concessions than he really desired in order to save what remained of communism in Hungary. Certainly he was struggling to keep up with events, after a short period of resisting even this. However, having taken the decisive steps, having crossed the Rubicon, Nagy was to throw himself into his new role as popular tribune and national leader with a verve and passion which was completely in opposition to his former reserve and hesitation. This was to lead Bela Kovacs, the Smallholders' Party leader and a member of Nagy's final government, to remark to a Western journalist on the very day the Russians renewed their onslaught on Budapest: "My fondest memory of Nagy will always be his transformation from an easygoing, jolly, studious professor into a flaming revolutionary."[32]

It seems to have been the great surge of popular opinion, represented in the unceasing flow of delegations coming to see Nagy, that convinced him both of the validity of the revolutionary cause, and the need for his government to step into stride with it. Quickly he came to feel that the spontaneous action of the masses had created a uniquely new situation, that what was emerging from the revolution was a national unity far surpassing previous political divisions. Casting aside his former hesitations, Nagy now assured the representatives of revolutionary committees from outside Budapest that not only was he in complete agreement with their demands, but he was preparing to go even further.

In the early morning of 28 October, Nagy prevented an attempt to wipe out an insurgent stonghold in the Corvin Alley, threatening his immediate resignation if the planned action was not called off. Then, at noon, he issued the order for an immediate ceasefire, and instructed the armed forces to fire only if attacked. Finally, in the evening, he declared in a radio broadcast that the government rejected the viewpoint that an attempt at counter-revolution had taken place. Rather:

> ". . . in these stirrings a great national and democratic movement, embracing and unifying all our people, developed with elemental force.
>
> . . . in the course of these battles was born the government of democratic national unity, independence, and socialism."[33]

This new government, Nagy promised, would begin at once to implement the people's just demands, first and foremost the dissolution of the AVH and the withdrawal of Soviet troops from Hungary.

With this speech, Nagy declared his solidarity with the basic demands of the revolution. In the next few days he was also to go along with the more radical demands for political democracy and national independence which had been raised by the revolution and which were also in line with the principles expressed in his own writings. Thus on 30 October, Nagy announced:

> "The Cabinet abolishes the one-party system and places the country's government on the basis of democratic co-operation between the coalition parties, reborn in 1945."[34]

At the same time he announced the formation of an Inner Cabinet designed to represent the new balance of forces. Its members were Imre Nagy, Janos Kadar and Geza Losonczy (Communists); Zoltan Tildy and Bela Kovacs (Smallholders); Ferenc Erdei (National Peasant Party), and "a person to be nominated by the Social Democratic Party".

The following day, in an impromptu yet passionate speech to an enthusiastic crowd outside the Parliament, Nagy announced that his government had opened negotiations for the withdrawal of Soviet troops and the renunciation of the Warsaw Pact. Passionately proclaiming his belief in an independent Hungary, Nagy declared:

> "We will tolerate no interference in our internal affairs.
>
> We stand on the principle of equality, national sovereignty, and national equality. . . . Long live the free, independent, democratic Hungarian Republic!"[35]

It is quite remarkable that this speech by Imre Nagy, in which he clearly states his government's intention to withdraw from the Warsaw Pact, was made before the rumours of new Soviet troop movements into Hungary had been confirmed, and a full day before the Politburo meeting at which the actual decision to withdraw from the Warsaw Pact was taken. Moreover, the following day when Nagy announced the decision to withdraw unilaterally from the Warsaw Pact and to declare Hungary's neutrality, he made no attempt to present this as a diplomatic move aimed at staving off a possible Soviet intervention, but spoke with the same fervour and passion as on the previous day. In a heroic struggle, he declared, the Hungarian people had realised a century-old dream, and achieved their fundamental national interest — neutrality.

Finally, on 3 November, the government announced the formation of a new enlarged Cabinet based on an even wider coalition of forces. Headed by Imre Nagy as Prime Minister and Minister of Foreign Affairs, the Cabinet included Pal Maleter as Minister of Defence and representative of the freedom fighters, as well as Geza Losonczy and Janos Kadar (Communists), Zoltan Tildy, Bela

Kovacs and Istvan B. Szabo (Smallholders), Istvan Bibo and Ferenc Farkas (Petofi Party), and Anna Kethly, Gyula Kelemen and Jozsef Fischer (Social Democrats).

Throughout the final days of the revolution Nagy and his ministers, while presenting themselves as a government "of democratic national unity", consistently stressed their adherence to the maintenance of socialism in Hungary. In his speech of 28 October, Nagy himself had warned against overlooking the achievements which the workers and peasants had gained over the past twelve years under the leadership of the Communist Party. In like manner, the leaders of the other parties in his government also declared their firm stand against any return to the old capitalist régime.

Bela Kovacs, the popular leader of the Smallholders' Party, declared: "No one must dream of going back to the world of counts, bankers and capitalists; that world is definitely over."

Anna Kethly, head of the Social Democratic Party, warned: "Freed from one prison, let us not allow the country to become a prison of another colour. Let us watch over the factories, the mines and the land, which must remain in the hands of the people."

Finally, at a press conference held on the eve of the second Soviet intervention, Minister of State Geza Losonczy warned of the dangers of counter-revolution, and affirmed the government's firm stand against them. "Counter-revolutionary forces are active," he acknowledged, but, "the government is determined not to tolerate the restoration of capitalism."[36]

While these statements provide some idea of how the men around Imre Nagy saw Hungary emerging from the revolution, other commentators went much further in claiming that the revolution was giving birth to a new and unique socio-economic system, combining the economic conquests of socialism with the political freedoms of democracy. In the words of the Polish communist journalist Wiktor Woroszylski:

> "It seems that we will be able to observe here a curious synthesis: a basic realisation of a popular democracy (land in the hands of the peasants, nationalisation of factories and banks) and of a pluralism of parties, freedom of press, and all the other liberties inherent in a liberal democracy."[37]

Imre Nagy: naive but defiant

"How naive Nagy was!" despairs one of his young followers, and even in the final days of the revolution, when he appeared at last to have become aware of the political consequences of his own position, his loyalties and trust in his communist colleagues and the Soviet leaders remained unruffled.

As rumours spread of renewed troop movements into Hungary, he at first refused to believe them. When they were confirmed, he still refused to believe that the Russians would really attack once again, preferring to accept their explanation that they were involved in manoeuvres to cover the withdrawal of their troops. Likewise, when informed of the curious disappearance of Janos Kadar and Ferenc Munnich on 1 November, Nagy was astonished but unable to believe in their treachery.

When the commander-in-chief of the National Guard, Bela Kiraly, telephoned Imre Nagy in the early hours of 4 November to tell him of the Soviet advance into Budapest, Nagy insisted that this must be an absurd mistake. Indeed the Soviet Ambassador Yuri Andropov was in Nagy's office, "trying to stop the slaughter"! As General Kiraly begged for permission to open fire, to defend the capital and issue a call for resistance, Imre Nagy angrily told him that only the government could make such decisions, and it had no intention of doing so. The freedom fighters, he insisted, must refrain even from returning enemy fire. "Up to the last minute," concludes General Kiraly, "Imre Nagy believed that he was not witnessing an act of infamy, but an unintentional disaster."[38]

Indeed, it was not to be until he could see with his own eyes the Soviet tanks lumbering into the very square before the Parliament building, that Imre Nagy went on the air to deliver his famous but brief announcement:

> "This is Imre Nagy speaking. . . . Today at daybreak Soviet troops attacked our capital with the obvious intent of overthrowing the legal democratic Hungarian government. Our troops are in combat. The government is at its post. I notify the people of our country and the entire world of this fact."[39]

The final sequel to this tale came some eighteen days later when Nagy and his colleagues prepared to leave the Yugoslav Embassy (where they had sought refuge at the time of the Soviet attack) after the Kadar government had promised them they would be allowed to return freely to their homes. The incident is reported by Miklos Molnar and Laszlo Nagy:

> "On 22 November a coach pulled up in front of the embassy building. An officer of the Hungarian police stepped out and informed the embassy officials that he had been sent by the Ministry of the Interior to conduct Nagy and his friends to

their homes. The officer made his way to the group of Hungarians, stopped in front of Nagy and came to attention, raising his hand to his cap. He then pronounced a few words in a lowered voice, which were as brief as they were unexpected: 'It's not to your home that you'll be going, Comrade Nagy. . . .'

The Prime Minister, taken aback by this declaration, returned into the building but, after a few minutes of discussion with his friends and the Yugoslavs, he came out again to get into the bus. Neither he, nor his friends, nor the Yugoslavs, had been able to believe the message which the police officer had delivered."[40]

After proceeding a short distance from the embassy, the coach was forced to a halt and surrounded by a number of Soviet tanks and police cars. The Yugoslav diplomats who were travelling with the Hungarians were roughly forced, over their protests, to leave the coach, which then drove off again escorted by Soviet tanks. The next morning a Hungarian government communiqué announced that Nagy and his friends had left Hungary — "at their own request" — for Rumania.

Besides his unshakable credulity and naivety, Nagy also stubbornly and defiantly maintained till the end of his life his conviction in the rightness of his own views and actions. Despite nineteen months of imprisonment and interrogation, he refused to "confess" to any errors or mistakes. Instead, he remained proudly loyal to his own beliefs which, we are told, throughout his prison days he feverishly continued to commit to paper. In the only sentence of these writings that has yet seen the light of day, he returns once more to his passionate belief in the national unity created during the revolution:

"This national unity (formed in the struggle for independence) embraced every class and every layer of society as well as every political tendency."[41]

Ever since his first return to Hungary in 1920, after the Russian revolution and civil war, Nagy had believed that he was the person chosen to reconcile the Hungarian people with communism. This belief stayed with him right to the end of his life. On the very day that he was sentenced to death, he proudly stood up and told the court that in his actions as Prime Minister during the revolution he had, for the second time in his life, offered the possibility of saving communism in Hungary. Moreover, he declared:

"I know that one day there will be another Imre Nagy

trial, in which I shall be rehabilitated, and three times as many will turn out to my funeral as went to Rajk's. The only thing I fear is that those who give the funeral orations will be those who now betray me."[42]

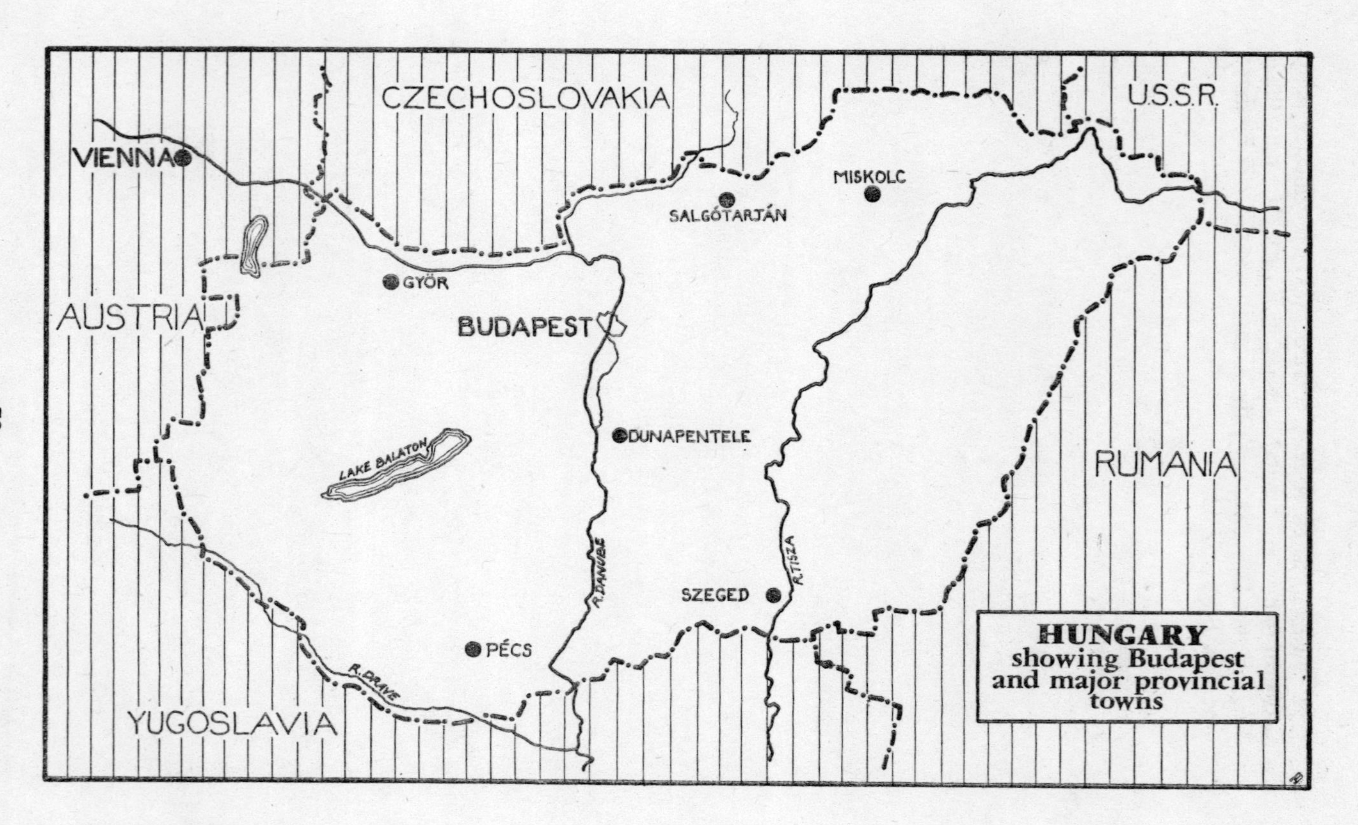

HUNGARY
showing Budapest
and major provincial
towns

3 The Provincial Towns: The Revolution Takes Shape

> "Socialism by its very nature cannot be decreed or introduced by *ukase*. . . . Only unobstructed, effervescing life falls into a thousand new forms and improvisations, brings to light creative force, itself corrects all mistaken attempts."
>
> *Rosa Luxemburg, 1918*

Most of the published studies of the Hungarian revolution have concentrated on the events in Budapest, the scene of dramatic armed combat between Hungarian freedom fighters and Soviet tanks, the scene of national political decisions and governmental changes. Little has been reported about events in the provincial towns, where the revolution developed a life of its own unrestrained by military conflict or political diplomacy. However, it is just possible — for the very reasons that made the events there different from those in Budapest — that a knowledge of the changes which took place in the provincial towns may provide a better key to an understanding of how the Hungarian revolution as a whole might have gone on to develop, had it not been suppressed by military force.

As in all true revolutions, the events taking place throughout the country did not fit neatly into any one pattern, but presented a multiplicity of disparate and diverse, spontaneous and often contradictory developments. Forces of reaction, of counter-revolution, were certainly present, though rarely predominant even in the more extremist mobs and fighting groups. Equally strong were the forces of socialist revolution — the students and youth, workers and intellectuals. In different towns, different forces came to the fore, different conflicts characterised the revolutionary upheaval.

In the following pages, illustrations drawn from the course of events in a number of different towns will be used to provide some pictures of the different social forces which were enmeshed in conflict, the different political tendencies at play, within the living turmoil of history presented by the revolution.

Szeged

The discontents of the students, which many observers have seen as the catalytic force that transformed covert dissent into manifest opposition, were first given open expression in the provincial town of Szeged, a university town situated on the banks of the river Tisza, which serves as the commercial and cultural centre of the southern part of the Great Hungarian Plain.

In the weeks before the revolution, the first demands for university reform at Szeged came, perhaps surprisingly, not from the students themselves but from the official authorities of the Communist Party and the university. At the beginning of the autumn term, the number of compulsory lectures was reduced, the students were offered a greater choice of courses, and arrangements were made for more student exchanges with other socialist countries. "All this came from above," we are told; but it seems to have sufficed to set in motion demands for further and more radical change.[1]

At the beginning of October, increasing discontent came to be expressed over the compulsory study of Russian by all students. It was particularly the students of law and medicine who objected to being forced to study a language which was of little use to their specialised studies. Similar complaints were expressed about the conditions of military service, and the hours of university time spent on National Defence training. The students were also dissatisfied with the DISZ (the communist youth league), an organisation in which they were grouped together with young workers and peasants. The students felt they needed a separate organisation to represent and defend the specific interests of university students. As one of them remarks, "I could never imagine a peasant boy representing university students."

The students held a meeting in the university on 16 October at which they decided to set up an independent student organisation (the MEFESZ) and to send delegates to other universities throughout the country to win their support. Meanwhile the activities of the Szeged students, together with equally strong if less organised discontent in Budapest and other university towns, was already calling forth a sympathetic response from the authorities. On 19 October, the Minister of Education announced the ending of compulsory Russian study, a re-examination of National Defence training, and a promise to send students on exchange scholarships to the West. By the time these reforms were announced, however, the demands of the students were becoming both more radical and more politicised.

The student movement in Szeged continued to gather strength

and, in co-operation with the recently created Szeged branch of the Petofi Circle, the students called a general assembly of all staff and students for 20 October. At midday handwritten leaflets were distributed in the university's central refectory, and in the afternoon the students marched from their hostels into the town centre for their meeting. The students were, "gay, self-confident, in holiday mood. . . . It was as unlike a political meeting as anything ever staged anywhere", recalls one Western journalist who was present. "Our aim," declared one of the students' leaders, "is the freeing of spirit . . . , the throwing off of the spiritual shackles with which Stalin and Rakosi have kept us in bondage."[2]

The meeting, at which the university rector and other professors supported the students, passed a resolution calling for withdrawal from the DISZ and the establishment of the MEFESZ as an independent body representing the students. Before the meeting had ended more political demands came to the fore, and a further resolution was passed which contained most of the points shortly to be demanded by the Budapest students. They included calls for a new government and party leadership, for new elections and the withdrawal of all foreign troops.

By the next day, however, the students of Szeged seemed somewhat dazed and nonplussed by the speed with which events had developed:

> "After the last big meeting we felt that: Tomorrow we colonise the moon!
>
> . . . Our demands were so far-reaching, we now felt them ridiculous, absurd . . . that everyone would laugh.
>
> . . . We felt our demands had been too high and too many. We didn't know what to do next."

Consequently the students of Szeged, whose initiative in setting up the MEFESZ has often been seen as the action that sparked off the revolution, were themselves taken by surprise when the revolution actually broke out.

The students heard of the demonstration in Budapest in the early evening of 23 October whereupon, assembling in front of their hostels, they marched into town and held a meeting in Kossuth Square. This first evening the police, the AVH, and the army all kept out of the way. On the next two days, however, troops guarded public buildings, and armed AVH men tried to break up crowds which assembled in the city centre, using tear gas to drive the demonstrators off the streets. Several student hostels were raided, and students questioned, searched and beaten up.

Only on 26 October did the armed forces withdraw from the

streets, whereupon the town hall, the AVH barracks, the newspaper offices and the radio were all taken over peaceably by student groups under the direction of a Student Revolutionary Committee which had been set up the previous day. Workers' councils were set up in the factories, and delegates from them united with representatives of the students and the town to set up a People's Revolutionary Council on 30 October. The Council co-ordinated strike action throughout the town, and declared its support for Imre Nagy. Student units were organised into a National Guard, and the forces of the Hungarian army in Szeged, though not coming out in open support of the revolution, co-operated with the Revolutionary Council in the maintenance of order.

A few days later, however, on 4 November, the city was occupied by Russian troops without any armed resistance, and the revolutionary organisations quietly disappeared.

All in all, the revolution at Szeged does not seem to have gone a great way beyond the actions of the students. Despite Szeged's reputation as a city of reactionaries, there is no evidence of any counter-revolutionary elements trying to take advantage of the situation. Nor does any really strong working-class presence seem to have been experienced here, and perhaps it is for this very reason that the revolution was to come to a standstill in the very town where it had been first set in motion. The students alone "didn't know what to do next".

Gyor

The events at Gyor, the largest provincial town in Western Hungary standing close to the Austrian border, provide one of the most fascinating and controversial episodes of the revolution. Indeed, Gyor has often been pictured as the foremost centre of open counter-revolution, and even such a critic of stalinism as Isaac Deutscher could write that at Gyor "the anti-communists — among whom the clergy were prominent — gained the upper hand". During the revolution itself the Polish communist journalist Wiktor Woroszylski visited Gyor to investigate reports he had received from Poland that "a Horthyite detachment coming from Austria had taken over here, that an autonomous government of clear-cut rightist character had been set up, and that it was headed by a fanatic Capuchin monk".

In the last days of October, similar reports appeared in the Western press to the effect that a "counter-government" had been set up in Gyor, that it had issued an ultimatum to Imre Nagy and was threatening to march on Budapest.[3]

In many ways, Gyor certainly provided the best opportunity for such developments. The natural centre of Western Hungary and so close to the Austrian border, it was perhaps inevitable that anti-communist sentiments should be most freely voiced here, and that counter-revolutionary adventurers should see it as a potential base for their ambitions.

It was not, however, only right-wing developments that were to be found in Gyor. In the early autumn a branch of the Petofi Circle had been established, and at a public meeting on 16 October addressed by the opposition writer Gyula Hay, outspoken demands were raised for the liberalisation of the régime and the withdrawal of Soviet troops. As one of those who was present has remarked, this meeting "prepared Gyor psychologically for the revolution; it literally revolutionised the city". Nevertheless, Gyor saw no scenes paralleling the student demonstrations in Szeged and Budapest, and as in Szeged the old régime was to continue without change through the first few days of the revolution.

The first small demonstration occurred on the afternoon of 24 October, when the young communist director of Gyor's local theatre, Gabor Foldes, led a group of twenty to thirty people into the town carrying a national flag and shouting, "We want freedom — Long live the Communist Party!" Joined by local high-school students and young apprentices, the demonstrators marched to the county offices of the Communist Party where Gabor Foldes gave a speech declaring that the students and workers fighting in Budapest were not fascists and counter-revolutionaries but honourable Hungarians fighting for freedom.

Meanwhile other sections of the crowd had been removing red stars and other communist emblems from public buildings, and had demolished the Soviet war memorial. In the evening another group of demonstrators broke into the local jail, disarming the prison commander and releasing the political prisoners. At this point AVH reinforcements arrived in trucks, and a conflict ensued in which the AVH eventually opened fire, killing some four people and wounding several more. During the evening they also arrested a number of students.

The next morning a crowd of several thousand gathered in front of the town hall, demanding the release of the students arrested the previous day, and the arrest of the AVH officer who had given the order to open fire. The ordinary police and local army units had now declared their support for the revolution, while the local Communist Party officials had slipped away over the Czechoslovak border. The only pillar of the old order still standing in Gyor was the AVH.

The crowd, which included many workers from the town's railway wagon factory as well as soldiers and peasants, lined up behind the students and apprentices and marched towards the barracks of the AVH. The AVH surrendered without resistance. The people then entered the barracks, released the prisoners, and seized a number of the officers whom they started to beat up. At this point some of the soldiers present rescued the AVH officers from the vengeance of the crowd, and took them into custody. The army also removed arms and ammunition from the barracks, to prevent them falling into the hands of the crowd.[4]

It was following these events, as the collapse of the old order in the town became clear to all, that the revolution in Gyor began to develop a momentum and organisation of its own. On the morning of 26 October, the strike became general throughout the town, and workers from all the town's major factories marched to the city hall where they elected a National Revolutionary Council to take over the town's administration. The majority of the Council's members were workers, several of them Communist Party members including the theatre director, Gabor Foldes.

Elected president of the Gyor National Council was Gyorgy Szabo, a skilled worker and foreman at the railway wagon works, and a former social democrat who had been imprisoned by the Hungarian fascists during the war. Vice-president of the National Council was Attila Szigethy, a former MP for the National Peasant Party and an old acquaintance and personal friend of Imre Nagy. He too had been imprisoned and in fact condemned to death by the Hungarian fascists, and since 1945 he had become a prominent local figure who had been able to co-operate with the country's communist rulers without losing the support and trust of the people of Gyor.

While Gyorgy Szabo was responsible for the organisational side of the National Council's work and was particularly active in the development of workers' councils throughout the town, Attila Szigethy was to emerge as the real figurehead of the revolution in Gyor. He became the main spokesman of the National Council, and when a National Council for the whole of Transdanubia (the Western half of Hungary) was created, he was to be elected as its president.[5]

Almost immediately upon its formation, the Gyor National Council was confronted with its first major test. News came of a massacre at the nearby village of Mosonmagyarovar, where the AVH had turned their machine-guns on an unarmed demonstration in the village square. The crowd had included many women and children, and almost a hundred people had been killed, some two hundred more wounded. When trucks carrying the wounded arrived in Gyor, the inflamed people seized cars and arms to rush to the scene of the fighting. Fearing an even greater tragedy if disorganised civilians joined in the fighting, Szigethy sent Gabor Foldes with an army detachment to disarm the AVH and try to prevent further bloodshed. Foldes' mission was successful, and the AVH surrendered without further resistance, though three or four of their officers who had been responsible for the bloodshed were seized upon and beaten to death by the angry crowd.[6]

Following its founding meeting the Gyor National Council broadcast a declaration over the radio to the Budapest government, calling for an end to the fighting and the withdrawal of Soviet troops from Hungary. The National Council based its political programme on the sixteen points of the Budapest students, adding to them demands for the disbanding of the AVH and the declaration of Hungarian neutrality. In support of these demands, the Council ordered that the general strike should continue throughout the county.

Meanwhile the network of local councils on which the National Council was based greatly expanded both in strength and organisation. The largest and most important workers' council was that of the railway wagon works, Hungary's largest railway wagon factory which employed over ten thousand workers. Other prominent workers' councils were those of the machine-tool factory, the textile factory and the printing works, as well as those set up by the miners of nearby Tatabanya and Balinka. It was in the course of organising the strike that the workers' councils were first established, but in the following days they quickly came to take over the functions previously performed by the trade union and Communist Party organisations in the factories. Section and personnel chiefs were almost everywhere dismissed, and new plant managers elected by the workers' councils. Similar councils were set up by the soldiers in the Hungarian army units stationed in Gyor. These soldiers' councils kept in contact with the workers' councils, while a Revolutionary Military Committee was established to coordinate their activities under the overall direction of the Gyor National Council. Still more councils were set up by the students and apprentices of the town's schools and technical colleges, as well as by committees of intellectuals and peasants.

All of these councils sent delegates to the Gyor National Council, which now took over complete control of the town's administration, appointing new people to replace the old officials who had mostly slipped quietly away. In this manner the local press was placed under the direction of the National Council, while the radio was placed in the hands of the theatre company under Gabor Foldes. Even the local Communist Party was re-formed and issued a proclamation declaring its support for the revolution and Imre Nagy, and calling for the disbanding of the AVH and the withdrawal of Soviet troops.

The National Council also entered into negotiations with the commander of the Soviet troops stationed at Gyor, who promised that the Soviet troops would not interfere in the Hungarians' affairs, so long as they were not attacked. Moreover, he declared that in his opinion the revolution was totally justified. In return for their neutrality, the National Council provided the Soviet forces with daily supplies of milk and food. By 27 October the National Council could justifiably claim that "in Gyor complete order and discipline reigns".

However, although the replacement of the old order by the new structure of councils appeared to have gone smoothly enough, many local people remained confused about just what was happening in Budapest, and what Nagy and his government were actually up to. This confusion was considerably increased by the broadcasts of Radio Free Europe, which announced that Imre Nagy had called in the Russian troops, that he and his government were murderers of the people, and that even the ceasefire was an act of treason. Moreover, quite a few people in Gyor had relatives who had been members of the fascist Arrow Cross Party during the war and who had fled to the West in 1945. Others came out on to the streets in their old army uniforms, in the belief that the collapse of the communist régime meant the return of the prewar system.[7]

The presence of these elements was no doubt responsible for the crowds occasionally developing bitter anti-communist moods, and they provided fertile soil for the activities of the small minority of extremist agitators who tried to exploit the situation. The combination of these circumstances led to a number of incidents which provided sensation-seeking Western journalists, and later the authorities of the Kadar régime, with grounds for allegations that in Gyor the "counter-revolutionaries" had gained the upper hand.

One of the first of such incidents occurred on 27 October, when a crowd demonstrated outside the town hall demanding the removal of Gabor Foldes from the National Council because he was a communist. Both Gyorgy Szabo and Attila Szigethy spoke out strongly in defence of Foldes and managed to quieten the crowd.

However, Foldes's somewhat melodramatic sense of his own importance seems even to have earned him the hostility of many of his colleagues on the National Council, and when a crowd again came to demand his dismissal the following day, Szigethy appears to have gratefully accepted his resignation. Indeed this time Foldes had to flee from the angry crowd who were threatening to lynch him.

Also on 27 October, a group of youths had demanded arms and trucks from the National Council to go to Budapest and take part in the fighting. Both Szabo and Szigethy had argued against such an expedition, warning that the road to Budapest was by no means safe. It was known that both Soviet and AVH troops might well be encountered, besides which the exact loyalty of the Hungarian army units in the area to be crossed was by no means certain. Some of the youths were dissuaded from going, but others commandeered a number of trucks and set out for Budapest. In the Pilis region, however, they were stopped by AVH and Russian troops who opened fire without warning. At least one truck returned to Gyor — "bloody and empty".

Up to this point, Attila Szigethy had been able to use his influence to dampen the wilder and less responsible spirits in the crowd, and to persuade the National Council to give its support to the government of Imre Nagy. Imagine his surprise, then, when on 28 October members of the government and the Writers' Association telephoned him and despairingly requested to know why he had set up a "counter-government" in Gyor in opposition to the Nagy government in Budapest.

The source of these rumours seems most likely to have been once again Radio Free Europe, and no doubt inspired by the same broadcasts a large crowd was to gather later in the same day outside the town hall where the National Council was in session. The crowd demanded the creation of just such a "counter-government", and the sending of military aid to the fighters in Budapest. This time many of the demonstrators were armed, and they sent a delegation into the town hall to press their demands on the National Council. Leading the delegation was a monk from the local Benedictine monastery, Father Iraneous Galambos — no doubt the basis for the stories that a "fanatic Capuchin monk" had taken over power in Gyor.

Attila Szigethy once more counselled against any military adventure, and argued that their forces might be needed to defend the revolution in Gyor itself. As for the demands for a counter-government, Szigethy declared, "That would be a cabaret, but no government!" and argued for a continued policy of conditional support for the Nagy government. Nevertheless, in order to meet the delegation's demands, the National Council agreed to send the government an ultimatum demanding that it bring an immediate end to the fighting. This action satisfied Father Galambos, who then returned to the crowd and helped dissuade them from attempting to implement their earlier demands. Father Galambos offered his help to Szigethy and was co-opted onto the National Council, while a number of the other protesters also placed themselves at its service.

In the evening, the idea of a counter-government was raised once again when Western journalists asked Szigethy why he continued to support Imre Nagy, and why he didn't set up a counter-government and ask for Western military help. Szigethy angrily replied that he had no intention of seeing Hungary sacrificed as a pawn in the cold war, and that he had every confidence in Imre Nagy.

However, the National Council received no direct reply to its ultimatum, and what news did come from Budapest was not terribly reassuring. Nor was the government's proclamation of 28 October, in which Nagy promised the disbanding of the AVH as well as the withdrawal of Soviet troops, deemed satisfactory. The people of Gyor wanted more definite action to end the fighting and implement the revolution's demands. Consequently, on 29 October the National Council broadcast a second ultimatum in which it threatened that if the government continued to ignore their demands for an end to the bloodshed, the people of Gyor would come to the assistance of those still fighting in Budapest. At the same time, Radio Gyor broadcast an appeal from a meeting of delegates from workers' councils throughout western Hungary calling for continued strike action until their demands were met, "until the last Soviet division has left Hungary!" Similar declarations in favour of continuing the strike were broadcast by several representatives of individual workers' councils, amongst them the coal miners of Balinka who declared, "Until these demands are met the miners of Balinka are not prepared to produce a single spadeful of coal."

Meanwhile the National Council at Gyor was establishing contacts with other revolutionary organisations in western Hungary, and it soon came to be felt desirable to set up a united political organisation to co-ordinate activities throughout Transdanubia. With this in view, invitations were sent out to every revolutionary committee in the area to send delegates to a meeting on 30 October to create a Transdanubian National Council. News of this meeting once again gave birth to rumours that an attempt was being made to set up a counter-government in Gyor, and also served to attract a handful of political adventurers who, no doubt encouraged by Western propaganda, saw themselves as its potential leaders. Thus it was that, as the delegates were arriving for their meeting on 30 October, the nearest thing to a counter-revolutionary putsch occurred in Gyor.

In the early afternoon three men arrived in a jeep from Budapest. Their leader, a man named Somogyvari, was wearing a white coat spattered with fresh blood, while his two companions carried machine guns. Gathering the crowd around him, Somogyvari explained that he had come directly from Budapest where the blood of patriotic Hungarians was still flowing. Imre Nagy, he declared, had lied on the radio: there was no ceasefire but continuing massacres of Hungarians by the state security force. He had come to tell the country the truth over the Gyor radio.[8]

Leading the crowd to the radio, Somogyvari forced his way into the director's office and demanded the right to broadcast. The radio's director explained that this first needed the authorisation of the president of the National Council, Gyorgy Szabo, but that Somogyvari could certainly record his broadcast on tape. This Somogyvari proceeded to do. His proclamation called upon the Transdanubian National Council to nominate him as Prime Minister of a counter-government which would launch a christian crusade against the Soviet Union. Somogyvari and his two companions then went to the town hall to find Gyorgy Szabo. Meanwhile, the radio director telephoned Szabo to warn him of his coming visitors and advised him to have them arrested. However, he added, Szabo should not worry if he were forced to give permission for the broadcast; the radio would not transmit it under any circumstances.

Somogyvari arrived at the town hall with a growing crowd he had succeeded in whipping up to near hysteria. His companions broke down the doors, forced their way into Szabo's office, and forced Szabo at gunpoint to telephone permission for the broadcast. Somogyvari then went out onto the balcony to listen with the crowd to his broadcast being relayed over the town hall loudspeaker. But after a short time, realising that his speech was not being transmitted, he began to harangue the crowd from the balcony. However, one member of the National Council managed to cut off his microphone, and members of the youth council began to circulate in the crowd arguing against Somogyvari's wild and irresponsible plans. Somogyvari now returned to the main hall of the building where, with the delegates to the Transdanubian National Council held at gunpoint by his aides, he started a tirade once more against "the traitorous Budapest government". Finally, he demanded that the Council should immediately declare itself a counter-government and appoint him its Prime Minister.

Meanwhile, amid the confusion, Gyorgy Szabo had managed to slip away to the railway wagon factory where the workers' council was in session, and where Attila Szigethy also happened to be. Szabo asked for help from the workers' council, and the workers led by their factory guards immediately set out for the town hall. "We don't want fascism," one worker is reported as saying. "We've had enough of tyranny, of whatever sort . . . and we won't renounce our newly-won liberty at any price." The workers' council also telephoned for reinforcements from the army command. A short while later, the soldiers and factory guards dispersed the crowd in the square, and when the armed workers entered the town hall, the aspiring Counter-Prime Minister and his henchmen smartly disappeared. The workers' council subsequently appealed over the radio to all workers to remain calm, "and not to listen to demagogues and provocateurs advocating the setting-up of a counter-government".[9]

With the afternoon's excitement at an end, the meeting of the Transdanubian National Council finally got under way at eight in the evening. Gyorgy Szabo opened the meeting, and Attila Szigethy gave a speech declaring the victory of the revolution at both the national and regional level. A long and stormy debate ensued over whether or not the new Council should proclaim itself an independent government, but Szigethy and others warned that any such action could only endanger the conquests of the revolution. Finally, the meeting decided to adopt a position of conditional support for the Nagy government, and to submit a programme of political demands to it. This programme was formulated in a fourteen-point resolution, which included demands for the fixing of a date for the withdrawal of Soviet troops, the declaration of Hungarian neutrality, the establishment of complete freedom of speech, of assembly and of the press, and the holding of free elections.

The Transdanubian National Council elected Attila Szigethy as its president, and Gyorgy Szabo as its vice-president. These two then led a delegation to Budapest the following day, presenting the Council's political demands to Imre Nagy, and returning to Gyor the same evening. Following Szigethy's report-back of his meeting with Nagy, the Council once again expressed its support for the government in Budapest, but resolved to continue the strike and withhold full recognition from the government until their demands had been met. Far from this action representing any lack of confidence in Imre Nagy, Szigethy is reported to have told the Council that Nagy had privately expressed himself in favour of such tactics as a means of keeping pressure on the Russians.

However, despite Szigethy's moderating role in the Council and his success in restraining the wilder hot-heads in the town, a number of unsavoury characters continued to put in an appearance at Gyor. These ranged from employees of Radio Free Europe, who continued to press Szigethy to set up a counter-government, to former Horthyite officers and Arrow Cross men who alternately offered their services to the National Council or sought to seize some public building, most frequently the radio station. One Hungarian source even claims that General Zako, the commander of the Hungarian fascist movement in exile, put in an appearance at Gyor.

Whatever truth there may or may not be in these various reports, the one thing that is certain is that neither Attila Szigethy nor the Transdanubian National Council allowed themselves to be influenced in any way by such incidents. Their real significance is well illustrated by the fate of a delegate from Jozsef Dudas's National Council in Budapest who turned up at the Transdanubian National Council on 1 November to propose that a counter-government be formed by uniting the forces of Transdanubia with those of Dudas in Budapest. Szigethy energetically denounced this latest proposal, and sent the delegate back to Dudas with a message that such action would be "treason against the country".

Finally on 3 November, after Imre Nagy's declaration of Hungary's neutrality and withdrawal from the Warsaw Pact, together with the formation of a new government and the opening of negotiations for the withdrawal of Soviet troops, the people of Gyor felt that their remaining apprehensions could be put aside. In this spirit a mass meeting of delegates from workers' councils throughout the town voted unanimously for a resolution proposed by the workers' council of the railway wagon factory for a return to work on the morning of Monday 5 November. Similarly the Transdanubian National Council, recognising that the policies of the Budapest government were now in line with the demands of Gyor, called for an end to the strike and the resumption of work.

"Just today," Szigethy told Wiktor Woroszylski who visited Gyor on 3 November, "we definitely recognised the government. Now it's the job of all revolutionary forces to rally around Nagy. . . . Beginning today this is a truly popular government."[10]

Thus by the first days of November the revolution in Gyor had clearly consolidated. Every single one of the attempts by right-wing agitators and adventurers to stir up trouble and give a counter-revolutionary turn to the events in Gyor had been defeated by popular leaders like Attila Szigethy and Gyorgy Szabo with the active support of the workers in the factories. The latter through their workers' councils had provided the real backbone of the revolution in Gyor, and the basis for the Transdanubian National Council.

However, on 4 November Soviet troops entered Gyor in force and occupied the major strategic points of the town. The people of Gyor could put up no effective armed resistance to the Russians, and the police and army soon returned to their former allegiance. Attila Szigethy and other leaders of the revolution at Gyor were taken into custody.

Owing to his local popularity, however, Szigethy was soon released and allowed to continue editing the local newspaper. The workers' council of the wagon factory also continued to function for a time and to issue its own paper. Between them these two papers were able to act as mouthpieces for the opposition to the Kadar régime in western Hungary for a few months following the suppression of the revolution. Before long, however, suppression turned to repression and what freedoms had at first been allowed to remain were soon crushed. A number of the leaders of the revolution in Gyor were now arrested, and some of them were executed. As for Attila Szigethy, after several attempts by the Kadar administration to win his co-operation, he was eventually arrested again in May 1957 and later committed suicide in prison.

Miskolc

The town of Miskolc in the north-east of Hungary, together with its industrial suburbs, is the country's largest industrial complex outside Budapest, with a population of almost two hundred thousand in 1956. The Borsod district, taking in the north-east of the town and the giant Dimavag iron-smelting works at Diosgyor, constitutes the largest continuous industrial neighbourhood in Hungary. In the county of Borsod around Miskolc are also to be found large paper, cement, and chemical factories and brickworks, as well as the iron furnaces and coalmines of the nearby industrial centre of Ozd. Miskolc also has its own technical university, attended by some two thousand students and occupying almost a separate quarter of the town.

The events in Miskolc, unlike those at Gyor, began well ahead of the outbreak of revolution in Budapest. The local Communist Party leadership included a number of people sympathetic to the ideas of Imre Nagy and the opposition, amongst them the party secretary for the County of Borsod, Rudolf Foldvari. The university also provided a breeding ground for dissent, while many workers from the town had attended evening courses there and come into contact with the students. Finally, in the Dimavag iron and steel foundry the workers held meetings on 21 and 22 October at which they set up a factory workers' council — perhaps the first in the whole country. Thus not only had a strong basis for future revolutionary organisations come into existence even before 23 October, but even more significantly the forces of communist reformists, students and workers were all acting in unison. This probably goes a long way to explain why the conflicts within the revolution at Miskolc never took on the same intensity as those at Gyor. At the same time the relative stability of events in Miskolc provides an illuminating instance of the evolution of political demands in the course of the revolution.

On 22 October the students of Miskolc met in a student parliament to discuss the appeal from Szeged to join in setting up the MEFESZ. In the debate political issues soon came to the fore, amongst them a call for a Danubian Federation of the peoples of Eastern Europe. 23 October itself passed fairly quietly and calmly in Miskolc. Meetings continued at the university, but news came only slowly from Budapest and most people sat glued to their radios. 24 October also started quietly, though quite a local sensation was created by an article in the local communist daily newspaper by Rudolf Foldvari, in which the party secretary bitterly attacked Gero's speech of the previous night and declared that the people of Borsod County supported neither the government nor the party. People also came out on to the streets at the sight of Russian tanks passing through the town — there are reports of demonstrations, even of people lying in front of the tanks to stop them going on to Budapest.

24 October also saw a meeting of the workers' council at the Dimavag iron foundry, at which a sixteen-point programme of demands was drawn up. On the morning of 25 October, the foundry workers led a march into the town. Carrying Hungarian flags, chanting slogans, and removing red stars everywhere, they were joined by many other workers and considerable numbers of students. A mass meeting was held in the student quarter of the town at which a larger workers' council was created to represent all the factories of Greater Miskolc, and the foundry workers' list of sixteen demands was extended into a twenty-one-point programme. The enlarged workers' council also proclaimed a general

strike, and demanded that the Russian troops should leave Hungary. Meanwhile, other demonstrators occupied the local printing press and ran off leaflets carrying the twenty-one-point demands. The radio station was also taken over and in its first broadcast declared on behalf of the workers of Miskolc: "We too want socialism, but according to our own special Hungarian conditions, reflecting the interests of the Hungarian working class and the Hungarian nation."[11]

A delegation from the workers' council presented their programme of demands to the party secretary, Rudolf Foldvari, who agreed to set off at once for Budapest to present their demands to the government. Later that day Radio Miskolc summarised the workers' council's programme in four main points — the immediate withdrawal of Soviet troops, the creation of a new government, the right of workers to strike, and a complete amnesty for those fighting in the revolution — and announced that it had called upon the people of the county to strike until these demands were fulfilled. The workers' council declared that they would press their demands whether or not Imre Nagy agreed with them, but at the same time called for calm, order and restraint.

On the morning of 26 October, a large crowd gathered before the police headquarters in the town centre, demanding the release of prisoners arrested during the previous days. From the first floor of the building the police chief, Gyula Gati, together with his wife and a number of AVH officers opened fire with machine guns and tossed hand grenades into the crowd, killing sixteen people. Ordinary police on the ground floor of the building, however, handed their weapons over to the crowd of miners, workers and students, who now broke into the building and captured many of the AVH officers inside. The police chief and several of his fellow officers were beaten up by the crowd and some six or seven of them lynched "in a hideous manner", although his pregnant wife was rescued from the crowd's wrath by a group of students.[12]

This incident in which the AVH's action in firing on unarmed civilians turned a peaceful crowd into an angry mob, and in which several criminals are suspected of having played a prominent role, has been described as "one of the bloodiest episodes of the counter-revolution". However, it is the only recorded instance of mob violence in Miskolc, and its lack of typicality can be seen by comparing it with the very different way in which a student group on the same day achieved the surrender of a separate AVH barracks without a single shot being fired. The barracks, a short way outside the town, were surrounded by about fifty lightly armed students who kept carefully out of sight. A delegation went into the building, convinced the AVH officers that they were surrounded by hundreds of armed students, and negotiated their surrender.

Meanwhile, under the auspices of the workers' council, smaller committees were set up to supervise the administration of the revolutionary forces, including the army and the police, and a National Guard began to be formed. Co-operation between the workers and the students — "the two authorities in the town" — is described as splendid. When later in the day a rumour spread that further AVH forces had surrounded the university, the entire shift of workers from a nearby factory marched on the university to liberate the students. Finding all was well, a mass rally was held in a jubilant spirit. The next day Radio Miskolc could confidently declare: "For two days the town of Miskolc has been under the leadership of the workers' council and the student parliament."

At noon on 26 October, Budapest Radio announced that the delegation from the Miskolc Workers' Council had met with Prime Minister Imre Nagy. The Council had presented their demands to Nagy, and he had expressed his agreement with them, even his belief that they could be surpassed. Promising that a new government would shortly be formed, he appealed to the people of Borsod for their support. On 27 October the delegation returned to Miskolc and the Workers' Council declared that it would support Nagy's new government, but that it would also continue the strike until its demands, above all the withdrawal of Soviet troops, had been fulfilled.

Over the following days, with the revolution in Miskolc stabilised and consolidated, its political form began to take on a more definite shape. New demands were expressed over the radio, addressed not only to the government but also to other revolutionary councils throughout the country. So far the major demands had been for the withdrawal of Soviet troops, the right to strike and higher basic wages. On 28 October a new policy declaration issued jointly by the Workers' Council and the Student Parliament demanded the formation of a new government excluding all the former stalinist ministers. It also demanded free and general elections with several competing political parties. Two days later, on 30 October, a further communiqué was issued calling for a revision of the Warsaw Pact, and declaring that the Soviet intervention was an open violation of the Pact. During these days Radio Miskolc also called for a Danubian Federation of the East European nations, and appealed to the surrounding countries to support the Hungarians, declaring, "We are fighting for you too, for peace, for socialist truth, for the guarantee of the free development of our peoples."

The Miskolc Workers' Council at no time declared itself opposed to the government of Imre Nagy. Rather it consistently expressed its confidence in Imre Nagy as Prime Minister, but criticised him for not acting firmly enough to replace the former stalinists and implement the revolution's demands. However, in the last days of October the Workers' Council of Miskolc became increasingly alarmed as it received reports of new Soviet troops moving into Hungary, and as it tried to bring this to the attention of the government. A series of almost despairing calls were issued over Radio Miskolc on 31 October, demanding to know what the government was doing to ensure that the Russian troops would actually leave Hungary.

However, Imre Nagy's declaration of Hungary's neutrality and withdrawal from the Warsaw Pact, and his announcement that negotiations had begun for the withdrawal of the Soviet troops, seems to have convinced the people of Miskolc of the sincerity of his government, and also to have put their minds temporarily at ease concerning the threatening Soviet troop movements. On 1 November a Workers' Council was formed for the whole of Borsod County and it sent a delegation of twenty-eight led by its president, Jozsef Kiss, to Budapest to meet again with Imre Nagy. This new countywide Workers' Council presented Nagy with a programme which included a demand for the Parliament to be replaced by a National Assembly made up of delegates from the workers' councils, and declared that the land, the factories and the mines must remain in the hands of the people. When the delegation reported back to Miskolc, the Workers' Council decided that it could now have every confidence in Imre Nagy and passed a unanimous vote of confidence in his government. They also voted to call off the strike.[13]

However, by midday on 3 November, Radio Miskolc was once more sounding a note of alarm as it reported massive Soviet troop movements into Hungary and the surrounding of several northern towns. Early in the morning of 4 November, the revolutionary council of the Miskolc garrison announced that the city was in a state of siege, but Radio Miskolc declared that the revolutionary and national councils would refuse to lay down their arms.

The revolutionary forces in Miskolc were unable to put up more than a short-lived and limited resistance to the Soviet forces, but in the weeks and months following the revolution's suppression the

Borsod Workers' Council, under the leadership of the former Communist Party secretary Rudolf Foldvari, was to remain as one of the strongest provincial bases of resistance to the Kadar régime and the Soviet occupying forces.

The unity and cohesion of the revolutionary forces in Miskolc rested on two main factors. The first was that the local Communist Party was already, before the revolution, sympathetic to Imre Nagy and his policies of reform. From the very start of the revolution the local party leadership declared its solidarity with the people's demands, and local party leaders and activists took a leading role in organising the revolution's forces. The second factor was that the strongest force of the revolution in Miskolc was provided by the workers organised in their workers' councils. Indeed, the first initiatives in raising the demands of the revolution and giving it organisational form had been taken by the workers' council of the Diosgyor iron foundry. In subsequent days the Borsod Workers' Council became the central power in the county.

Throughout the revolution, the demands of the communists, students and workers of Miskolc never wavered from their assertion of "socialism . . . reflecting the interests of the Hungarian working class". When the Russian leaders talked of a counter-revolutionary danger in Budapest, of threats to the workers' power, and of capitalist restoration, delegates from the Borsod Workers' Council told the Nagy government that they would lead the workers of Borsod to Budapest to demonstrate just who was leading the revolution. "You have only to pick up the telephone," they promised, "and in three hours we will be there, the workers of Ozd, Diosgyor and Miskolc, all twenty thousand and armed."[14]

The sequel to this story was played out some several months later when Sandor Kopacsi, the son of a Diosgyor family, who was head of the Budapest police force, and who had played a prominent role in the revolution, was put on trial and condemned to death. At this, the promise previously made to the Nagy government was repeated as a threat to the Kadar régime. Kopacsi was speedily reprieved.

Pecs

In the towns that have been looked at so far, the officials of the old stalinist régime, with the noted exception of the AVH, put up little if any resistance to the revolution. In many places the old authorities disintegrated almost overnight. But this was not the case in every part of the country.

In Pecs, a beautiful old town lying at the foot of the Mecsek hills in southern Hungary, the stalinist functionaries in both the town and party administration and in the factories sought to maintain control for several days with the support of a force of over a thousand armed AVH men. A secondary result of this was that while the motive forces of the revolution in Pecs were the workers' councils in the recently-opened uranium mine and the nearby coal-mines, the leadership of the revolution in the town passed into the hands of somewhat more reactionary forces than was the pattern elsewhere.[15]

Little news came to Pecs from Budapest on 23 October, but in the early evening the AVH imposed a six o'clock curfew, and by the next morning a number of prominent local citizens had been taken into custody. On the next day, by which time the radio had brought news of the events in Budapest, many people were out on the streets of Pecs, but so were numerous AVH patrols, moving the people on and continually breaking up the crowds. In the mines and factories, however, all work came to a halt.

On 25 October the university students held a meeting at which they denounced the communist university authorities and elected a MEFESZ committee. The students also called a meeting in the main square of the town for the afternoon. Several thousand people attended, mostly workers, miners and soldiers, and the meeting elected a provisional revolutionary committee for the town. Meanwhile a number of student groups toured the local factories and mines, calling upon the workers to strike in support of the revolution. One group of students went to the nearby mining town of Komlo and helped to organise a meeting at which the miners elected a revolutionary committee.

The authorities in the town, however, refused to make way for the revolution. On 26 October the commander of the AVH announced over Radio Pecs that "there is no such thing as a revolutionary committee", and that "all state and social organs of the city of Pecs stand firmly on the side of the people's democracy". Over the next two days, however, even their determination began to weaken.

By the twenty-sixth, workers' councils had been formed in almost all the factories and mines, and the strike had become universal. Somewhat paradoxically, the first intiative to set up workers' councils had come from the factory directors and party officials themselves who, following directives from Budapest, had put forward party lists for the election of workers' councils. The workers, however, almost everywhere rejected the party lists in favour of candidates they put forward themselves. It was likewise in vain that the local party authorities and the AVH leaders tried to force the men back to work. In the uranium mines, for instance, a force of three hundred AVH guards rebelled against their officers and declared their support for the revolution.

On 28 October, a meeting of delegates from all the local workers' councils and revolutionary committees elected revolutionary committees for both Pecs itself and the county of Baranya. At this meeting, representatives of the army and the police declared their support for the revolution. On 29 October the AVH barracks were occupied, their leaders arrested and their forces disarmed. A number of local Communist Party leaders were also taken into custody. A National Guard was set up composed of students, soldiers and police, and in the following days order was almost completely restored in Pecs.

At the same time, aware of the large number of Soviet troops in the vicinity, the revolutionaries in Pecs took measures to prepare against a possible Soviet attack. A military council was formed under the leadership of Professor Kalman Csikor, a former Horthyite officer and a specialist in military science at the university. While it was considered unrealistic to attempt to defend the town, plans were made for small brigades of soldiers and police, workers, miners and students, to withdraw into the Mecsek hills and hold out as long as possible. All told, some fifteen hundred men were expected to take part in this action, and preparations were made to hold off the Soviet forces from the roads into the the hills while they retreated.

When the Russians did move in to occupy the town on 4 November a large number of volunteers, particularly students and young miners, did take up arms and retreat into the hills. Fighting in small bands fifteen to twenty strong, they put up considerable resistance for about ten days to the Soviet tank forces sent to drive them out. Most of the resistance collapsed when the Russians sent in infantry forces backed by aircraft and bombs, but even after that a force of soldiers and miners in the eastern region of the Mecsek hills carried on guerrilla activity against the Soviet forces for several weeks.

Salgotarjan

Salgotarjan is the small county town of Nograd county lying to the north of Budapest, close to the Czechoslovak border. The industrial centres of the county are made up of the iron and steel foundry and the metallurgical and glass works in Salgotarjan, and the coalmines at Nagybatony.

The events at Salgotarjan offer a fascinating illustration of the conflict at a local level between the forces of the old stalinist régime and the new forces arising from the revolution. As in Pecs, the stalinist leaders of the local Communist Party and the AVH tried to keep the county under their control despite the revolution. But later, after the imposition of the Kadar régime in Budapest, the leaders of the revolution at Salgotarjan were to resist for several weeks the efforts of the Kadar régime to impose its authority on the county of Nograd.[16]

There being no university in Nograd county, there was no student agitation to disturb the relative peace in the county which prevailed on 23 October. News of the events in Budapest only came to Salgotarjan over the radio on the morning of 24 October, and the first to take note of it were the local stalinist authorities themselves. The AVH at once set up controls over all road and rail transport into the county, and at Balassagyarmat eleven Budapest students were turned off the bus to Salgotarjan. The first person in Salgotarjan to circulate demands in favour of the revolution, a long-standing Communist Party member, Istvan Mlinarik, was immediately arrested.

In the following days, however, local opponents of the old régime began to mobilise their forces. They included a number of left-wing schoolteachers, old social democrats in the steel foundry, a group of pro-Nagy communists amongst the coalminers, and others in the transport services. These people took the lead in setting up workers' councils and revolutionary committees in the factories and offices, and organising the strike.

From 25 October work came to a halt in most of the town's factories, and on the morning of the twenty-seventh workers from the steel foundry marched into town, stopping at the metallurgical works and the glass factory to gain the support of the workers there. Marching through the town centre, they removed the red stars from public buildings, released the political prisoners from the police headquarters and demolished the local Soviet war memorial. Meanwhile the local police and AVH refrained from interfering.

The local communist authorities, however, still hoped to keep control in the town. Copies of the communist paper for the Hungarian minority in Slovakia, which denounced the revolution as a fascist attempt to overthrow socialism, were brought from Czechoslovakia and distributed in the town. The Communist Party even called a meeting for 30 October to elect a National Revolutionary Council.

But it was this meeting which finally showed the door to the old stalinist functionaries. The delegates elected a National Council for the county, and passed a policy statement the first point of which was a call for the immediate withdrawal of Soviet troops. Istvan Mlinarik was elected president of the Council, and alongside him a four-man executive was elected, representing the parties of the postwar coalition period. Representatives of the army and the police declared their support for the revolution, and a National Guard was set up to maintain public order. The National Council appointed people to take over the direction of the local press and radio. Workers' councils had by now taken over most of the factories and mines, and they worked to co-ordinate the strike throughout the county. The premises of the Communist Party were taken over, with the intention of converting them into workers' flats.

The revolution, however, had been slow to organise in Salgotarjan, and following the renewed Soviet attack on 4 November and the formation of Janos Kadar's Revolutionary Worker-Peasant Government, a small AVH force under the direction of a group of the party's former stalinist leaders took the National Council by surprise, easily overpowering its guards and taking over the town hall. The National Council members were not arrested, but thrown out of the town hall which was placed under AVH guard.

A Revolutionary Worker-Peasant Committee for Nograd County was now formed by the latest occupants of the town hall, its president being a man named Janos Mrazik. But no Soviet forces entered the town, and the new administration at first sought to win the co-operation of those who had taken part in the revolution. Three members of the National Council were even taken as members of a delegation from the Revolutionary Worker-Peasant Committee which went to Budapest to meet Kadar on 9 November.

However, the National Council was reconstituted at the steel foundry, which had throughout been the real stronghold of the revolution. An assembly of workers' delegates met there on 13 November and declared its continued support for the National Council and its refusal to recognise the Revolutionary Worker-Peasant Committee. The events of 5 November were then repeated in reverse. A well-armed force from the steel foundry surprised the forces of the Revolutionary Worker-Peasant Committee, took over the town hall without firing a shot, and reinstalled the National Council. The press and radio again came into the revolutionaries' hands, the army once more supported the National Council, and the National Guard was organised anew.

In the face of the total inability of the local stalinists to maintain their power, Soviet armoured units entered and occupied Salgotarjan on 16 November. The town hall was now placed once more in the hands of the Revolutionary Worker-Peasant Committee, but the force of foreign arms could not confer any authority on this body. Two rival centres of power existed — the National Council had the overwhelming support of the people, the Revolutionary Worker-Peasant Committee the support of the Soviet armed forces. This very balance of forces meant that neither side could exercise effective power.

In an attempt to counter this new situation, two hundred delegates from workers' councils throughout the county met on 21 and 23 November to elect a County Workers' Council. Its president was Ervin Szabo, the communist president of the workers' council of the Nagybatony miners. This County Workers' Council quickly became the most important centre of power in the county, being recognised as such by both the Budapest and Soviet authorities, and it resisted all attempts by the local stalinists to win its collaboration.

Faced with this continued resistance to its authority, on 1 December the Revolutionary Worker-Peasant Committee arrested the president and three vice-presidents of the National Council of Salgotarjan. At this provocation protests poured in from throughout the county, and the town's workers marched on the police headquarters. The four arrested were released immediately, making it clear once again exactly where power lay in Salgotarjan. In protest against the arrests, and to express its dissatisfaction with the Kadar government, the County Workers' Council called a two-day general strike for 3 and 4 December. The complete success of the strike, followed by a huge mass meeting of the Nagybatony miners, demonstrated the continuing unity of the people of Nograd against the Kadar régime, and the total failure of its local supporters to win the slightest degree of popular confidence.

The Revolutionary Worker-Peasant Committee now finally gave up even the pretence of seeking a political solution, and arrested two leading members of the County Workers' Council on 7 December. In answer to this attack on their elected organisations, workers and miners poured into Salgotarjan from all parts of the county. 8 December saw the largest demonstration so far as several thousand people marched on the town hall and the police headquarters. This time, however, Soviet tanks and Hungarian state security forces fired on the unarmed crowds, leaving several dozen dead and many more wounded.

The following day Soviet troops entered and occupied the steel foundry, thus bringing a final end to the resistance and at last imposing the authority of the Revolutionary Worker-Peasant Committee on the town, but in the very act of so doing, clearly and dramatically illustrating the real conflict of social forces which had taken place in Salgotarjan.

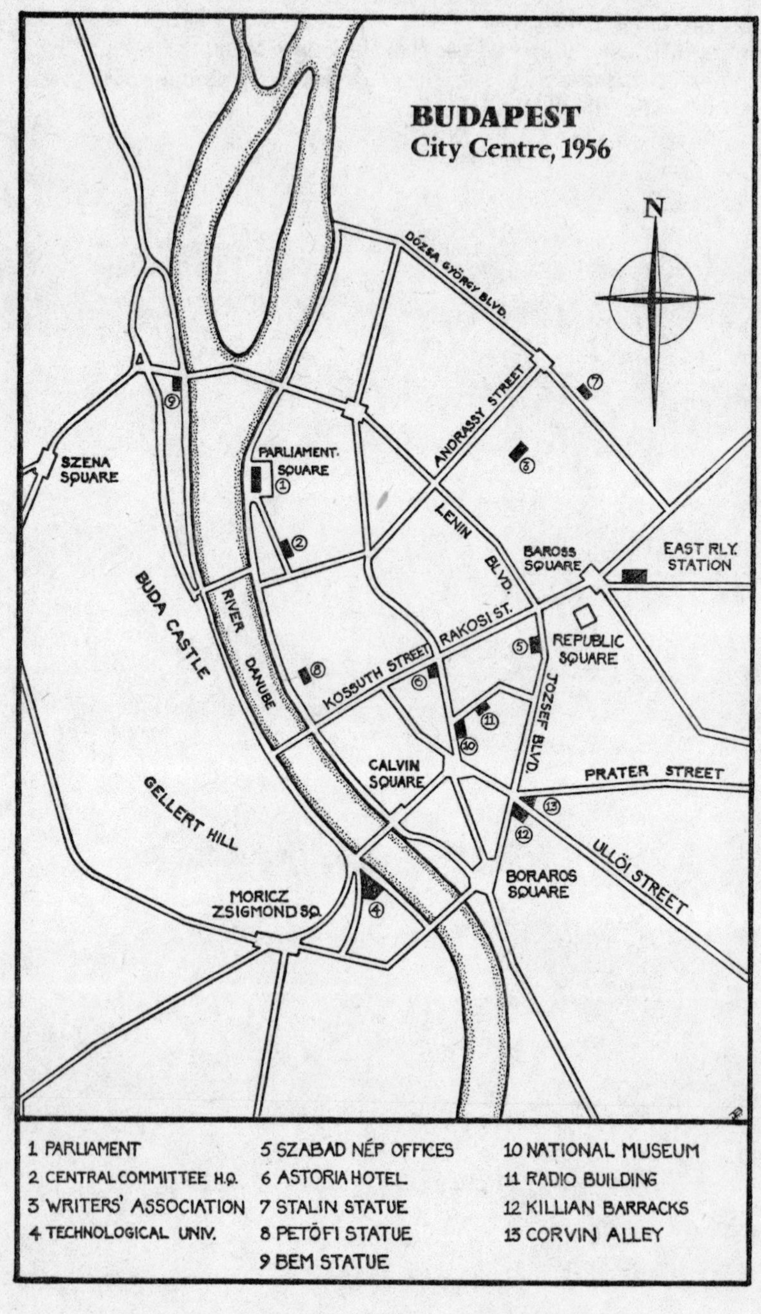
BUDAPEST
City Centre, 1956
N
DÓZSA GYÖRGY BLVD.
ANDRASSY STREET
SZENA SQUARE
PARLIAMENT. SQUARE
LENIN BLVD.
BAROSS SQUARE
EAST RLY. STATION
BUDA CASTLE
RIVER DANUBE
RAKOSI ST.
KOSSUTH STREET
REPUBLIC SQUARE
JOZSEF BLVD.
CALVIN SQUARE
PRATER STREET
GELLERT HILL
ULLÖI STREET
BORAROS SQUARE
MORICZ ZSIGMOND SQ.
1 PARLIAMENT
2 CENTRAL COMMITTEE H.Q.
3 WRITERS' ASSOCIATION
4 TECHNOLOGICAL UNIV.
5 SZABAD NÉP OFFICES
6 ASTORIA HOTEL
7 STALIN STATUE
8 PETŐFI STATUE
9 BEM STATUE
10 NATIONAL MUSEUM
11 RADIO BUILDING
12 KILLIAN BARRACKS
13 CORVIN ALLEY

4 Budapest: Between Revolution and Counter-Revolution

"Then what are we supposed to fight with?"

"I don't know — pikes, swords, homemade weapons, anything you can make in your own factories."

"You mean we should fight tanks with spears?"

"You'll have to do the best you can. You can make fire bombs out of bottles of petrol or kerosene and throw them at the tanks."

Malenkov replying to Khrushchev, 1941

Many of the accounts of Budapest in 1956 — written in the heat of political emotion following the Russian suppression of the revolution — have represented the events which took place there in far too black-and-white terms as constituting either an unblemished revolution for freedom and liberty, or a dastardly counter-revolution directed by American agents and former fascists. Each of these approaches fails to do justice to the full richness and variety — let alone the chaos and confusion — of the revolutionary events.

Hungarian reactionaries and fascists, Western agents and spies too, certainly played their part, yet even amongst the most counter-revolutionary forces and events they were probably more often than not outnumbered by plain fools and common thugs. But it is even more absurd to deny the leading role played by longstanding communists and socialists in the mainstream of events, let alone the actions of the working class in providing the revolution with its major social base.

Moreover, when the Soviet tanks returned to crush the Hungarian revolution in the early morning hours of 4 November, the actual development of the revolutionary situation was cut short long before its final outcome had been resolved. To try and predict what might otherwise have happened is really a task for the astrologist, rather than the historian or even the political scientist or sociologist. Consequently, what I shall attempt to do in this chapter is to provide a picture of the different social forces and political tendencies at work within the revolutionary situation. In this way it may well prove possible to portray the different alternatives which were presented by the revolution; but which of them would finally have prevailed would have depended on the decisions and actions of many different individuals, the living men who by their own actions make history — never more so than in times of revolution.

The students light the blue touchpaper

If the actual starting point of the Hungarian revolution could be placed at any particular time, it would undoubtedly be at the students' meeting at the Technological University of Budapest on the night of 22 October.

It was on this occasion that the students first publicly expressed the revolutionary demands for the withdrawal of Soviet troops from Hungary, for the dismissal of the former stalinist leaders, for free elections and a free press. These demands went far beyond the possible limits of internal reform; they were symbolised in the demand for the removal of the Stalin statue, itself the symbol of an entire régime. And indeed, on the following day this immense statue — "the symbol of stalinist tyranny and political oppression", as the students described it — was to be pulled down by the workers of Budapest before a single shot had been fired by the AVH, before a single Russian tank had even started on its way towards the city. When Gero denounced the students as enemies of the people, when the AVH fired upon unarmed crowds, and when the stalinist leaders called in the Russian tanks, their actions may have strengthened the resolve of the demonstrators but they did not cause the revolution.

Following the initiative of the Szeged students in setting up the independent student organisation MEFESZ, several meetings were held in the various faculties of Budapest University at which the students expressed their discontent both with aspects of university education and with the official youth organisation DISZ. "We wanted to get out of DISZ," recalls one student, "and set up MEFESZ within our university too." In an attempt to head off these rapidly growing demands, to "take the wind out of the sails of MEFESZ", it was the official communist organisers of DISZ who proposed the convening of a special mass meeting of the students of the Technological University to debate their demands and discontents. It was also they who proposed that workers from the Budapest factories be invited to take part in the meeting, no doubt hoping to pull out loyal party forces to counteract the students. The students, however, took up these challenges with enthusiasm. They went out to the factories and appealed to the workers to come to the meeting and support their demands.

Long before the meeting was due to commence, several thousand students had massed in the main hall of the university and were energetically discussing the issues to be raised. When the meeting began, the Executive Committee of DISZ put forward a twenty-five-point resolution which expressed not only student demands for university reform but also called for a complete change in the party leadership, the reinstatement of Imre Nagy, and a revision of Hungarian-Soviet relations. But because of the resolution's appeal for continuing support of DISZ, it was unable to win the support of a majority of the students present. Indeed, not only the DISZ secretary but also the rector of the university were shouted down when they appealed to the students not to withdraw from DISZ. The students then voted by an overwhelming majority to leave DISZ and set up MEFESZ.

The debate itself moved on very quickly from issues of primarily student concern to ones of a general political nature. Soon the demand was raised for the withdrawal of the Russian troops and the ending of Hungary's rule "by an imperialist tyranny", and eventually these demands were put before the meeting in the form of a ten-point resolution which combined them with the call for the creation of MEFESZ. The provisional draft of this first resolution reads as follows:

> Introduction: MEFESZ (League of Hungarian University and College Students' Associations) established. This organisation is competent to solve the problems of the students.
>
> 1. A new Central Committee and new leadership for the party.
> 2. A government under the leadership of Imre Nagy.
> 3. Hungarian-Soviet friendship (and Hungarian-Yugoslav), and the withdrawal of the Soviet troops.
> 4. New elections.
> 5. New economic policy. Uranium, foreign trade, etc.
> 6. Readjustment of the norms of workers, and workers' autonomy in the factories.
> 7. Improvement of the situation of agricultural workers and of peasants farming individually.
> 8. Revision of political and economic trials and the granting of an amnesty.
> 9. 15 March, 6 October. The old coat of arms.
> 10. Freedom of the press, and an official newspaper for MEFESZ. Destruction of the personal "screening" files.

Declaration: Full solidarity with Warsaw and with the Polish independence movement.[1]

Even this early draft embraced a wide range of demands, expressing the discontents of workers and peasants as well as students. It is also interesting to note that in this first version the demand for the withdrawal of Soviet troops was only put in as an addition to a point on Hungarian-Soviet relations. During the course of the debate, however, it was soon to be raised to a point in its own right, and finally into the very first point of the resolution.

While the debate continued, increasing attention was given to the problem of getting the decisions of the meeting publicised. Delegations went to the radio, the newspapers and the student and youth journals in an effort to get the students' demands printed. But they were met everywhere with refusals to print their demands in full, particularly the call for the withdrawal of Soviet troops. The rector refused even to let them run off their demands on the university's own duplicating machines. When the student leaders then proposed toning down the resolution to enable it to be published, the mass meeting rejected any such compromise, insisting that their demands remain full and clear.

Meanwhile in the course of the debate, the students had decided — again against the advice of both DISZ and party officials as well as that of the rector — to call a demonstration the following day in support of their demands and for the return to power of Imre Nagy. Once they had done so, it became even more important for their demands to be clearly formulated and publicised. The demands had now expanded to some sixteen points, and these were now read out over the microphone so that all those present could write them down and spread them further in handwritten and typed copies. These points constituted what has subsequently come to be known as the students' sixteen-point resolution, and the manner in which it was originally formulated accounts for the numerous versions in which it has subsequently been recorded.[2]

Around midnight, some students suggested they should break into a nearby printing shop and print their demands themselves, while others called for a demonstration outside the radio station. This time, however, the more moderate counsels of their leaders prevailed when it was pointed out that such a step was just what the AVH would be waiting for. The students also agreed to confine the following day's demonstration to a silent procession, and to post guards at all entrances to the university to ensure that neither provocateurs nor police informers could find their way in.

It was almost 2 a.m. on the morning of 23 October when the meeting finally came to an end, but many of the students stayed on throughout the night, typing and retyping copies of their resolution. Eventually some of them secured the use of the university's duplicating machinery previously denied to them, while others made their way into the university printing shop where they reset the type for the first page of the student paper *Jovo Mernoke* ("The Engineer of the Future"), replacing it with a shortened version of their demands. By dawn they were ready with bundles of their proclamations to take out and distribute to the workers at the factory gates.

On the morning of 23 October all the university centres of Budapest were centres of feverish activity, from which students emerged to distribute their leaflets outside the factories and in the city's streets. The pupils of the city's high schools were also preparing to participate in the demonstration, and even the young officer cadets of the Hungarian army's Petofi Academy decided to take part. A number of factories, amongst them the giant Mavag and Ganz works, sent busloads of workers to the Technological University to express their solidarity with the students and join in the demonstration. When the Minister of the Interior announced that the demonstration would not be permitted, delegations from the Petofi Circle and the Writers' Association went to the ministry and party headquarters appealing for the ban to be lifted, but the students declared they would march regardless.

By early afternoon thousands of students were gathering at a number of assembly points outside the different university faculties, whence they converged on Petofi Square on the banks of the Danube. Only then did news arrive that the ban on the demonstration had been lifted. Some ten thousand people, still mostly students, had by then gathered around the bronze statue of Petofi. They carried Hungarian and Polish flags, and banners bearing such slogans as "Long live Polish youth", and "We trust Imre Nagy". Even an official contingent from the DISZ Central Committee joined the gathering, as well as a group of students from the party's Lenin Institute who arrived marching behind a red flag and huge portraits of Lenin.

The whole crowd joined in as a popular young actor, Imre Sinkovits, recited the famous poem of Petofi which had become Hungary's national song, "Arise Hungarians". Then they cheered a brief greeting from the Writers' Association delivered by Tibor Dery, and listened as a student read out the sixteen points. Then they marched off up the main street of Budapest, Lajos Kossuth

Street, singing the Kossuth song, the Marseillaise and the International. Soon they were shouting slogans such as "Poland has shown the way, let us follow the Hungarian road", and uttering cries of "Independence" and "Freedom". Increasingly a sharper tone came to be adopted, and as the demonstrators crossed Stalin street they raised the cry, "Down with the Stalin statue!" As for their own Hungarian dictator, their cries ranged from "Into the Danube with Rakosi!" to "Boiling water for baldie!" Then there arose what was soon to become the most popular slogan of the revolution, "Let the soldier of every country return to his own land", or more pointedly expressed, "Let the Soviet Army go home and take the Stalin statue with them!"[3]

At the corner of Vaci road, by the Western railway station, the ranks of the crowd were swelled by many workers returning from the day's work. Growing numbers of Hungarian national flags with the Soviet emblem cut out were now raised amongst the demonstrators, and hung out from the windows of houses and offices under which the crowd passed. When the marchers had crossed over the Danube and were approaching Bem Square, a great cheer went up as the soldiers of the nearby Bem barracks also hung out a national flag. Arriving in Bem Square, the crowd against listened to representatives of the writers and the students, and once more sang their national song which ended with the refrain,

"By the God of the Hungarians, we swear, we swear,
No more shall we be slaves — no more!"

With the ceremony over, the majority of the crowd headed back into the town centre, many of them singing an old revolutionary song of the People's Colleges, "Tomorrow we shall change the world", and shouting, "We want a Hungarian government! We want Imre Nagy!" By 6 p.m. some two or three hundred thousand people had converged on the Hungarian Parliament, demanding that Imre Nagy come to speak to them. But they grew increasingly restless and frustrated, and when Imre Nagy did eventually appear some two hours later the last thing they were prepared to hear was the word "comrades" with which he started to address them, and the square was filled with the sound of derisive whistling.

At this point the students were finding themselves suddenly and speedily overtaken by the very masses they had mobilised. In the crowd outside the parliament, with its increasingly anti-communist mood, students constituted but a fifth or quarter of its number, and some were to feel themselves quite uncomfortable amongst it. In subsequent days, as demonstrations were replaced by street battles fought arms in hand against Soviet tanks, secondary school students and young workers came to take a much greater part in events than the university and high-school students. Indeed, many of the students from more middle-class or professional families were ordered not to go out into the streets and not to leave their homes, while one even reports being locked up in his bedroom by his parents. When these students did venture out on to the streets, it was more often as individual voyeurs than as revolutionary combatants. Those who were more active were more likely to be found distributing leaflets and posters, acting as couriers between different groups or helping out in hospitals, than actually fighting on the streets.[4]

More prominent amongst those who took up the fight against the Russian tanks were the rough, working-class youths of the Budapest slums, the tough-guys, leather-jacketed "yobos" and hooligans from Angyalfold and Ferencvaros. Uncultivated, rude, often anti-semitic, many of them joined for the adventure and sport of the fight. It is with a strange mixture of shame and admiration that the students themselves refer to this development. One of them, for instance, remarks, "It is touching that it was the hooligans of Ferencvaros who created ethics out of nothing during the revolution", and another adds, "Painful as it is to acknowledge it, it is nevertheless true that they were the real heroes."

All of the official information subsequently released concerning casualties during the revolution confirms that it was young people, and young workers in particular, who took the main part in the fighting. A clue to the motivation of many of them is provided by a Hungarian doctor who treated a large number of wounded insurgents, and who has been quoted as saying:

> "There was any number of youngsters amongst the fighters who knew nothing about the Petofi Circle or who for that matter hadn't even heard of it, to whom Gomulka's name was equally unknown, and who replied to the question as to why they had risked their lives in the fighting with such answers as, 'Well, is it really worth living for six hundred forints* a month?' "[5]

The night of 23 October

While the majority of the demonstrators on 23 October had ended up in Parliament Square, other groups had headed for the Stalin statue on the edge of the city park intent on implementing

*£9.26 at the official rate of exchange in 1956.

the most immediately realisable of the students' demands. Many of those who came here were industrial workers; as one observer remarks, "It was at the Stalin statue that the workers of Budapest appeared on the scene." And already someone had hung around Stalin's neck a placard with the inscription: "Russians, however great your hurry to leave, don't forget to take me with you."

Efforts to pull down the statue with ropes and steel cables fastened to tractors and lorries were all in vain, but eventually two workers brought an acetylene welding torch and at last the massive statue gave way, leaving just a mammoth pair of boots on the former dictator's pedestal. Amid scenes of great jubilation, the gigantic statue of the former Russian leader was dragged behind a lorry through the streets of Budapest, to be left outside the National Theatre in the very centre of the town. On the side of Stalin's head were inscribed the internationally recognisable initials "W.C.".

In another part of the city a more serious conflict was building up outside the radio building in Sandor Brody street, just behind the National Museum. Many of the students from the afternoon's demonstration had marched here directly from Bem Square to demand that their sixteen-point resolution be broadcast. Officials of the radio had first pleaded with the students to leave, but later invited them to send in a delegation to negotiate about a broadcast. The negotiations dragged on for some time, with the result that a rumour spread that the delegation were being held captive by the AVH, and the crowd started to throw stones and pebbles at the windows of the building.

The radio authorities had agreed to broadcast a version of the students' demands omitting the call for the withdrawal of the Soviet troops, but when the delegation tried to explain this compromise to the crowd, even they were shouted down. In the street confusion reigned, and many could not hear the speeches from the building's balcony. The crowd grew in size, becoming both more tense and angry, and more militant and uncompromising. But during the first hours the crowd was far from violent, as evidenced by the fact that more than one group of AVH reinforcements was able to enter the radio.

One demand of the crowd was for a microphone to be placed in the street to let the voice of the people be freely heard, and eventually a radio car was brought out and the demonstrators invited to read their demands into the microphone. The demonstrators, however, soon discovered that their speeches were not being transmitted live and, suspecting trickery, they angrily chased away the car's operators. After this their temper grew increasingly angry, and the building was now showered not only with stones but also with "pots and pans . . . coal, china, bricks, anything". Their mood now became so wild and threatening that even leading members of the opposition, amongst them Geza Losonczy, Miklos Vasarhelyi and Zoltan Szanto, who came to the radio at the request of its director, didn't dare to address them.

At 8 p.m. Erno Gero, the First Secretary of the Communist Party who had returned to Budapest only that morning from an official visit to Yugoslavia, made a radio broadcast in which many of the demonstrators had been hoping he would promise changes and reforms. In his speech, however, Gero denounced the demonstration as a manifestation of chauvinism and nationalism inspired by hostile propaganda and enemies of the people, and he made absolutely no concessions to the popular demands of the demonstrators. The whole tone of his speech angered the people and did much to exacerbate the already tense situation. Indeed the speech itself no doubt contributed to the outbreak of violence, and some commentators have even suggested that it was a deliberate act of provocation.

Certainly, when the crowd in Sandor Brody Street heard the broadcast over radios placed in the windows of apartments in the street, they became even more angry and embittered than earlier, and attempted to force their way into the Radio building through the ground floor windows. The AVH guards used fire hoses and threw hand grenades in attempts to hold the crowd at bay, but this only provoked them still further. Using the abandoned radio car as a battering ram, they broke down the main outside door of the radio. At this point, at about 9 p.m., the AVH charged out into the street with fixed bayonets and drove the crowd temporarily out of Sandor Brody Street.

Varying and conflicting reports exist as to whether in this charge the AVH refrained from firing, fired blanks, fired warning shots into the air, or actually fired into the crowd. Certainly it was at this time that a number of people on both sides were injured. One eye-witness reports an army captain being killed when a tear-gas grenade exploded in his face. Others report that a young army officer was shot down when he went up to try and reason with the guards. Possibly the first shot was accidental — in fact an official Hungarian account reports that the machine gun of one of the radio's defenders may have gone off by accident. Whatever the exact circumstances, the atmosphere now changed dramatically, and cries arose of "The AVH are murderers! — Death to the

AVH!" The word also quickly spread throughout the city that "the AVH are shooting on the students at the radio", and more and more people converged on Sandor Brody Street.

Up to this point the demonstrators had been throwing little more than bricks, bottles and unexploded tear gas bombs. They appear to have first come into possession of firearms when, on stopping two ambulances that were trying to enter the radio, they found them full of arms and ammunition for its defenders. Also there were a number of soldiers and police amongst the crowd, and naturally enough they were carrying arms. Now too a succession of further AVH contingents, military cadets and regular army troops were sent to reinforce the radio's defence, but wherever they appeared they were surrounded by the crowd chanting "The army is with us!" and "Long live the people's army!" Most of them handed over their weapons to the demonstrators, or themselves joined in the attack. Between 9 and 10 p.m. sporadic but increasing small-arms fire — rifles and revolvers — was exchanged between the radio's defenders and the crowd, and by 10 p.m. the radio was the scene of a full-scale gun battle.[6]

Some time between 10 and 11 p.m. an armoured tank regiment from Piliscsaba arrived at the radio building. The regiment had been summoned to the defence of the radio but on being greeted jubilantly by the crowd, its commander refused to join forces with the AVH and went to report the situation to his ministry. Shortly afterwards one of his company commanders, a major, declared to the crowd that he himself was a worker from Csepel and that he would never order his men to fire on the workers. Some reports say that he went up to the building in an attempt to negotiate, others that he was standing on his tank addressing the crowd, when he was shot down in a volley of machine-gun fire. With their commander's death, the Piliscsaba troops joined forces with the crowd in the assault on the building.

Towards midnight the ranks of demonstrators who had come chiefly as spectators were thinning out. At the same time a number of lorry loads of workers arrived from the industrial suburbs of Csepel and Ujpest, bringing heavier arms and ammunition obtained from the arms stores in the factories, and the attack on the radio building turned into a complete siege. In the early morning hours the attackers gradually penetrated into the building, and by 9 a.m. the insurgents were in complete control.

On the night of 23 October, while the fighting at the radio building had been getting under way, almost the entire population of Budapest had been out on the streets of the city. Crowds gathered at almost all of the major intersections of the town, and one journalist who had walked across the city centre in these hours described its atmosphere in the following words:

> "This was a real revolution without inhibitions and barriers. . . . The crowd forgot everything, ran out and fought, shouted slogans about which it hadn't heard a moment ago, overturned streetcars, etc. . . . This was a form of drunkenness like a genius in the act of creation."[7]

Far from being a revolutionary coup in which organised bands of insurgents seize the focal points of power and communications — government ministries, party offices, police stations and post offices — this was a spontaneous revolutionary mass movement in which the people threw themselves at the symbols of the old régime: first the Stalin statue had fallen, then red stars were removed from public buildings.

Another leading symbol of the communist régime was provided by the offices of the party's daily newspaper *Szabad Nep*, in the very centre of the city. Crowds gathered here throughout the evening, demanding that the students' demands be printed, roaring "Down with the lies of *Szabad Nep*", and calling for the removal of the red star from the building's roof. Inside the building a number of journalists from the former opposition, amongst them Miklos Gimes and Pal Locsei, ran off leaflets proclaiming their solidarity with the demonstrators and threw them down into the street. The crowd, however, set fire to the leaflets without even reading them. Others broke into the bookshop on the ground floor of the building, throwing the works of Marx, Lenin and Stalin out into the street and setting them ablaze. Huge pictures of Stalin and Rakosi were joyously added to the flames. One member of the opposition who went down to try and calm the crowd was himself set upon and beaten up.

Shortly after nine a group of demonstrators came from the radio carrying the corpse of the first person killed there by the AVH. This raised the crowd's fury and anger to an uncontrollable rage — cars were turned over and set on fire in the street, the ground floor rooms of the building were broken into and everything in them, books and furniture, thrown on to the bonfires in the street. Meanwhile up in the editorial offices on the third floor, the party leader Jozsef Revai had arrived to supervise the next day's issue of the paper — a strictly party-line edition to be headed by Gero's speech. Now, however, Revai had to be helped to safety through a back door of the building by the very journalists he had come to dictate to.

So far most of the street crowds and demonstrations had been unarmed, but between 10 p.m. and midnight, as word spread throughout the city that the AVH were murdering people at the radio, cries arose of "Get weapons! Get weapons!" Buses and lorries were commandeered in the streets and driven to armaments factories or depots where arms were stored. Similarly, workers in the industrial suburbs seized lorries from their factories and local transport depots and rushed into the city, stopping on the way wherever arms could be procured. At first most of the arms came from the Hungarian Civil Defence organisation which had arms stores in each district of Budapest, as well as in the factories and university faculties.

Later in the night other groups went to military barracks, arsenals and armaments factories to collect arms. In many instances the arms were gladly handed over to them. As one participant in the fighting explains, "What weapons we possessed we got from Hungarian army arsenals and warehouses, an operation facilitated and made possible by the Hungarian army itself." The great majority of these attacks on barracks and arms stores were first made by unarmed crowds. It was only on subsequent nights, when the insurgents desperately sought weapons to fight against the Soviet tanks, that far more intensive armed raids were made on places where armaments and munitions were thought to be stored.

The armed fighting groups

In the early morning hours of 24 October, columns of Soviet tanks poured into Budapest. It was at this point that the Hungarians threw up barricades at major points of the city — at the Moricz Zsigmond and Szena Squares in Buda, at the Baross and Boraros Squares and in the narrow streets of the eighth and ninth districts of Pest — and that organised fighting groups began to emerge. Many of these groups arose as completely ad hoc formations, coming together for a particular engagement, their personnel continually changing. Two participants recall their groups in the following words:

> "Some people got together, fought, went home, then others came and continued the fight. People changed all the time. . . ."
>
> "There was no organisation whatsoever, consequently there was no discipline either, but there was astonishingly good teamwork."[8]

Most of their weapons came from the Hungarian army itself, and some of the first organised centres of resistance were set up in students' and workers' hostels. The major fighting groups came together at the main intersections of the city, at Szena Square in Buda and in the Corvin Alley in Pest.

One of the earliest groups to be formed came together in the half-built underground station at the Szena Square on the morning of 24 October. Using barrels and drums from a nearby garage, they set up barricades and fought a fierce battle throughout the afternoon in which they prevented Russian tank forces from breaking through the square. On the following day the group was reorganised under the command of a former Yugoslav partisan, Kemal Ekren, and a fifty-nine-year-old bus driver and former soldier, Janos Szabo. "Uncle Szabo", as he was known to his men, seems to have been very popular amongst the fighters of Szena Square. They described him as "a peasant with a big moustache — honesty and decency radiated from him", "a simple, uneducated man, a man who evoked confidence in everybody", "a very competent and skilful organiser, respected by all both as a man and a leader, almost as a father".

Most of those who fought under Uncle Szabo's command were young workers and students — even many schoolchildren, boys and girls in their early teens. On 26 October the soldiers of the Petofi military academy threw in their lot with the Szena Square fighters, and on the twenty-seventh their numbers were further swelled by released prisoners from the forced labour mines at Piliszentivan. In the last days of October the group participated in the organisation of the National Guard, transferring its headquarters to Maros Street police station. Throughout the revolution the group's strategy and tactics were decided upon at public and democratic meetings of all its members.

A number of small armed groups which had taken part in the siege of the radio and in attacks on nearby arsenals came together in the early morning of 24 October at Baross Square, by the Eastern railway station. Unable to resist the advance of Russian tanks, they were split up and driven into the narrow backstreets behind the station. By the twenty-sixth they were able to form up once again in Baross Square under the leadership of Laszlo Nickelsburg, a thirty-two-year-old factory worker, a Communist Party member and a Jew whose mother had perished together with her other three children in a German concentration camp. Other smaller armed groups also operated throughout the area of small backstreets which lay behind the Eastern station. Official Hungarian reports have gone out of their way to point out that these groups included many underworld criminals, petty thieves, prostitutes, "notorious tavern loafers" and delinquent youths. Indeed, the area in which they operated was one of the seamiest districts of the city, long known in Budapest slang as "Chicago".

The largest and most important of the insurgent fighting groups arose in the Corvin Alley on the corner of the Jozsef Boulevard in Pest. Gathering here on the morning of 24 October, they occupied the Corvin cinema and a number of the houses surrounding it. At first only a small group sniping at Soviet tanks with rifles and attacking them with hand grenades and Molotov cocktails, they were fortunate enough to come into possession of a couple of anti-tank guns with which they put a number of Soviet tanks out of action. Their numbers now grew much more quickly, approaching a thousand by 30 October, and on 1 November the leadership of the group was taken over by Gergely Pongracz, one of five rough and enthusiastic "dare-devil" brothers who provided the main inspiration of the Corvin Alley group.

Almost next door to the Corvin Alley was the Prater Street school which was also taken over by insurgents on the morning of 24 October. Though relatively small, it was in this group that the famed Budapest underworld achieved its greatest notoriety. Their leader was Janos Mesz, commonly known as "Peg-Leg Janko", and described by the Hungarian authorities as an "inveterate criminal . . . convicted sixteen times for theft, violence, vagrancy, intoxication, robbery etc." Next in command was Gabor Dilinko, nicknamed "Jewel", one of Janko's former cellmates. This group, calling itself the Petofi Brigade, became a refuge for many escaped criminals who were provided with clothes in exchange for their prison uniform.

Just opposite the Corvin Alley stood the Kilian barracks, which became one of the most famous centres of the Hungarian armed resistance. On the night of the twenty-third an unarmed crowd from the radio building had come to the barracks, breaking down the main door and taking what few weapons they could find. Apart from a small number of young conscript soldiers and a group of officers, the main force in the barracks was an unarmed labour battalion, many of whom left with the crowd. On the morning of the twenty-fourth the soldiers still in the barracks refrained from any action. However, they found it hard to disguise their jubilation when two Soviet tanks approaching and firing on the insurgents' stronghold in the Corvin Alley were seen to go up in sheets of flame. In fact a number of soldiers then went out to join forces with the insurgents, and by noon the Kilian's officers were instructing the latter in the use of machine-guns and hand grenades, and the Corvin Alley "counter-revolutionaries" were lunching in the barracks' canteen.

During the night, however, a group of political officers in the Kilian took it into their heads to make surprise attacks on the insurgents' patrols and capture some ten of their number. This led the Corvin group to lay siege to the barracks on the morning of the twenty-fifth in the belief that it had been taken over by AVH forces. It was in these circumstances that Colonel Pal Maleter was sent from the Ministry of Defence with a force of five tanks to relieve the barracks. On arrival, his forces took up the fight with the insurgents, but Maleter himself went into the barracks to question the prisoners taken the previous night. On being assured by them that they were neither fascists nor counter-revolutionaries, he sent three of them back to the Corvin with the offer of a ceasefire. Within a short while the Kossuth arms had been raised above the barrack gates, Hungarian flags were hung out from the windows, and the insurgents from the Corvin Alley were out in the street, cheering the Hungarian army and their new hero, Colonel Maleter.[9]

On the twenty-sixth, Maleter at first tried to maintain the Kilian's policy of neutrality in the armed combat, though many of his soldiers joined in the battle on the side of the Corvin Alley insurgents. As increasing Soviet forces came into action against the Corvin, and the Kilian barracks also suffered damage and injuries, Maleter called upon the Ministry of Defence to have the Soviet forces withdrawn from the area and thus avoid needless bloodshed. When his request was denied he replied, "In that case, I must inform you that I shall open fire on the first Soviet tank to approach the Kilian barracks." For the rest of that day and the following two, Soviet forces unceasingly attacked the Corvin Alley and the Kilian barracks. Under Maleter's command the Kilian held out against the Russian attacks until the ceasefire on 28 October, and in so doing gave a great psychological impetus to other fighting groups throughout the city. At the same time, Maleter became a symbol and a legend of the Hungarian resistance, and the most popular hero of the revolution.

Pal Maleter, thirty-nine years old in 1956, had been captured on the Russian front in the second world war, then thrown his lot in with the Communists and become a partisan fighter against the Germans in Transylvania. Returning to Hungary in 1945, he joined the Communist Party and participated in the postwar reorganisation of the Hungarian army. Throughout the revolution, he continued to wear a partisan red star on his uniform, and emphasised to all comers that he remained a committed communist. As he explained to one Western journalist, "If we get rid of the Russians don't think we're going back to the old days. And if there's people who do want to go back, we'll see!" To emphasise the last remark, he reached for his revolver holster and repeated, "We don't mean to go back to capitalism. We want socialism in Hungary."[10]

The Soviet troops

The first Russian tank units entered Budapest in the early hours of 24 October, having been told they were being sent to put down a fascist uprising. But they had not been given orders to open fire, since it was thought that a display of overwhelming force would suffice to end the disturbances. Moreover, these troops had been stationed in Hungary for some time and were reluctant to fire on the Hungarian people whom they had come to know.

The Hungarians did not see events in quite the same light. They presumed that the Russian tanks had been sent in to support the AVH and the Gero régime in their stubborn resistance to the people's demands for change. At the main strategic intersections of the town they set up barricades and fired upon the approaching tanks, or attacked them with petrol bombs. After their leading tanks were in many cases burned out, and their occupants mercilessly shot down on emerging, the Russians started to fire back. Only now, as the fear of being burned alive in their tanks was starkly brought home to them, did they begin to fire savagely and sometimes indiscriminately. As one of them later argued before a crowd of Hungarians: "How do you think we felt, cooped up in a tank, with people dropping bombs of liquid fuel, grenades, and anti-tank mines on us from the houses?"[11]

Despite the bitter fighting there were also numerous scenes where Russian tanks were to be found surrounded by unarmed crowds, with young students passionately arguing with the soldiers in Russian. More than one Russian commander was to declare to such a crowd that he had been told that counter-revolutionaries and fascist bandits were on the rampage in Budapest, but that he could now see this was false, and he would not shoot upon the Hungarian people. Such declarations were met with displays of great emotion and jubilation. Soviet soldiers were embraced by the crowd, they exchanged their caps with those of Hungarian soldiers, and the Hungarians draped their national flags over the Soviet tanks.

Other reports speak of Russian troops only passively carrying out their orders, of them handing over weapons, sometimes even their tanks themselves, in exchange for food and liquor. Some of the Soviet soldiers even deserted and fought on the side of the Hungarians, amongst them many members of national minorities within the Soviet Union. One Armenian major went over to the Hungarian side on the first day of the fighting and helped to print and distribute leaflets in Russian to the Soviet troops. One such leaflet declared:

> "Friends! Don't fire on us!
>
> Refuse the hateful role of executioners! You helped to overthrow the fascist dictatorship, but now you yourselves are serving dictatorship!
>
> Friends! You are serving red imperialism and not the just cause of socialism!"[12]

Meanwhile, those Hungarians who had been the first to grab eagerly for their weapons, seeing the Russian soldiers as their natural and hated enemies, also began to see things in a different light. As one young fighter recalls:

> "I found myself shooting at bewildered Ukrainian peasant boys who had as much reason to hate what we fought as we had. . . . It was an embittering shock to find that one can't confront the real enemy even in a revolution."[13]

The growing incidents of fraternisation, however, were brought to a sudden and tragic end in an incident which occurred on 25 October. Early in the morning a large crowd had gathered around some five or six Russian tanks outside the Astoria Hotel. When a Russian officer climbed out of his tank he was surrounded by Hungarians demanding to know, "Why have you come here? What do you want? Why don't you go home?" The Russian officer explained that he had been sent to liberate the city from fascist bandits. Then, looking around him, he declared, "I can't see any fascists. It's the people who are here . . . workers . . . women . . . and youngsters, who have every right to decide for themselves how they want to live." At this, the Hungarians thronged on to the Soviet tanks, embracing the Russian soldiers and covering the tanks with flowers and Hungarian flags. One American journalist who witnessed the event described it as "the most joyous fraternisation between a populace and foreign troops I had ever seen".[14]

When another Russian tank appeared from round the street corner, similarly bedecked with flags and with Hungarians all over it, the crowd's ecstasy became uncontrollable. "The Russians are on our side!" they shouted, "Let's show the whole town our friendship! Let's go together to the Parliament!" Within minutes the whole town was alive with the news that Soviet troops had joined the revolution, and thousands of people began streaming towards the Parliament. "We are not fascists, we are workers," they shouted, and demanded, "We want Imre Nagy!" Surging into Parliament Square, the crowds swarmed around further Soviet tanks in front of the Parliament, embracing the Soviet soldiers and climbing onto the tanks.

Suddenly this amazing scene was shattered by bursts of machine-gun fire. Dead and wounded fell to the ground, the rest rushed frantically for safety. Not knowing who was firing, where from, or why, a frenzied panic gripped the crowd. The Russian soldiers were equally confused, but did their best to defend the crowd, and fired back at the rooftops of the ministry buildings surrounding the square from where the firing appeared to be coming. The murderous fire lasted for a good ten minutes, until the snipers' guns were put out of action by the Soviet tanks. When the shooting stopped, about a hundred dead as well as many wounded lay in the square, including several Soviet soldiers and a number of Hungarian policemen who had been on duty outside the Parliament.

Exactly who fired on the crowd outside the Parliament building has never been conclusively established. The Hungarian authorities insist that it was counter-revolutionaries seeking to launch an attack on the Parliament under the cover of an unarmed demonstration. This account, however, does not explain why even fascist elements would have fired directly into the crowd, and it is certainly a suspicious circumstance that this should be the only instance of "fascist atrocity" where the Hungarian authorities have been unable to identify a single one of the alleged bandits. It seems more likely that the AVH had set up machine-gun nests on the rooftops of the buildings around the Parliament, in anticipation of a possible attack. On being unexpectedly confronted by a massive crowd advancing on the Parliament with a number of tanks, and apparently overpowering the Soviet guard, they could well have thought the Parliament was under attack and therefore have opened fire.

One result of the bloodshed arose from the fact that the demonstrators themselves were not really aware who had done the shooting. Many thought it was the Soviet tanks that had fired into the crowd, or even that their previous fraternisation had been a trick, that they had deliberately led the people into a trap. By evening Budapest was alive with rumours, whipped on by Western radio broadcasts, that Soviet tanks had opened fire on a peaceful demonstration, murdering hundreds of unarmed civilians. In this work of distortion and propaganda, the British diplomatic service played no small part, announcing that more than twelve truckloads of corpses had been seen removed from the square, while the BBC reported the slaughter of over six hundred unarmed Hungarians.

Up to this point popular feeling towards the Russians had been growing more and more friendly, but the spread of exaggerated tales of the massacre was now to fill the Hungarian people with a bitter hatred. The same journalist who had witnessed the earlier scenes of fraternisation now reported:

> "Like a black whirlwind descending out of the sunny skies that morning, an incredible revulsion and a feverish desire for revenge enveloped everyone. . . . The revolution became a blind, merciless war between half-armed people and the Soviet Army."[15]

The next two days, up to the declaration of a ceasefire on 28 October, saw the heaviest fighting and the most vicious battles of the first Soviet intervention, in which many Hungarians lost their lives, and scores of Soviet tanks were destroyed. But there are no reports of Soviet soldiers being lynched, or of their corpses being disfigured, as did happen in the case of the occasional AVH man who fell into the hands of an angry crowd. Nor on the other hand were there any Soviet atrocities, many Western reporters confirming that the Soviet troops behaved with considerable restraint. Even during the second intervention, when the resistance they met from the Hungarians was far more bitter and determined, they did not seem to like the dirty job they were called upon to do.

In the face of the horror stories about the Russian troops later whipped up by unscrupulous Western propagandists, it was left to a Hungarian émigré himself to argue that "most of them did not indulge in personal cruelty, and some of them, in their clumsy and puzzled ways, tried to be kind to the people they met".[16]

The terror of the mob

The massacre in the Parliament Square on 25 October also led to a rising anger and hatred against the Hungarian state security force. In subsequent days a number of Western newspapers, particularly the more right-wing press (which seemed to have forgotten that this was one revolution they were supposed to be in favour of) spread salacious tales of horror around the world purporting to be eyewitness accounts of the vengeance being taken by the Hungarian people on the representatives of the communist state. Such stories spoke of "unrestrained popular violence" (*Daily Telegraph*) and of "the terror of the mob . . . imposing on Budapest a system of lynch-law" (*Daily Express*), while even the normally restrained

Reuters could report "the beginning of a manhunt in the streets of Budapest. Members of the security police are being killed like dogs, they are hanging from the lampposts and balconies".[17]

Although these reports were later to be picked up with great glee by the Kadar régime, the true extent of such atrocities is probably even less than it has commonly been the practice to concede in accounts published in the West — even in those by Hungarian émigrés themselves. Indeed, if we leave out those killed at the scene of major armed engagements, even the Hungarian government's own series of White Books only instance three cases of individual AVH men being seized and killed by street mobs. The first concerns an AVH lieutenant, pulled from his car at an insurgent checkpoint on Margaret Bridge on the night of 23 October, being beaten unconscious by the crowd and thrown into the Danube. The second instance involved the beating up of an AVH captain, Ferenc Brodovics, outside the Prater Street school on 25 October. He is said to have been taken inside the school and later thrown to his death from a fourth-floor window. On the third occasion, 31 October, an AVH captain named Ferenc Toth is said to have panicked and shot at random into a crowd near the Western railway station. He was seized and beaten by the crowd, then hung from a lamp-post with a placard around his neck bearing the words, "The same fate awaits every secret policeman".[18]

Apart from these three incidents, the claims of the Hungarian authorities that a new "white terror" comparable to that of the early days of the Horthy régime in 1919 was enveloping the streets of Budapest are based almost exclusively on the one indeed gruesome armed confrontation which took place on 30 October in Republic Square, when armed insurgents laid siege to the headquarters of the Budapest City Communist Party.

The massacre of Republic Square was to take the whole of Budapest by surprise. Neither Imre Nagy nor the commanders of the armed forces, Pal Maleter and Bela Kiraly, learned about it before it was all over. Nor did any of the larger fighting groups take any organised part in the attack. The Hungarian court proceedings against those subsequently charged with the killings in Republic Square make it clear beyond almost all doubt that the unruly mob which stormed the City Party headquarters was headed by the small armed groups which operated in the backstreets behind the Eastern railway station, the roughest area of Budapest. Another group which took a prominent part in the final killings was that from the Prater Street school led by "Peg-Leg Janko". It was these groups that many escaped criminals had joined, as well as several former members of the Hungarian fascist party, the Arrow Cross. Theirs was indeed the lumpenproletariat's contribution to the revolution.[19]

It was in the early morning of 30 October that these groups, under the direction of leaders from Baross Square, prepared for their attack on the headquarters of the Budapest City Communist Party. Republic Square was kept under watch from dawn, and during the early hours of the morning small groups of armed insurgents were to be seen gathering in the area. Shortly after ten o'clock they approached the party headquarters from all sides, and a small group some five or six in number forced their way into the building but were quickly driven out. Following this incident, in which the first shots were fired, the attackers opened fire on the party building from all sides, one group firing with a machine gun which they had set up on the roof of the Erkel Theatre. Shortly afterwards the AVH inside the building started to fire back, and a battle began which was to last for over three hours.

Inside the party headquarters was an AVH guard made up of forty-six young conscripts all in their early twenties, under the command of two lieutenants. There were also some five or six army colonels and three or four policemen, as well as the civilian staff of the party headquarters some thirty or forty in number, many of whom were women. The acting first secretary of the City Party Committee was Imre Mezo, a devoted communist who had fought with the International Brigades in Spain and who was an old and loyal friend of Imre Nagy. When the party building came under attack, Imre Mezo called together the party workers and warned them to be prepared for a long drawn out siege while they waited for help to be sent by party or government forces.

The siege continued for over three hours. Many of the attackers were youngsters in their early teens who, with little cover except the trees on the square, suffered many casualties. Shortly after noon, one Western journalist present reported that the attackers were "falling like flies". Even Red Cross nurses trying to rescue the injured youngsters were fired upon — such incidents increasing the fury and determination of the attackers yet further. The defenders would probably have been able to hold off the attack but for the sudden arrival shortly after 1 p.m. of the help they had been waiting for — three Hungarian army tanks which, to their dismay and horror, joined forces with the insurgents and opened fire on the party headquarters. The stunned horror of the defenders was equalled only by the jubilation of the attackers who now threw aside all restraint and surged forward in a direct assault on the building.

At this point, hoping to prevent further bloodshed, Imre Mezo ordered his men to cease fire and, together with two of the army colonels, prepared to go out to meet the insurgents under a white flag of truce. Tragically, however, he was not even to gain the street. Stepping into the hallway at precisely the same time as the first attackers burst through the doorway firing their weapons in all directions, he collapsed with a stomach wound from which he later died. The two army colonels stepped out into the street, only to fall before a hail of bullets. Two AVH conscripts following behind them with hands raised met the same fate. A further eight AVH conscripts were then marched out of the building and stood with their backs to the wall. While still trying to protest that they were only conscripts and not terrorists, these youngsters too were shot down in cold blood by repeated bursts of machine-gun fire.

Those who shot them down were a gang of some fifteen or so armed insurgents, amongst them the leaders of the Baross Square group and the notorious "Peg-Leg Janko", as well as a number of former fascists and escaped criminals. Despite shouts from the crowd that these were unarmed prisoners and should not be shot, two more AVH conscripts were pushed into the street, then shot in the back as they tried to run for safety, and yet another five were also brought out to be stood against the wall and mercilessly mown down.

The brutality, however, had even now not reached its peak. As more of the defenders emerged from the building, some were shot and others viciously beaten up by the crowd. Even the dead bodies were now seized and sadistically mutilated. A hand was cut off one, the head off another, while yet another corpse had its heart cut out. One officer's body was dragged around the square by the mob, then hung up by the feet from a tree, while another's, also hung up by the feet, was soaked in petrol and set on fire. Red flags were brought out from the party building and set on fire, and for some time the mob continued to kick and spit upon the disfigured corpses.

When the siege ended, many of the inhabitants of the nearby streets had flooded onto Republic Square, and some of these unarmed onlookers had taken part in the final atrocities. But not all those there approved of the events, and from the very start there had been protests against the killings. Then violent arguments broke out between the different groups of rebels, in which the most prominent in trying to stop further killings were the leaders of the

Corvin Alley fighters who had arrived on the scene at the very last moment. On managing to save a few of the captives from the wrath of the mob, they themselves were accused of being secret police, and Gergely Pongracz recalls: "It was simply not possible to do anything with the crowd. Our National Guard detachment tried to intervene to safeguard the prisoners, but in the end we were glad to be able to get back to the Corvin in one piece."[20]

Nevertheless, many of those in the party building were helped away to safety, and several of the injured were rescued from the mob and taken to a nearby hospital. Miraculously enough, even two of the young AVH conscripts, the first to be mercilessly shot down and machine-gunned, survived and recovered from their ordeal. At the final count, out of the eighty to a hundred people in the party headquarters only twenty-five had lost their lives. Over two-thirds of the defenders survived, including thirty of the forty-eight AVH men.

While the Hungarian authorities have tried to suggest that the massacre of Republic Square was just the start of a white terror which would far exceed these events, it led on the contrary to a feeling of horror and revulsion amongst the revolutionaries who did not hesitate to express their condemnation of the atrocities. Even the relatively right-wing *Magyar Fuggetlenseg* ("Hungarian Independence")* was to declare:

> "We must raise our voices against those who stoked the fires of anarchy, who circulated slogans of fascist inspiration, who incited the throng to press this fratricidal struggle, and who took delight in the devastation and destruction that resulted."[21]

Undoubtedly the Hungarian revolution was not completely without blemishes. During these days, many common criminals had been freed from their cells and several of them had gone round in their own armed bands plundering and looting. Some ultra-nationalist, fascist and anti-semitic slogans had occasionally been heard on Budapest's street corners. A number of district party headquarters and local police stations were attacked and sacked. Other groups had even taken it into their own hands to seek out particularly detested communist functionaries, or to settle personal grievances.

But the extent of such incidents should not be exaggerated, for although the Hungarian authorities have no hesitation in speaking

---

*The paper of Jozsef Dudas's "National Revolutionary Council" discussed in more detail below, pp. 130-32.

of "the murderous manhunt to which hundreds and thousands of communists and democratically minded people fell victim", the only figure they have ever produced for these victims is one of 234 deaths adduced in the judgment at the end of the Imre Nagy trial in 1958. In the White Books themselves, further particulars are given of 220 of these victims, of whom 164 or over three-quarters were members of the armed forces of the state (85 AVH, 40 army soldiers, 27 police and 12 frontier guards). These figures are not only for Budapest but for the whole country, and include those who died in armed defence of party and AVH strongholds, and even several who themselves fell victim to AVH bullets. Even compared to the figure of 2,700 deaths, which is the Hungarian authorities' own estimate of Hungarian fatalities during the revolution (Western estimates suggest much higher figures), the number of 234 representatives of the forces of oppression to fall victim to popular vengeance represents a relatively small proportion. Indeed, it would seem to establish the Hungarian revolution as one of the most bloodless revolutions of all time.

Western agents

While the activities of agents sent into Hungary by Western espionage services had little real influence on the actual development of the revolution, it would be absurd to deny that they existed at all. But they were more often the unfortunate victims of these agencies than James Bond-style anti-communist crusaders.

Following the Soviet Twentieth Party Congress, the mines and barbed-wire fences lining the Hungarian-Austrian border had been removed, resulting in an increase in the number of refugees escaping to the West. Many of these Hungarians ended up in refugee camps in Austria where they would often be approached by agents of both Radio Free Europe and the West German intelligence agency of General Gehlen (propaganda and espionage set-ups supported by the American CIA) with lucrative cash offers if they would make trips into Hungary and bring back information about the siting of industrial concerns and military installations. When the Hungarian revolution broke out, many of these refugees were provided with money and weapons to return to Hungary and take part in the fighting. Some of them got to Budapest and joined in the activities of the fighting groups, and a handful were later captured and imprisoned by the Kadar régime.

An older generation of refugees, fascist exiles who had fled Hungary at the end of the second world war, and who had maintained exile centres and even military training camps in France and

Spain, West Germany and Austria, were also mobilised when the revolution broke out. Most prominent amongst these private fascist armies was the Fraternal Society of Hungarian Fighters under the command of General Andras Zako, which moved its headquarters to a Vienna hotel at the time of the revolution. In broadcasts to Hungary, issued over the American propaganda station Radio Liberty, they called on the insurgents to send representatives to meet them at the Austrian frontier, and promised: "The Western world's material aid is on its way to you." They may also have sent a number of small armed detachments over the border into western Hungary.

Agents and employees of Radio Free Europe also entered the country and met with leaders of insurgent groups in both Gyor and Budapest. Finally, a few prominent figures of the Horthyite emigration also turned up in Budapest during the revolution, amongst them the former landowner and Horthyite minister Baron Tibor Collas, Prince Hubertus Lowenstein and the Countess Beatrix Szechenyi.

But the influence of these Western agents, and of previously exiled fascists and aristocrats, should not be seen as having had any real significance on the development of events. Even the fullest study published in Kadar's Hungary concludes that "it was not the elements that came in from the West that played the decisive role", and certainly the leaders of the revolution wanted nothing to do with these ghosts of the past. Their attitude was most clearly expressed by Colonel Maleter at a meeting in the Kilian barracks, when he declared:

> "If there are any Western volunteers at the Austrian border desiring to join our fight, we have to ask them very politely but very firmly to abandon their plans. The frontier guards of freedom-fighting Hungary have been ordered to prevent such volunteer troops from entering the country."[22]

The Jozsef Dudas group

Unlike most of the revolutionary groups we have examined so far, the group led by Jozsef Dudas was not primarily a fighting group but one which issued a political programme and sought to win a political role for itself in the revolution.

Jozsef Dudas had been an active member of the prewar underground Communist Party, and a member of the armistice delegation sent to Moscow by Horthy in 1944. After the war he left the communists and became active on the left wing of the Smallholders' Party, but was arrested in late 1946 and charged with conspiracy.

Subsequently he spent eight years in a number of prisons and forced labour camps, where he made a wide variety of contacts and became very popular amongst the prisoners. Released in 1954, he went to work in a Budapest factory and here too won a great deal of respect from his fellow workers.

When the revolution broke out, Dudas called together a number of his former friends from both factory and prison life and organised a fighting group in the second district of Budapest. On 28 October, Dudas and his closest followers crossed into Pest and occupied a large part of the *Szabad Nep* building, where he was to proclaim the formation of a Hungarian National Revolutionary Council and publish his own daily newspaper *Mayyar Fuggetlenseg* ("Hungarian Independence"). In these headquarters, Dudas's control over the telephone exchange of the former Communist Party daily, with its direct lines to party and government offices, enabled him to achieve a prominence far out of proportion to the real strength of his group.

Subsequently Dudas was to be cast by both the Hungarian and Soviet authorities as one of the principal leaders of the forces of counter-revolution. However, those journalists from both Western and communist countries to whom he gave interviews during the revolution saw him not as some potential fascist tyrant but as a well-intentioned and enthusiastic if somewhat over-ambitious political adventurer. The Polish journalist Wiktor Woroszylski described his appearance as follows:

> "Tall, flushed, black-haired, with a large, expressive but repulsive face and mildly protruding cheek bones. A Tyrolean hat, a coat thrown over his shoulders like an imaginary cape, a revolver at his belt, and wearing black riding-breeches."[23]

His flamboyant and swashbuckling appearance seems to have given a fair representation of his character too, at least as François Fejto saw it:

> "He was somewhat confused ideologically, but a sincere patriot, an excellent organiser, and a courageous soldier; he was overflowing with vitality, and capable of communicating his enthusiasm to others."[24]

His sincerity and enthusiasm certainly won him the loyalty and devotion of his supporters, one of whom recalls: "He was such a brave man. The boys around him lived and died for him. . . . He was such a daredevil."

Dudas was not only adept at inspiring his followers; he proved also quite a dab hand at public relations, sending his representatives to the hotels where foreign journalists were staying and inviting them to press conferences in his "revolutionary headquarters". On 28 October he issued a twenty-five-point political programme declaring that his men would continue to fight, regardless of the ceasefire, until the Soviet troops had completely left Hungary. On 30 October, Dudas brought out the first issue of his own newspaper *Magyar Fuggetlenseg,* in which he reprinted his demands under the banner headline, WE REFUSE TO RECOGNISE THE PRESENT GOVERNMENT. Dudas sent delegates to revolutionary committees and workers' councils throughout the capital and the country, calling upon them to recognise his National Revolutionary Council as representing all the nation's freedom fighters. He demanded that six ministerial posts be allocated to his council, and that he himself be made Minister of Foreign Affairs. Finally he even appealed to the United Nations to recognise his National Revolutionary Council as a belligerent party in a state of war with the Soviet Union, and to send UN troops into Hungary.

In the event, however, Dudas's political posturing seems to have met with little success. His demands for a place in the government do not seem to have been taken seriously by anyone except himself. While he managed to secure audiences with both Geza Losonczy and Imre Nagy, they refused pointblank to recognise him as representative of all the rebels, let alone to accede to any of his wilder demands. His group was not represented at the founding meeting of the National Guard on 31 October, but on that occasion considerable distrust of his ambitions was expressed by both the major fighting groups and by Colonel Maleter himself. All in all, Dudas's often spectacular show was little more than a one-man band. There is no record of any member of his National Revolutionary Council besides Dudas himself, and when he convened a conference to establish a countrywide National Council, it appears that nobody even bothered to turn up.

The most serious incident caused by Dudas's activities was his seizure of the Ministry of Foreign Affairs on the night of 2 November, which some observers even saw as an attempted "putsch" to overthrow the Nagy government. The attack was carried out by a small armed group under the leadership of a certain Tibor Szeifert, whom Dudas had appointed as a lieutenant-colonel, and on the basis of rumours that AVH troops were stationed there. On hearing of the action, Colonel Maleter telephoned to the Foreign Ministry and ordered Szeifert to withdraw his men immediately. On Maleter's instructions Bela Kiraly then surrounded the Ministry with National Guard troops, disarmed the occupiers and publicly stripped the "lieutenant-colonel" of his rank in front of his men.

Dudas was arrested by the police the same night, but released after denying any connection with the attack. The following day, however, rumours spread that Dudas's men had held up the National Bank and robbed it of some two million forints. As a result Dudas was arrested again, held for several hours, and then again released, only to be arrested once more on 4 November, this time by his own men!

Despite his far-flung ambitions and his demagogic posturings, Dudas never expressed any particularly reactionary, let alone fascist ideas or slogans. On the contrary, he had described his movement to Wiktor Woroszylski as, "national, revolutionary, democratic and socialist", declaring both that "socialism must be preserved" and that "fascist or extreme right-wing groups could not be tolerated". Equally clearly, he had rejected all calls for the banning of the Communist Party, insisting that the communists must be allowed to participate in the new elections. Indeed, he had permitted the two communist papers *Nepszabadsag* ("People's Freedom") and *Magyar Szabadsag* ("Hungarian Freedom") to be printed on the *Szabad Nep* presses alongside his own. Even though for a long time he refused to recognise the government, he consistently supported Imre Nagy, declaring at one point that "the leaders of the revolutionary forces must have faith in Nagy, even if the people have lost it". Finally, in the last days of the revolution, he was to declare his support for the new coalition government of Imre Nagy, and to join in the call for an end to the strike and a return to work.

The political parties

While the armed fighting groups we have looked at so far may be seen as having occasionally displayed limited counter-revolutionary tendencies, these represented the "lumpen" counter-revolution, the counter-revolution of the uneducated and underprivileged, rather than that of a group seeking to win or regain a privileged position in society, that of the "bourgeois" counter-revolution. The bourgeois counter-revolution, in the limited extent to which it too existed, found expression in the re-emergence of the political parties which had been banned since the days of the communist seizure of total power in 1948.

First to reappear were the parties of the coalition period of 1945-48, the Smallholders, the Social Democrats, and the National Peasant Party. Undoubtedly some of their leaders such as Bela Kovacs of the Smallholders, Anna Kethly of the Social Democrats, and Istvan Bibo of the National Peasants were held in wide popular esteem, and were sincerely committed to maintaining the socialist achievements of the postwar years. The majority of those in the middle ranks of these parties, however, were less ideologically committed to preserving the socialist régime, and far more concerned with gaining the positions and privileges of office which their parties' reconstitution opened up to them.

These people had made little contribution to the actual revolution or to the resistance to the Soviet attack, let alone to the earlier opposition movement against the Rakosi régime. Both their members and their ideas were of a past generation. Yet they appeared, as the fighting died down and the Russians withdrew, preparing to step into the political arena, and to move in above the directly created organs of popular power — the workers' councils and revolutionary committees — formed during the revolution. The students in particular protested at the unmerited rise to prominence of these former middle-class politicians, fearing that those who had done most in making the revolution might now be excluded from influence by an older and more conservative generation. The general public also feared that the unity of the revolution might be undermined by the introduction of partisanship and party bickering, with the result that even such disparate figures as Maleter, Mindszenty and Dudas raised their voices against the re-emergence of the old party system.

The first of the parties to re-form itself, and the one which presented the most potential danger of leading a bourgeois-conservative reaction, was the Smallholders' Party. While Bela Kovacs was elected chairman of the party, he seems to have kept his distance from those most active in its reorganisation, who were certainly the more right-wing leaders like Jozsef Kovago, and Istvan B. Szabo who declared, in direct contradiction to the expressed views of Bela Kovacs, that the Smallholders' Party stood on the basis of its 1930 programme. Subsequently, Bela Kovacs was to recall that he had felt unhappy at the way things were turning out:

> "I disapproved of the return to the multi-party system. I said it at that time in Semmelweis Street where I found, in general, a mixed gang struggling against each other for office desks and power; longing for the return to the old world so hated by me, and saying that 'they are organising a Smallholders' Party'."[25]

Another caller at the party headquarters was similarly to remark:

> "Semmelweis Street once again had the appearance with

which it had started out in 1945: everybody was there, it was just peasants who were hard to find."[26]

The Smallholders' Party was by all accounts the most active in "bounty seeking" — claiming back their former political headquarters, dividing up leading positions in the ministries amongst themselves, and scrambling after perks from offices and desks to motor cars. They also played the leading part in establishing a so-called Metropolitan National Committee which elected their general secretary, Jozsef Kovago, as Mayor of Budapest, and began replacing the municipal officials appointed by the communists.

Less concerned with gathering the fruits and spoils of office, and undeniably committed to a radical and socialist programme, was the National Peasant Party. Renamed the Petofi Party, its executive committee read like a roll-call of Hungarian literature, including amongst its members Laszlo Nemeth, Janos Kodalanyi, Peter Veres and Gyula Illyes. The Petofi Party also supported the more left-wing Smallholders who belonged to the Peasant Alliance of Sandor Kiss, which favoured uniting the two peasant parties. While their appeals for unity were opposed by the most influential of the Smallholders' leaders and thus unlikely to meet with any immediate success, they might have led to a realignment of forces in which the more radical Smallholders could have come together with the Petofi Party and the Peasant Alliance, leaving the more right-wing rump of the Smallholders deprived of any real popular base.

Last of the coalition parties to reconstitute itself was the Social Democratic Party. This party had been the one most seriously damaged in the course of its conflicts and eventual fusion with the communists, while its unshakable dedication to bureaucratic procedures caused it to proceed very slowly in taking up any standpoint towards the revolutionary events. Anna Kethly, elected president of the Social Democratic Party, has described in her own words how she "constantly and most firmly rejected the idea of participating in the government" right up to 1 November. Her party eventually agreed to join the government on 2 November, after it had finally gone through all the requisite procedures for reconstituting itself.

Besides the coalition parties, there was a multitude of smaller and generally more reactionary parties calling for the restoration of private ownership and capitalism. One group of these were parties similar to the conservative parties of the West, such as the Democratic People's Party, the Hungarian Independence Party and the Hungarian Radical Party. Other parties were of a directly religious inspiration such as the Christian Democratic Party, set up on the model of Adenauer's CDU in West Germany, the Catholic People's Party and the Christian People's Party. A third group consisted of parties calling openly for the restoration of the prewar Horthy régime, such as the Hungarian Freedom Party and the Hungarian Christian Party. While few of these right-wing parties were of any real size or influence, moves were set in motion to unite them all within an all-embracing Christian Front, though whether such a unity could really have been achieved remained a much disputed point.

Finally, way out on the extremist fringe of the parties of bourgeois reaction, were a number of even more reactionary neo-fascist parties, movements of a very shadowy nature and perhaps equally tentative existence. On 31 October a demonstration was held in front of the Hungarian parliament in the name of a self-styled Party of Hungarian Revolutionaries, calling for a government headed by Cardinal Mindszenty. On 1 November a considerably more sinister meeting was held in the Urania Cinema to reconstitute the prewar fascist Arrow Cross Party, but the meeting is reported to have been a sparsely attended and highly confused organisational fiasco. Other attempts to re-form branches of the Arrow Cross Party seem to have been equally unsuccessful.

The one person who could perhaps have succeeded in uniting the many and diverse conservative, Christian, Horthyite and neo-fascist parties into a reactionary clerical coalition opposed not only to the socialist régime but also to the democratic coalition parties was Cardinal Jozsef Mindszenty. Primate of the Hungarian Catholic Church, Cardinal Mindszenty had been sentenced to life imprisonment in 1949 for his persistent championing of opposition to the communist régime. Mindszenty certainly provided the focal point around which any truly reactionary and counter-revolutionary forces could have gathered. Even such a moderate observer as Hugh Seton-Watson describes him as "an old reactionary, a narrow Hungarian nationalist and anti-socialist", while to the opposition intellectuals who supported Imre Nagy he was "a stupid, feudal cretin and idiot".

The real danger of Mindszenty arose from the fact that, by persecuting him, the communists had turned him into something of a popular martyr. One result of this was that, had the army detachment which freed him from his chateau-prison at Felsopeteny arrived a mere hour or so later than they did, this reactionary Catholic cardinal would have been liberated and brought triumphantly back to Budapest by a delegation of armed workers who had already set out by car from the revolutionary workers' council of Ujpest.

As for his political ambitions, some accounts suggest that he hoped to head a Christian Democratic Party formed on the model of the West German CDU, others that he would have become the leader of a united Christian Front set up to contest the claims to power of the Nagy government. Such accounts are lent some credence by Mindszenty's uncompromising declaration, "I shall carry on where I left off eight years ago," as well as by reports that he appealed to America for Western military intervention, and that he told Adenauer's representative in Budapest, Prince Lowenstein, that the only hope for Eastern Europe lay in a united and rearmed Germany "ready to repulse the Soviet danger by all means".

But despite these allegations, in his brief public statements Mindszenty went out of his way to avoid all questions of his participation in the government, implying that he saw his role as a spiritual but not a political leader, and leading one Italian journalist to inform his readers that "the obvious irritation in which he left us, after the so controversial question of his eventually succeeding to power, shows that he has no intentions at all along these lines".[27]

When Mindszenty did eventually make a public broadcast to the nation on the night of 3 November, his speech appeared deliberately vague and ambiguous, if not openly self-contradictory. While refraining from actually opposing the Nagy government, he referred to its members as "the successors of the fallen régime" which had been forced on Hungary in 1945 and now swept away for ever. While proclaiming his wish for Hungary to live in peace with all her neighbours, he spoke derogatorily of the Soviet Union as "the Russian Empire". While declaring his wish to live in "a society without classes", he affirmed his belief in "private ownership rightly and justly limited by social interests". And finally, while not making clear whether he was referring to its former schools and estates, he called for "the restitution of the institutions and societies of the Catholic Church". At the same time he warned against "party struggle and disagreement", asserting that he himself was "independent of any party, and — because of my office — also above it".[28]

Mindszenty's speech has meant all things to all men. The Hungarian authorities have interpreted it as an outright call for the restoration of Horthyite capitalism. Western commentators have preferred to see in it a recognition of the necessity of reconciling the interests of the Church with democratic and social progress. Others, on the other hand, have suggested that by the very fact of hinting at the possibility of restoring capitalism, and in particular the large landed estates formerly owned by the Church, Mindszenty had placed in jeopardy his earlier support amongst working people.

All that can definitely be said is that while Mindszenty's exact position was by no means clear because, in his own words, he "deliberately refrained from mentioning other details", and while his speech came too late to influence either the development of the revolution or the Soviet decision to suppress it, there can be no doubt that he was potentially the most likely standard-bearer around whom the reactionary and counter-revolutionary forces might subsequently have gathered.

Writers — students — youth

While the university students had played a much smaller role in the fighting than the young workers, they themselves did not hesitate to criticise in turn the more middle-class writers' and intellectuals' even greater impotence during the revolutionary events. One of them remarks that "most intellectuals were either organising the political parties and newspapers or sitting at home in their well-equipped apartments". Another student, who spent a large part of the first days of the uprising at the headquarters of the Writers' Association, reports: "There was a frustrated feeling . . . a feeling of 'what are we supposed to be doing here?' Everyone came to the Writers' Association for advice, but in practice the Association was impotent."[29]

Yet, as the students at least were aware, during these first days of the revolution, when the government was still far from placing itself at the head of the revolt, when the intellectuals and writers were debating what to do in their apartments and offices, while the more politically inclined of them stood around in the corridors of Parliament or the party headquarters trying to influence the "men of power", it was the power of the men in the street, the youth and workers in particular, that resisted and repulsed a mighty invading force of Soviet tanks. It was these same workers who, in the following days, were to bring into being a network of workers' councils, a new structuring of social and economic power throughout the industrial factories and workers' districts of the city.

These developments, however, were ones whose significance the writers and intellectuals were slow to appreciate. Few indeed of the former oppositionists thought for even a moment of turning anywhere other than towards the existing political leadership in an attempt to bring the situation under control. In such a spirit, a number of opposition spokesmen went on the radio to call upon the insurgents to stop fighting and lay down their arms. Thus Gabor Tancsos issued an appeal on behalf of the Petofi Circle, declaring that further progress could not be made "while the guns are roaring", and the writer Gyula Hay went so far as to demand on 25 October, at the height of the armed conflict: "We must immediately revert to peaceful methods; fighting must stop immediately. Even peaceful demonstrations should not now be undertaken."[80]

In view of these statements it is hardly surprising that when the fighting did die down and the Soviet troops pulled out of Budapest, it was not the writers but the students who went out to join forces with the young workers who had been fighting in the streets. In fact it was students distributing leaflets in the working-class suburbs of Budapest who provided the inspiration for the creation of the first revolutionary committees in the industrial districts of Csepel and Ujpest. The students recognised the importance of the new organisations created by the workers in the factories, and they joined with the young workers in raising the slogan of the revolutionary alliance of students and working youth, in proclamations such as the following statement issued on 2 November:

> "The revolutionary youth committees which have sprung up in the factories are the representatives of this significant new alliance. They are the new revolutionary organisations, independent of the party."[81]

The students themselves organised a Students' Revolutionary Committee under the leadership of the young communist psychology professor, Ferenc Merei, and published the journals *Egyetemi Ifjusag* ("University Youth") and *Magyar Jovo* ("Hungarian Future"). They also co-operated closely with the Revolutionary Committee of Hungarian Intellectuals which was set up in the University, and whose chairman was Professor Gyorgy Adam, a former communist militant who had been imprisoned under both the Horthy and the Rakosi régimes. Besides these bodies, two other national organisations of revolutionary youth were set up, these also publishing their own journals.

The students also took an active part in persuading some of the former sympathisers with the opposition to support the revolution, amongst them the Budapest police chief, Sandor Kopacsi, who had at first considered the uprising to be "in its essentials a counter-revolution". A few days later he told them:

> "The events have proved you right. I myself have learned a lot of things during the last three days. This is really a revolution of the people and, what is more, a victorious revolution."[32]

After this, the students acted in close co-operation with Kopacsi and the city police in setting up student units of the National Guard.

The students were equally in the forefront of those opposing any counter-revolutionary tendencies. Following the massacre on Republic Square, they sent a delegation to Imre Nagy to warn against the counter-revolutionary danger, and they strongly condemned "those who want to besmirch the sacred ideals and heroic days of our revolution by fishing in troubled waters, committing atrocities and resorting to arbitrary force".[33]

Student and youth journals bravely raised their voices against summary executions, robberies and lootings, declaring, "We will let no one soil *our* October revolution," and: "We do not want the return of the Horthy régime." Several foreign journalists were greatly impressed by the sincerity and idealism of these young students and workers. Even one British communist, who was in the end to support the Russian suppression of the revolution, could not hide his admiration for the students' struggle "for a really independent, democratic Hungary building socialism".[34]

The students were perturbed by the rise to prominence of the bourgeois political parties, and appealed to them to put aside their partisan interests for the sake of revolutionary unity. But as the surge forward of the parties appeared ever less resistible, some of the students, amongst them the daughter of the communist philosopher Georg Lukács, decided to set up their own Revolutionary Youth Party, which they explained would be "a party rising out of the democratic movement of the past months and of the insurrection — a party dedicated to humane socialism".[35]

The workers' councils

Behind the students stood the workers of Budapest who were quick to move into action, setting up their own organisations in the factories. The first workers' council was established on 24 October at Egyesult Izzo ("the United Lamp Factory"), one of the largest factories in Budapest employing over ten thousand workers and situated in the northern industrial district of Ujpest. The workers' council of the United Lamp Factory issued a ten-point declaration which made clear its intention of replacing the previous bureaucratic administration by a structure of workers' councils at each level, headed by a factory workers' council which would direct the entire enterprise. The declaration ended with an appeal to the workers to "show that we can manage things better than our former blind and domineering bosses".[36]

In the following days similar workers' councils were set up in the large Beloiannis electrical equipment factory and the Gamma optical works, in the Ganz electrical, wagon and machine works, in the Lang and Danuvia machine-tool factories, in the Matyas Rakosi iron and steel works in Csepel, in the Klement Gottwald electrical appliances factory, in the Obuda and Gheorghiu Dej shipbuilding yards, in the rubberware, leather and clothing factories, in the cotton mill Magyar Pamut and the Goldberger textile factory, as well as in the MAVAG, MOM, Orion, Chinoin and Ikarus concerns, to mention only some of the most prominent.[37]

Most of these workers' councils passed resolutions proclaiming their political demands, at the forefront of which stood the call for the immediate withdrawal of the Soviet troops. Many sent delegations to see Imre Nagy, and in support of their demands they launched a general strike throughout the city. When a few days later the government, the Communist Party, and the Central Council of Trade Unions called in turn for the creation of workers' councils, they were merely giving official recognition to an already accomplished fact.

When the fighting died down, the workers' councils set about grouping themselves together in district workers' councils. On 29 October delegates from some nine major factories in Ujpest met together at the United Lamp Factory, while several meetings were held in the Beloiannis factory of representatives from workers' councils in the ninth district of Budapest. Similar efforts towards co-ordination and joint action also took place in Obuda and Angyalfold, while on 30 October representatives of workers' councils in nineteen of the larger Csepel factories set up the Central Workers' Council of Csepel.

Finally on 31 October, a Parliament of Workers' Councils was convened for the whole of Budapest at which delegates from some two dozen of the city's largest factories were present. The meeting drew up a statement of the basic rights and duties of the workers' councils, which were formulated in the following nine points:

1. The factory belongs to the workers. The latter should pay to the state a levy calculated on the basis of the output and a portion of the profits.

2. The supreme controlling body of the factory is the Workers' Council democratically elected by the workers.
3. The Workers' Council elects its own executive committee composed of 3-9 members, which acts as the executive body of the Workers' Council, carrying out the decisions and tasks laid down by it.
4. The director is employed by the factory. The director and the highest employees are to be elected by the Workers' Council. This election will take place after a public general meeting called by the executive committee.
5. The director is responsible to the Workers' Council in every matter which concerns the factory.
6. The Workers' Council itself reserves all rights to:
   (a) Approve and ratify all projects concerning the enterprise.
   (b) Decide basic wage levels and the methods by which these are to be assessed.
   (c) Decide on all matters concerning foreign contracts.
   (d) Decide on the conduct of all operations involving credit.
7. In the same way, the Workers' Council resolves any conflicts concerning the hiring and firing of all workers employed in the enterprise.
8. The Workers' Council has the right to examine the balance sheets and to decide on the use to which the profits are to be put.
9. The Workers' Council handles all social questions in the enterprise.[38]

This resolution represents one of the clearest formulas for establishing a structure of workers' control of the factory ever to have been put forward. That it could be formulated in so clear and concise a form only two or three days after the fighting had died down does much to refute the Kadar régime's claims that the workers' councils were largely dominated by politically reactionary elements which sought the restoration of capitalism. Indeed, it shows not only that there was a strong and determined proletarian aspect to the revolution, but that this proletarian movement was able to express quite clearly how it sought to take power out of the hands of the Communist Party bosses and bureaucrats and place it firmly in those of the workers themselves. The real strength and determination of this movement, however, was only to be fully displayed after the Soviet tanks had crushed the revolution, when the workers' councils remained as the only organised force capable of resisting the efforts of the Soviet leaders to reimpose their rule on Hungary.

On the morning of 1 November the students' and intellectuals' organisations arranged a meeting between delegates of the workers' councils and representatives of the Nagy government in the Hungarian Parliament. Following these preliminary discussions, a further meeting was convened for the same evening in the headquarters of the Building Trade Unions, and was attended by delegates from the workers' councils of all the large Budapest factories. The meeting was addressed by Ferenc Erdei and Zoltan Vas for the government, who appealed to the workers' delegates to call off the strike. After a lively debate, the delegates expressed their confidence in the Nagy government, and decided to call for an immediate return to work.

The remaining few days of the revolution saw this debate continuing at grass-roots level, and a growing movement in favour of the return to work. In many cases there were disagreements between factory workers' councils, more concerned with securing the industrial achievements of the revolution and favouring a return to work, and district revolutionary committees often linked with armed fighting groups, which wanted to continue the strike until all their political demands had been met. Nevertheless, on 3 November two of the most prominent district councils, the Central Workers' Council of Csepel and the Ujpest Revolutionary Committee, voted to call off the strike. All was set for a united resumption of work on the morning of Monday, 5 November.

The communist opposition

Geza Losonczy and Ferenc Donath, the two most prominent opposition politicians after Imre Nagy himself, spent the first two days of the revolution secluded in their homes and out of touch with their friends. On the morning of 25 October they went to the Central Committee headquarters but rejected the party's interpretation of the events as a counter-revolution, and declared their intention of resigning from the posts allocated to them on the Central Committee. However, before they could actually hand in their resignations, the replacement of Gero by Janos Kadar was announced, and they then agreed to take part in the Central Committee's deliberations. In the following days, Losonczy and Donath were to argue in the Central Committee for the recognition of the events as a national democratic revolution, and for the Communist Party to adopt as its own the popular demands of the revolution, but they were consistently and overwhelmingly voted down.

Meanwhile a number of the opposition journalists assisted with the publication of the party daily *Szabad Nep*, bringing out its first issue of the revolution on 26 October. Within the paper's editorial board the opposition faction gradually gained the upper hand, and on 28 October *Szabad Nep* carried a leading article entitled "Faithful to the Truth", which rejected the condemnation of the recent events as a fascist counter-revolution and declared that "a great national democratic movement has developed in our country which embraces and welds together our people as a whole". On the following day, in an article written by Miklos Molnar, *Szabad Nep* even dared to publicly repudiate the views of the official Soviet paper *Pravda* which had carried an article entitled "Collapse of the Antipopular Adventure in Hungary". In the opinion of *Szabad Nep*:

> "What happened in Budapest was neither antipopular nor an adventure. What is more, it did not collapse. . . .The slogans of socialist democracy were the loudest to be heard and not those of the reaction and counter-revolution."[39]

Finally, on 1 November Janos Kadar, the new First Secretary of the Communist Party, announced the dissolution of the former party and the formation of a totally new one, to be called the Hungarian Socialist Workers' Party, and declared in a radio broadcast:

> "In a glorious uprising, our people have shaken off the Rakosi régime. They have achieved freedom for the people and independence for the country, without which there can be no socialism."[40]

Outlining his views further to an Italian journalist, Kadar declared his commitment to a "new type" of communism, which he described as "Hungarian national communism". He also pointed out that this had "emerged from our revolution, during the course of which, as you know, numerous communists fought at the side of students, workers and the people."[41]

Kadar also announced the creation of a preparatory committee to organise the new party which included, besides Kadar himself, some of the most prominent members of the former opposition — Imre Nagy, Zoltan Szanto, Georg Lukács, Sandor Kopacsi, Geza Losonczy and Ferenc Donath. The new party also published its own newspaper *Nepszabadsag* ("People's Freedom") which was edited by Sandor Haraszti, and which declared its wholehearted support for the demands of the revolution and the government of Imre Nagy.

Several other members of the opposition, however, refused to join the new party even though Nagy, Losonczy and Donath were amongst its leaders. Considering themselves as the real socialist wing of the revolution, these people wanted to establish, "a national, non-communist but socialist, revolutionary party". They included many of the former opposition journalists such as Miklos Gimes, Peter Kende, Miklos Molnar, Pal Locsei and Sandor Fekete, and on 30 October they brought out their own independent socialist paper *Magyar Szabadsag* ("Hungarian Freedom"), which they saw as representing "the independent left-wing of the revolution". The first issues of *Magyar Szabadsag* called upon the government to accept the revolution's demands for a restoration of the multi-party system and the declaration of Hungarian neutrality.

The most proletarian voice of the revolution was raised by an independent radio station called Radio Rajk, which expressed its dismay that the Communist Party had been forced to consent to the reorganisation of the bourgeois parties, but declared that the maintenance of socialism was a task for the Hungarian communists themselves, and not one calling for outside intervention. Socialism, it declared, could not be achieved by the use of bayonets, and the Hungarian communists could only regain respect for themselves and for the ideas of marxist-leninism by facing up bravely to the new situation and adopting a clear and sincere stand. In the words of Radio Rajk: "The Hungarian Communist Party is now fighting for its survival, and it can only survive in the new situation if it serves the interests of the Hungarian people."[42]

Similar views to these were shared by one of the most illustrious intellectual leaders of the new Communist Party, Georg Lukács, who told the Polish journalist Wiktor Woroszylski that in free elections the new party would get, at the most, ten percent of the votes and might have to pass into the opposition:

> "The new party cannot count on any rapid success, because communism is completely compromised in Hungary. . . . But the party will exist to safeguard its ideals, to be an intellectual centre, and in a few years, or dozens of years, who knows . . . ?"[43]

These were also the ideals expressed by many young Hungarian communists in the days of the revolution, one of whom explained to a Yugoslav journalist: "As soon as peace is restored, we've got to start from the very beginning, all over again. We have to gain the confidence of the masses through an honest, truly socialist policy."[44]

The dedication of these young Hungarian communists to the

ideals of socialism remained steadfast if not strengthened when the Russians returned to finally crush the revolution. On 5 November, as the workers of Budapest continued to resist the onslaught of the Soviet tanks, Radio Rajk declared that the Soviet leaders had "convinced not only the whole world, but also all communists, that they do not care for communism at all". At the same time, these Hungarian communists even in this dark hour did not for one moment give up their belief in the struggle to realise their communist ideals. While vehemently denouncing Janos Kadar as a traitor to his country and a servant of Russian imperialism, Radio Rajk also issued the following appeal:

> "Comrades, join the pseudo-Communist Party of Janos Kadar immediately, possibly in leading positions, and do your best to make a truly Communist Party of it. However long and hard this task may be, turn it into a Hungarian Communist Party."[45]

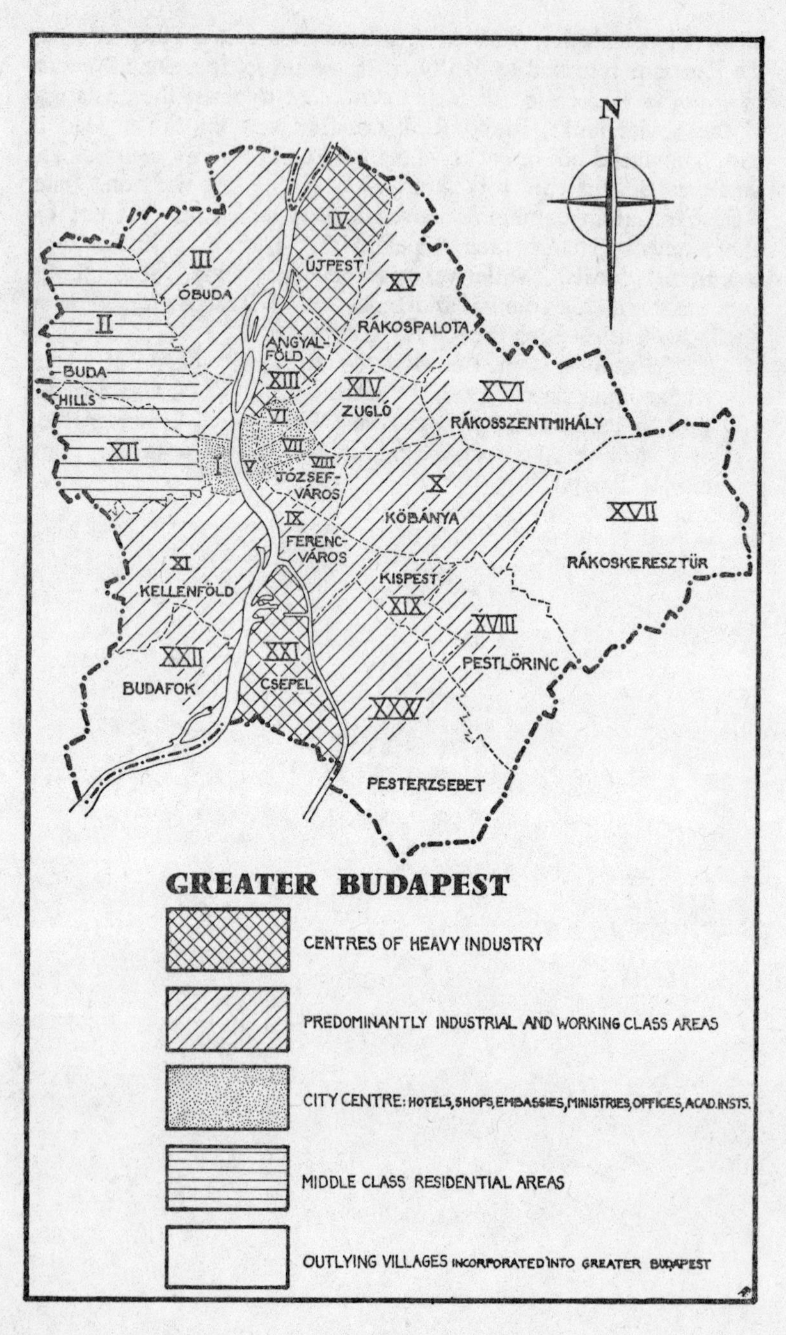
N
III
ÓBUDA
IV
ÚJPEST
XV
RÁKOSPALOTA
II
ANGYALFÖLD
BUDA
HILLS
XIII
XIV
ZUGLÓ
XVI
RÁKOSSZENTMIHÁLY
VI
VII
XII
I
V
VIII
JÓZSEFVÁROS
X
KÖBÁNYA
XVII
IX
FERENCVÁROS
RÁKOSKERESZTÚR
XI
KELLENFÖLD
KISPEST
XIX
XVIII
XXII
XXI
PESTLÖRINC
BUDAFOK
CSEPEL
XX
PESTERZSEBET
GREATER BUDAPEST
CENTRES OF HEAVY INDUSTRY
PREDOMINANTLY INDUSTRIAL AND WORKING CLASS AREAS
CITY CENTRE: HOTELS, SHOPS, EMBASSIES, MINISTRIES, OFFICES, ACAD. INSTS.
MIDDLE CLASS RESIDENTIAL AREAS
OUTLYING VILLAGES INCORPORATED INTO GREATER BUDAPEST

5 The Workers' Councils of Greater Budapest

> "We may not be able to hold out for long, so let us do such things during our brief tenure of power that the working classes of the world will remember them for ever."
>
> *V. I. Lenin, October 1917*

With the second Soviet intervention of 4 November the first phase of the Hungarian revolution was brought to a sudden and violent end. The government of Imre Nagy collapsed, and he and his leading supporters sought refuge in the Yugoslav Embassy. The leaders and spokesmen of the various political parties disappeared from the scene even more quickly than they had arrived upon it. The armed forces of the revolution put up a last ditch defence in both the towns and the countryside, but soon they were either defeated or forced to flee to the West. But the revolution was still far from over. Instead it was to develop into a new phase, a phase in which the leading role was to be taken by the Hungarian working class.

Unable to keep up armed resistance in the face of overwhelming military supremacy, the workers of Hungary now turned to the most basic and traditional weapon of the working class — to a general strike which was to become one of the most total and united in the whole history of the world working-class movement. Their strike was even to lead one Western academic to remark:

> "This was the first time in history that the syndicalist myth of the revolutionary general strike . . . actually became the basis of sustained political action by the entire industrial population of a country."[1]

The strike, lasting for well over a month, was in its very essence a political strike, employed as a weapon against both the Soviet military occupation and the new Kadar régime. It demonstrated that despite the paper existence of the Kadar government, despite the very concrete existence of the Soviet armed forces, power in Hungary remained where it had been ever since 23 October — in the hands of the ordinary people, and first and foremost in the hands of the workers.

In the following weeks, the power of the working class was to achieve an even greater strength and consolidation. In its beginnings, the strike had been an instinctive reaction of the working class, completely spontaneous and neither centrally directed nor organised. Having realised their power, however, the workers proceeded to consolidate and organise it in a revolutionary structure of workers' councils set up at the level of the factory, the district, the city and eventually the country itself.

Thus while the Soviet military intervention had crushed overnight the purely political achievements of the revolution, it led at the same time to the strengthening of the real social base of the revolution. In the weeks which followed 4 November, the Hungarian workers seized the opportunity to establish a revolutionary structure of workers' councils which would ensure that power remained in the hands of the working people themselves .

The workers' resistance

When Janos Kadar announced the formation of his Revolutionary Worker-Peasant Government on 4 November at the same time as the Russians launched their second armed invasion of Hungary, it was the committed Hungarian socialists and the Hungarian working class who turned most strongly against him. And it was in the working-class districts of Budapest, and in the industrial centres of the countryside, that the Soviet forces were to meet with the strongest resistance.

On 5 November Radio Rajk issued an appeal to resistance, declaring: "Comrades! The place of every true Hungarian communist today is on the barricades!" On 7 November the workers' council of the huge iron and steel complex of Dunapentele, formerly Stalinvaros, the great new industrial city built under the communist régime, announced that it was being attacked from all sides by Soviet forces:

> "Dunapentele is the leading socialist town in Hungary. In this town all the inhabitants are workers and they hold the power in their hands.
>
> . . . The population of the town is under arms . . . they will not give in because they have erected the factories and homes of the town with their own hands. . . . The workers will defend the town against fascism — but also against the Soviet troops."[2]

A week later it was the turn of the workers' council of Ozd, an industrial centre in north-east Hungary, to defiantly reject the appeal of Kadar's government for the support of the Hungarian workers:

"No! The working class wants Kadar and his colleagues to know that they will never under any circumstances work together with traitors.

The workers from Ozd, Diosgyor, Kazinbarcika, Borsodnadas and Salgotarjan, the miners of the coalfields of Borsod and Ozd stand firm and united against Kadar and Co."[3]

Similar rebuttals were received by the Kadar régime from all the leading working-class centres of the country. The greatest armed resistance to the Soviet forces occurred in the large iron and steel centres of Dunapentele, Ozd and Miskolc, and in the mining regions of Borsod, Dorog, Tatabanya and Pecs.

In Budapest itself the Soviet military authorities had to concentrate their heaviest armoured units on the workers' suburbs of Kobanya and Csepel, where the workers had occupied their factories and continued to defend them for several days against the Soviet tanks. One writer claims that hospital figures show that eighty to ninety percent of the wounded were young workers, while the Kadar régime's own reports show that the greatest damage to buildings and the greatest number of deaths occurred in the predominantly working-class districts of the city. The stately villas and gardened houses of the fashionable middle-class districts on the slopes of the Buda hills were hardly touched by the fighting.[4]

The major organised centres of resistance in Budapest — the Kilian barracks and the Corvin cinema, the citadel on Gellert hill and Buda castle, as well as such prominent intersections as the Moricz Zsigmond, Szena and Marx Squares — were the first targets of the Soviet assault, but even so they were not put out of action until 6 or 7 November after three days and nights of heavy fighting. In the outlying districts of Ujpest and Kobanya fighting continued for a few days more. "Red Csepel" was the last workers' district to fall but then only when, having put down resistance in the rest of the city, the Soviets could move all their major units against Csepel on 10 and 11 November.

The military defeat of the workers, however, by no means assured the immediate victory of the new authorities, for the workers still held the trump card — their control over production. Following the Soviet ocupation the workers refused to return to work, and in the course of the ensuing general strike they organised themselves in workers' councils at factory, district, city, and eventually national level. Through the strike and the workers' councils, they were to carry on the struggle of the revolution and to withstand for several weeks the counter-revolutionary assault of both the Kadar régime and the Soviet authorities.

The development of district workers' councils

Those workers' councils which had been in an active stage of development before 4 November were also the first to reorganise as the fighting died down. They were also the first to realise that to defend the achievements of the revolution they would have to co-operate with one another and co-ordinate their activities. With this aim in view, the workers' councils of the the larger factories took the lead in setting up district workers' councils in their local neighbourhoods. The first of these was probably that in the Kellenfold district of Budapest, where the lead was taken by the workers of the Beloiannis electrical equipment factory. As early as 8 November, a delegation from this district workers' council was even received by General Grebennik, the commander-in-chief of the occupying Soviet forces.

The Ganz electrical works in Csepel took a similar lead in the creation of a Csepel Workers' Council, which also sent delegations both to the Soviet Commander and to Kadar. Between 8 and 12 November, further local workers' councils were established in the districts of Kispest, Zuglo, Obuda, Angyalfold and Ujpest.

In slight contrast to the factory workers' councils, whose major task had been to take over the management of their enterprises, these district workers' councils were from the start essentially political organs. They saw their role as to defend what they could of the achievements of the revolution, and to represent the interests of the workers in dealings with the Kadar government and the Soviet military authorities. But there was a common demand unifying the two, and this was that the factories should be the common property of those who worked in them, that production should be managed by the democratically elected organs of the workers themselves, by the workers' councils.

The first statement of the political demands of the workers to be made after 4 November was put forward in a resolution of delegates from workers' councils of the Kellenfold district at a meeting on 12 November. This resolution declared the readiness of the workers to return to work and to negotiate with the Kadar régime, on condition that certain of their political demands were met. In the forefront of these demands stood the immediate release of Imre Nagy and his supporters, an immediate ceasefire, and a commitment to the withdrawal of the Soviet troops and the holding of free and democratic elections. At the same time, the workers emphasised that the factories and the land must remain in the hands of the working people, and called for the enlargement and strengthening of the power and authority of the workers' councils.[5]

The creation of the Central Workers' Council

It was also on 12 November, at a meeting of the Revolutionary Workers' Council of Ujpest, that the first move was made towards the creation of a central body to co-ordinate the activities of workers' councils throughout the whole of Budapest. The meeting was also attended by workers' delegates from the neighbouring district of Angyalfold, and by a few students and young intellectuals.

It was a young Budapest intellectual, Miklos Krasso, who called upon the Ujpest workers' council to take the lead in issuing an appeal for the formation of a central workers' council which would represent the workers of the whole of Budapest, and be able to negotiate in their name directly with the Kadar régime and the Soviet authorities. The suggestion received support from the older workers present, and the workers' council agreed to call upon other workers' councils throughout the city to send delegates to a meeting in the town hall of Ujpest the following afternoon in order to set up a central workers' council.[6]

The students attending the meeting agreed to arrange for the duplication of the appeal, and its distribution throughout the city. Indeed, two of those present left the Ujpest meeting to proceed directly to the district workers' councils in Csepel and Kellenfold.

However, on the morning of 13 November, several members of the Ujpest workers' council were arrested, and delegates arriving for the meeting to set up a central council found the town hall of Ujpest surrounded by Soviet tanks. Many of them, nevertheless, were directed to the nearby United Lamp Factory, Egyesult Izzo, but since many of the districts and large factories were not represented there, it was decided to put off the founding meeting of the central council until the following day.

On the afternoon of 14 November, the founding meeting of the Central Workers' Council of Greater Budapest finally took place in the Egyesult Izzo factory. Some fifty delegates were present, representing all the major factories and districts of Budapest. Delegates also attended from the provincial centres of Miskolc and Gyor.

Some confusion now arose from the fact that the proceedings were not presided over by the members of the Ujpest workers' council who had originally convened the meeting, but the leaders of the workers' council of the Egyesult Izzo factory in their capacity as hosts. Consequently, when the young intellectual who had originally proposed the creation of a central workers' council two days earlier rose to expand on his ideas, he was pulled up short by those now present who argued that they had not come to be lectured to, least of all by someone who was neither a worker nor a representative of any workers' organisation. Then, while a lively debate ensued in which the workers' delegates were quite clear and united in their political demands and in their will to create a central organisation, they were vague and unsure about the form of organisation they required and the strategy to adopt for the realisation of their demands.

It was Sandor Bali, a delegate from the Beloiannis electrical equipment factory, who was the first to impose any real direction on the meeting. Bali argued that the workers' councils should not recognise the Kadar government, but that they should be prepared to parley and negotiate with it. To this end he proposed the creation of a central workers' council which, at the same time as giving overall direction to the general strike, would be able to represent the demands of the workers and win concessions from the Kadar government.

Bali's proposal was accepted by the meeting, which declared the establishment of the Central Workers' Council of Greater Budapest with the authority to negotiate in the name of the workers of all the factories of Budapest. The meeting also called for the election of district workers' councils throughout the city, and for new elections to the factory workers' councils as soon as possible. Finally, the meeting passed a resolution which declared the workers' loyalty to the principles of socialism and their determination to defend the collective ownership of the means of production. The resolution went on to outline the workers' political demands which included a general amnesty, a government under Imre Nagy, the withdrawal of the Soviet troops and the abolition of the one-party system. Until these demands were met, they declared, the general strike would continue.[7]

The Central Workers' Council: composition and organisation

The delegates to the founding meeting of the Central Workers' Council made up an interesting selection of workers from the major local districts and the larger factories of Budapest. Many of them were long-standing members of the working-class movement, with past political experience in either the Social Democratic or the Communist Party, and often both. Several of the older workers had also been active in the militant prewar Metalworkers' Union. At the same time, the meeting was remarkable for the strong representation of young workers, with almost half of the delegates aged between twenty-three and twenty-eight. These younger workers added enthusiasm and dynamism to the experience and responsibility of the older delegates. There was also, within both age groups, a very strong representation of skilled workers — engineers, metalworkers, toolmakers and electricians. A number of students and young intellectuals also attended the meeting as observers.

Following the debate and the decision to set up the Central Workers' Council, it became increasingly clear that some more formal structure was necessary to give order and direction to the proceedings. Consequently the meeting elected a provisional committee of some twenty-odd members, whom it authorised to draw up a more orderly and precise programme of action. Amongst the members of this provisional committee were to be found most of those who were subsequently to become the effective leaders of the Central Workers' Council. Though the exact composition of this committee has never actually been documented, we do know the identity of a good half of its members, who may not be unrepresentative of the body as a whole. They included:

Istvan Babay: Delegate of the Municipal Company of Tramways.

Arpad Balazs: Delegate from Ujpest, and a worker in the mining machinery factory.

Jozsef Balazs: Delegate from Angyalfold and a turner in the steel works Magyar Aczel. Veteran of the Metalworkers' Union, and Communist Party member since 1945.

Sandor Balazs: Delegate of Egyesult Izzo, toolmaker and veteran of the Metalworkers' Union.

Sandor Bali: Delegate of the Beloiannis factory and the Kellenfold district. A forty-year-old toolmaker, veteran of the Metalworkers' Union, member of the Social Democratic Party before the war and of the Communist Party since 1945.

Jozsef Devenyi: Delegate of the workers' council of the Csepel iron and steel works.

Gyorgy Kalocsai: Delegate from Csepel, and a thirty-two-year-old chemical engineer in the Vegetable Oil Factory.

Sandor Karsai: Delegate from Kobanya, and a twenty-six-year-old metal engineer in a factory producing radiators.

Miklos Sebestyen: Delegate of the Hungarian Optical Works, and a twenty-six-year-old metallurgist.

Ferenc Toke: Delegate from Zuglo, and of the workers' council of the Telephone Apparatus Factory. A twenty-six-year-old toolmaker, and former member of the Social

Democratic Party.

From the very start the most prominent of these individuals was Sandor Bali, who had given both drive and direction to the creation of the Central Workers' Council. It was also he who was to provide the larger political conceptions within the framework of which the Central Workers' Council was to develop and organise. It was characteristic of his personal honesty and socialist spirit that, despite being an active member of the Communist Party since 1945 and a more than able toolmaker, he had remained amongst the workers on the shopfloor when many others were seeking positions of management and privilege. Now too, though the undisputed driving spirit of the Central Council and frequently its most prominent spokesman, he was content to remain with the position of a simple member.

Shortly to achieve an equal prominence to that of Sandor Bali was Sandor Racz, another toolmaker at the Beloiannis factory and the president of its workers' council. Only twenty-three years old, Sandor Racz was the most active representative of the younger workers, and a man whose character combined profound sincerity with both dynamism and determination. Somewhat more militant than Sandor Bali, he was a vocal advocate of the creation of a national workers' council, and was later to be elected president of the Central Workers' Council.

Elected secretary of the Central Workers' Council was Istvan Babay, a delegate of the Company of Tramways. The Council's headquarters were shortly to be moved to the city centre offices of the Company of Tramways, and Istvan Babay was to perform the day-to-day administrative tasks involved in running the Council.

Sandor Karsai, a young fitter who had worked his way up to become a metal engineer at a factory producing radiators in Kobanya, was very popular with the workers and became head of the political commission of the Central Council. He had insisted from the start on the importance of formulating a long-term perspective for the workers' councils, and of clarifying their proper role within the economic and political system.

Two other members of the provisional committee, Miklos Sebestyen and Ferenc Toke, are also worthy of special note since they have both subsequently provided accounts of the activities of the Central Workers' Council. Miklos Sebestyen, a young engineer who had learned a number of Western languages, became head of the Council's press commission and assumed responsibility both for holding press conferences for foreign journalists, and for producing the Council's information bulletin. Ferenc Toke, a young worker who had attended evening classes at the Technological University where he had come into contact with the students' movement, was made responsible for organisational matters.

Besides those already mentioned, amongst others who joined later in the work of the Central Council was Lajos Varga, a worker from the workers' council of the Zuglo district who could speak Russian, and who took charge of the Council's relations with the Soviet military command.

The plenary meeting of the Central Workers' Council, however, was not a permanent body but a delegate assembly, made up of two representatives from each of the district workers' councils of Greater Budapest. Consequently, the delegates attending its different meetings were not necessarily always the same people. At first the only appointed official was the secretary, Istvan Babay, and members of the Council took it in turn to preside over its meetings. This arrangement, however, proved to present a number of problems, and eventually Sandor Racz was to be appointed as a permanent president, with Gyorgy Kalocsai as vice-president.

The Central Workers' Council also set up a secretariat with seven commissions for the supervision of particular fields of its activities. Their heads were Sandor Racz, Sandor Bali, Gyorgy Kalocsai, Sandor Karsai, Istvan Babay, Miklos Sebestyen and Ferenc Toke. Since they included the three permanent officials of the Central Council, it is obvious that these seven constituted the effective leadership or working executive of the Central Workers' Council of Greater Budapest.[8]

The strike issue

Having created a working executive and prepared a platform of political demands, the Central Workers' Council appointed a nineteen-man delegation under the leadership of a Csepel delegate, Jozsef Devenyi, to present the demands of the workers of Budapest to the Kadar government. This delegation met with Kadar in the parliament building on the evening of 14 November.

Kadar, in a most remarkable speech, declared his agreement in principle with most of the demands of the delegation, namely Imre Nagy's participation in the government, democratic elections with several political parties, and the eventual withdrawal of the Soviet troops. In the same breath, however, he argued that these demands could not be met immediately under the prevailing circumstances, and while calling upon the workers to first return to work, he offered no guarantee that their demands would be implemented. Thus, while appearing conciliatory, Kadar did not in fact give way on a single point. Consequently, the Central Council delegates felt that they could not make any concessions either, and the meeting broke up with no obvious results or achievements.[9]

Meanwhile, the initial informality of both the structure and proceedings of the Central Workers' Council was giving rise to a number of problems. At first the Council had no permanent chairman or president, or even an officially appointed spokesman. The first meeting had been chaired by an Ujpest delegate Arpad Balazs, and he was then mandated to act as spokesman to make known the Central Council's standpoint to the public. Arpad Balazs, however, used the opportunity to issue a radio appeal that same evening, 14 November, calling for an unconditional return to work in the name of the Central Workers' Council. Learning of his action, other members of the Council concluded that he was a government agent who had infiltrated the Council, and he was removed from its membership.

Arpad Balazs was then replaced by Jozsef Devenyi, who had led the delegation to Kadar on 14 November, but in subsequent days he too took up an almost equally equivocal attitude towards the strike, and generally acted in a rather indecisive manner. Consequently he soon came to be regarded as an opportunist who was inclined to compromise with the Kadar régime, and he too was removed from the Central Council. The situation was eventually resolved by the election of the more militant and combative Sandor Racz as a permanent president of the Central Council.

Meanwhile, the debate continued within the Central Council over the attitude to adopt towards the Kadar government and towards the continuation of the strike. The Central Workers' Council had now moved its headquarters to the offices of the Municipal Company of Tramways in central Budapest, and a second meeting was held there on 15 November which was considerably more representative of the workers of the whole of Budapest. More district workers' councils had sent their delegates to this meeting, while a meeting of delegates from the workers' councils of another twenty-five large factories had also voted to join forces with the Central Workers' Council. Several delegates from workers' councils in the provinces also took part in this session.

The main issue before the meeting arose from the failure of the meeting with Kadar. While some delegates called for outright opposition to the new authorities — "We have no need of the government! We are and shall remain the leaders here in Hungary!" declared Sandor Racz — the majority of delegates favoured seeking a compromise settlement with the government. It was Sandor Bali who proposed that while refusing to grant *de jure* recognition to the Kadar government, they should not hold back from establishing a *de facto* relationship with it.

The central question, however, remained that of the strike. A number of delegations, most notably those from Csepel and Gyor, favoured an unconditional return to work designed to give the government time to prove the sincerity of its intentions. Others, in contrast, argued for a total and resolute strike, refusing all offers of compromise and holding out for the full implementation of their demands. Once again, Sandor Bali won support for a policy of moderation. The country, he declared, was in a condition of severe devastation, and the workers' councils had no reserves to draw on for a long strike. In this situation, he suggested, the workers should offer to return to work in return for substantial concessions from the Kadar government. Moreover, by such action they could demonstrate that the strike was not just a spontaneous and unorganised reaction of the workers, but an organised and formidable weapon consciously directed for the implementation of the workers' demands.

A new delegation was formed and sent again to Kadar in a deliberate spirit of conciliation. However, this delegation met with just the same rebuttal as the earlier one. While Kadar appealed to the Central Workers' Council to call off the strike, he would not, or could not, offer any guarantees for the satisfaction of their demands.

Nevertheless, pressures for a return to work were building up throughout the city. As the bitter Hungarian winter approached, the general strike came to be seen as a lethal weapon to those who used it as well as to those against whom it was directed. On 15 November, the Central Workers' Council of Csepel had called for a return to work. The next day, the Central Workers' Council of Greater Budapest followed suit, and agreed to call for the resumption of work throughout the city on Monday 19 November. At the same time, they insisted that they were not abandoning any of the popular demands of the revolution.

Not everyone, however, was happy with the decision to call off the strike. Far from having been pressganged into going on strike by the Central Workers' Council, as the Kadar régime tried to make out, many of the workers were bitterly opposed to the return to work, and felt that the Central Council had betrayed the strikers. Indeed, some members of the Central Council were almost beaten up by angry crowds of workers protesting outside the Council's headquarters. When other delegates arrived later from the countryside, several of them turned angrily on the leaders of the Central Council, "calling us all possible names: scoundrels, traitors, etc".[10]

Relations with the Soviet military command

Besides attempting to negotiate with the Kadar government, the Central Workers' Council also entered into direct contact with the Soviet military authorities under the command of General Grebennik. The first contacts were made in an effort to prevent deportations, and to secure the release of Hungarians arrested by the Russians. An agreement was reached whereby the Central Workers' Council presented the Soviet military command each day with a list of missing workers' council members, and the Russians then saw to their release from prison. The workers' councils also acted as intermediaries in the distribution of provisions and medical supplies to the population.

In these arrangements, the Soviet command dealt directly with the Central Workers' Council, completely over the heads of the Kadar government, and in so doing effectively recognised the Central Council as the representative organ of the Hungarian workers. Indeed, each member of the Central Council was even issued with a special Soviet pass authorising the bearer to travel freely after curfew, as well as a permit to carry arms.

At first, representatives of the Central Council would go to the Soviet military headquarters for talks, but later on Soviet officers were sent to attend the sessions of the Central Council. Eventually the Russians actually delegated a Soviet colonel with an interpreter as a permanent representative to the Central Workers' Council, and on one occasion a group of Soviet officers accepted an invitation to visit a local factory and hear the Hungarian workers express their views.

On the whole, the Soviet representatives acted very correctly and with apparent sympathy for the workers' councils. Most reports, however, suggest that they were somewhat confused as to just what role the workers' councils were seeking to perform, and it is very probable that their conciliatory attitude had been ordered from above. Certainly their attitude was quick to change at the beginning of December when General Grebennik was recalled to Moscow and replaced by the Russian secret police chief, General Ivan Serov.

The National Workers' Council

Proposals to create a National Workers' Council had been put forward at several meetings of the Central Workers' Council ever since its foundation, but the action had been put off until a meeting could be held of democratically elected delegates from the workers' councils of the whole country.

A detailed plan for the constitution of a National Council which would serve as a "Parliament of Workers' Councils" was put before the Central Workers' Council on 18 November. The plan proposed the creation of a 156-member assembly of delegates from the workers' councils of the districts of Budapest, and of the counties, as well as from a number of the largest factories. This assembly would elect a thirty-member presidium which would have the right to co-opt up to twenty further representatives of the universities, the army, the police, the intellectuals' organisations and the political parties. The Central Workers' Council approved the plan and on 19 November issued an appeal to all workers' councils in Hungary to send delegates to a conference in the Budapest sports stadium on 21 November to set up a National Workers' Council. "The principal task of this national conference," states one of the signatories to the appeal, "was to create a power under the direction of the workers, and in opposition to the government." Invitations to attend the meeting were also issued to both the Kadar government and the Soviet military authorities.[11]

At 8 a.m. on the morning of 21 November it almost looked as though General Grebennik had accepted the invitation to the conference — some four hundred Soviet tanks had appeared on the streets, surrounding the sports stadium, and blocking off all the roads leading to it. Delegates arriving for the conference, however, were quietly redirected to the headquarters of the Central Workers' Council in the city centre, where the national conference was able to take place after all, despite the Soviet display of force. Besides the representatives of Budapest, delegates arrived from workers' councils in Gyor and Veszprem, Tatabanya, Pecs and Komlo, Ozd and Salgotarjan. There were also a number of peasants' delegations from smaller villages.

Many of these delegates had arrived in an angry mood, believing that the leaders in Budapest had betrayed them by calling off the strike. The miners' delegates from Tatabanya, Pecs and Salgotarjan were the most angry and uncompromising. "You can work if you want," they declared, "but we shall provide neither coal nor electricity, we shall flood all the mines!" The sending of Soviet tanks to prevent the meeting of the national conference showed what one could expect from negotiations with Kadar. The only answer to such people, they declared, was to maintain the general strike.

With some difficulty, the leaders of the Central Workers' Council managed to convince the delegates from the provinces that they were not collaborating with the government, and that a continuation of the strike in Budapest would only cause misery to the population and disorganise the workers' forces. At the same time, the meeting decided not to officially constitute a National Workers' Council for fear that this might serve as a pretext for the Kadar régime to ban the Central Workers' Council too and clamp down on the workers' councils elsewhere. Nevertheless, the meeting had in fact established the basis for a permanent liaison between the Central Workers' Council and the workers' councils in the provinces, and in this way a National Council had in effect been brought into being. Finally, the meeting issued a proclamation restating the workers' demands and declaring that their full co-operation with the government could not be assured until their demands were met.

Meanwhile, the news that the sports stadium had been surrounded by Russian tanks had given birth to rumours throughout the city that the national conference had been prevented from meeting and the delegates arrested. Before the national conference had completed its deliberations, the workers had launched a protest strike, and by the time the Central Workers' Council learned about it, the strike was almost total throughout the city. Faced with the reality of the strike, the leaders of the Central Council agreed to give their backing to it, in protest against the attempt to prevent the national conference from meeting. Acting partly in solidarity with the strikers, partly under the pressure of the delegates from the provinces, they declared an official forty-eight-hour protest strike.

From the very beginning, the Central Workers' Council of Csepel had acted in a somewhat independent fashion. They had from the first been opposed to the strike, and in favour of a more trusting attitude towards the government. At the same time, though, they were just as adamant as the Central Council in Budapest in demanding the withdrawal of Soviet troops and free elections with a plurality of political parties. Equally resolutely, they condemned the attempt to prevent the meeting of the national conference on 21 November and the continuing arrests of members of workers' councils.

However, on 22 November the workers' council of the Csepel iron and steel works went a good step further out of line in condemning the call of the Central Workers' Council of Greater Budapest for a forty-eight-hour protest strike. The time for such head-on collisions with the government had, they declared, passed. Nevertheless, the Csepel workers themselves proved as ready as those in the rest of Budapest to answer the strike call. In view of this situation, the Central Workers' Council decided to send a special three-man commission to Csepel to investigate the local workers' councils' opposition to the strike and to the Central Council. But in the days which followed, the workers of Csepel themselves set matters right in new elections to their workers' councils. In these elections those leaders who had opposed the strike, including the former president of the Central Workers' Council of Csepel, lost their positions and were replaced by more militant workers prepared to act in greater solidarity with the Central Workers' Council of Greater Budapest.

Following the over-reaction of the Soviet authorities in sending tanks to prevent the meeting of the national conference on 21 November, the Central Workers' Council went out of its way to avoid any action that might be taken as a provocation and prejudice the attempt to reach a compromise settlement with the Kadar government. With such considerations foremost, the Central Council's activity turned increasingly to the organisation of passive resistance. One of the first instances of this was the silent demonstration on 23 November, in commemoration of the revolution. The suggestion that no one should go out on to the streets of Budapest between 2 and 3 p.m. in the afternoon was put forward by the Revolutionary Council of Intellectuals and taken over by the Central Workers' Council. The call to the people of Budapest was followed unanimously, perhaps particularly so because on this very day came the news of the abduction of Imre Nagy and his companions from the Yugoslav Embassy. The occasion is recalled by an eye-witness:

> "Budapest, in a matter of one second, became a haunted city. Haunted only by the Russian armoured cars driving from one place to the other, but to no avail. The silence was more eloquent than any shot which might have been fired at them."[12]

The most significant attempt to reach some form of agreement between the Central Workers' Council and the Kadar government occurred on 25 November, when a conference between the two sides was held in the parliament building. In speeches to the workers' leaders, Janos Kadar, Gyorgy Marosan and Antal Apro appealed to the workers' councils to help the government in the establishment of order and the resumption of production. The workers, Kadar argued, were confused and did not know which road to follow. It was the duty of the workers' councils, he continued, to support the government in leading the workers away from the counter-revolution. To this, Sandor Bali replied: "There is no confusion in the spirit of the workers, but rather in yours!"

"You ruffians!" exclaimed Marosan in return, "To think you can give us a lecture! You call yourselves prolos! But what have you in common with the workers?"[13]

In such an atmosphere it is hardly surprising that the conference ended without any agreement being achieved, and if anything the two sides moved further apart. Having failed to win the co-operation of the workers' leaders, the government was increasingly to charge the workers' councils with being unrepresentative of the working class as a whole, and to use force and coercion against them. At the same time the confrontation hardened the views of the workers' leaders, and strengthened the arguments of those calling upon the Central Workers' Council to act as an independent political force. This standpoint was made clear in a speech to the conference by Sandor Bali, who asserted "it is the Hungarian working class which has set on foot the workers' councils, which for the moment are the economic and political organisations that have behind them the working class."[14]

In similar tones, in an appeal to all workers' councils throughout Hungary issued on 27 November, the Central Workers' Council proclaimed: "We reaffirm that we have received our mission from the working class . . . and we shall work with all our might for the strengthening of the workers' power".[15]

"The time had now come," recalls Miklos Sebestyen, "to strengthen the activity of the Central Workers' Council and to assert ourselves as a political force recognised as such by the people."[16]

A workers' journal

The last week of November saw increasing efforts by the authorities to misrepresent and undermine the workers' councils. For instance, at the parliamentary conference Gyorgy Kalocsai had denounced provocative actions by stalinist elements in the factories, but his speech was reported on the radio as an attack on "provocative fascist elements". The Central Workers' Council took even greater exception to the overall picture of the parliamentary conference given by Kadar in a radio broadcast on 26 November, in which he attacked the workers' councils as counter-revolutionary forces, and said they would either have to support the government or shut up shop.

The re-formed AVH also set to work to undermine the workers' councils, and forged leaflets in the name of the Central Workers' Council calling both for a continuation of the strike and for armed action against the Soviet authorities. These provocations were obviously aimed both at disrupting the unity of the workers' councils, and at lending support to allegations that they were instigating counter-revolutionary actions.

In view of these incidents, the Central Workers' Council came to the conclusion that it would have to issue a journal to keep the factories and the country truly informed of its activities. Most of the printing shops, however, were occupied by the Soviet forces, and the government was adamant in refusing the Central Council any authority to publish its own journal. Despite this, the Central Council set up a press commission under Miklos Sebestyen who got together with a number of young journalists, intellectuals and students to bring out a paper under the simple title of *Munkasujsag*, or "Workers' News". They even arranged with the workers' council of a small printing shop to print the paper without official authorisation.

The first numbers of the *Workers' News* were already coming off the press when leading members of the Central Council arrived to announce that the government had made it known that it would regard such activities as a provocation, and so the Central Council had decided not to go ahead with publication. Instead, they agreed to continue with the duplicated *Information Bulletin* which was already being produced and distributed through the workers' councils.

Despite the stepdown by the Central Council, the Hungarian authorities still raided the printing works, seizing the few copies of the *Workers' News* that had been printed, and trying unsuccessfully to arrest Sebestyen. At the same time the Soviet authorities seized the duplicating machines in a number of large factories, in an attempt to prevent the propagation of the Central Council's bulletin. These actions, however, served only to increase the workers' interest in the *Information Bulletin*, typed copies of which were now passed from hand to hand in the factories, read out to workers' meetings, and relayed to provincial towns over the telephone. The Central Workers' Council called upon the workers to boycott the Communist Party daily *Nepszabadsag*, and all other official papers with the exception of the *Sports News*.

The battle for control in the factories

Meetings between the Central Workers' Council and the Kadar government continued almost daily, but while Kadar continued to express his agreement in principle with the workers' demands, he insisted that in the existing situation the first task had to be the restoration of order, i.e. the strengthening of his government's power. In practice, however, the more the authority of the government was increased, the more it sought to restrict the activities and competence of the workers' councils. In this spirit, a decree on the workers' councils was issued on 22 November which sought to restrict their activity to purely economic and not political functions.

At other times Kadar seems to have been on the verge of reaching some compromise with the Central Workers' Council, but to have been overruled by the hardliners in the government and party leadership. For instance, at one point Kadar offered to recognise the Central Workers' Council as a national council of producers which would have a leading role in the administration of the economy, but the decree effecting this proposal was vetoed by the stalinist members of his government.

For a time the government sought to persuade the workers' councils to function within the framework of the official trade unions, but the Central Workers' Council categorically refused even to negotiate with the official trade unions which they regarded as bureaucratic organs of party control in no way representative of the workers. As Sandor Bali explained: "We mustn't, indeed we cannot, talk about trade unions until the Hungarian workers have themselves built up their organisations from the base up, and have won back the right to strike."[17]

The Central Workers' Council, its leaders explained, was ready and willing to co-operate with independent and democratic trade unions which represented the interests of the workers. To make the unions into such organisations, the Central Council demanded new democratic elections within the trade unions. Such elections had been agreed to before the second Soviet intervention, but after 4 November the official union leadership continually postponed the elections, contending that "the atmosphere in the factories . . . was not conducive to the holding of democratic and secret elections".[18]

The end of November also saw the intensification of conflict at the level of production itself, as the Communist Party attempted to rebuild its organs of control within the factories, to deny the workers' councils the right to appoint and dismiss factory directors, and to reorganise the trade unions and the AVH.

The workers' councils had been unanimous that they would allow no party organisations within the factories, and when Communist Party officials sought to return and re-establish their organisations that had existed before the revolution, many were banned or even physically prevented from entering the factories. With reregard to the trade unions, the workers' attitude varied from place to place. Where the unions had remained under the control of former stalinist functionaries, they too were banned from the factories, and the workers demanded that they be represented either by the workers' councils themselves or by unions independent of party control. In other cases, where local union leaders had supported the revolution and now refused to join Kadar's Communist Party, the unions were able to retain the confidence and support of the workers.

During the revolution or shortly afterwards, a large number of workers' councils had dismissed and replaced their communist factory directors. Now, however, the Kadar régime declared that it alone, not the workers' councils, had the right to appoint or dismiss leading executives, and sought to reinstall those factory directors who had been replaced.[19]

Finally, Kadar had repeatedly asserted that the hated AVH would not be re-formed, and that the workers themselves would be incorporated into the new organs of public security. From the first days of his régime, numerous workers' councils had offered to assist Kadar in his proposal to arm the workers — offering to provide the workers to be armed — but they had been totally ignored, and as the new security force was established it was not units of factory workers' guards but members of the former AVH who provided its mainstay.

In this battle for control of the factories, a battle which was fought for no less than direct control of the means of production, and fought out at the very point of production itself, the workers succeeded for a considerable time in resisting the onslaught of the party bureaucracy. In the terminology of the latter, "for several days at the end of November the counter-revolution ruled over a significant proportion of the factories". But, aware of their structural weaknesses and their total lack of any base amongst the workers themselves, the communist authorities came increasingly to use intimidatory and coercive measures against the workers' councils. Verbal attacks on the councils' "anti-government policy and anti-party campaign" were stepped up, and in the first days of December some two hundred members of various workers' councils were arrested.[20]

In this atmosphere of growing repression, calls were increasingly raised for more determined and open resistance to the Kadar régime, and for a new general strike. This placed the Central Workers' Council in a somewhat awkward position. While its power was being undermined by the coercive actions of the government, it was coming under increasing pressure from below to take firmer and more energetic action. While fearing it might lose the confidence of the workers if it did not act strongly enough, it was also aware that almost any action might be considered by the government as a provocation and an excuse for even more coercive measures.

Meanwhile, proposals were being aired for some action to commemorate the victims of the second Soviet intervention of 4 November. One plan which had been drawn up was for a great workers' demonstration through the streets of Budapest on 4 December. The Central Workers' Council firmly rejected this idea for fear of bloodshed and further repression, and decided instead on a silent procession of women, dressed in black and carrying flowers, who would march to the Tomb of the Unknown Soldier in Heroes' Square. The Central Workers' Council also called upon the rest of the population to demonstrate their solidarity by placing lighted candles in their windows at midnight.

The women's procession took place despite the presence of Soviet tanks and armed troops trying to disperse them, and although the government had withdrawn all candles from the shops, almost every window of Budapest was lit up that night.

Kadar and his government were evidently outraged by this open flouting of their authority. The Central Workers' Council, they declared, was now "in the tow of the counter-revolution". The Central Council's leaders gained the impression that the government was now preparing for a final blow against them, and in view of their good relationship up till now with the Soviet authorities, they decided to appeal for help to none other than the Soviet Government. A delegation from the Central Workers' Council went to the Soviet military command and asked them to inform the Soviet ambassador that the Central Council would like the opportunity to present its case before representatives of the Soviet Government. They also sent a letter to the Soviet Premier, Bulganin, with a similar request, in which they declared that "the various measures of the government . . . against the revolutionary elements serve only to splinter the best and most progressive forces of socialism in Hungary".[21]

The dissolution of the Central Workers' Council

In the first weeks of December, faced with increasing attacks from the government, with many members of workers' councils disappearing daily and increasing demands from the provinces for action, the Central Workers' Council recognised the necessity, come what may, of calling a further national conference of workers' councils.

A secret and extraordinary session of the Central Workers' Council was held on 6 December, at which plans were discussed to create a National Workers' Council with a definite political programme. The proposals envisioned the extension of the Central Workers' Council of Greater Budapest into a National Workers' Council with a permanent presidium, secretariat and committee structure. In addition, a provisional Workers' Parliament would be set up, composed of representatives of workers' councils throughout the country, which would replace the National Assembly until 23 October 1957, on which date free national elections would be held between the democratic political parties.

The Central Council also adopted a memorandum addressed to the government, in which it protested that while it had been prepared to negotiate with the régime and work for the resumption of production, it had met with only force and intimidation from the authorities. Repeating once again the fundamental demands of the workers' councils, the Central Council demanded a public reply from the government saying what steps it would take to meet the workers' demands.[22]

Finally, the Central Workers' Council arranged to secretly convene a meeting to create the National Workers' Council on 9 December. But the Kadar régime learned of these plans from AVH agents who had infiltrated the Central Council, and in the early hours of 9 December the government arrested a majority of the Central Council's members and issued a decree declaring its dissolution.

Nevertheless, several members of the Central Council as well as a number of delegates from provincial towns had already arrived at the headquarters of the Central Council on the evening of 8 December. Learning that their plans were about to be forestalled, they went into immediate session. In fact a member of the Central Council was called to the telephone by a representative of the government who demanded to know if they really were planning to create a National Council. "Yes," he replied, "we are already in session. . . . We shall continue."[23]

A few moments later, news came that Soviet troops had opened fire on demonstrating miners in Salgotarjan. The atmosphere, relates Ferenc Toke, became "a tempest of indignation". Without hesitation, the delegates declared a forty-eight-hour protest strike against the terroristic and intimidatory actions of the government. "Let the lights go out, let there be no gas, let there be nothing!" declared one delegate. "Strike till the spring, or even till our lives end!" called another.[24]

Finally, the meeting issued a proclamation in support of the strike in which it declared that the Kadar government was no longer capable of resolving the country's troubles, and called upon trade unions throughout the world to hold strikes in solidarity with that of the Hungarian workers.

As already planned, the government replied to the strike call by outlawing the Central Workers' Council and arresting the majority of its members. Two of its most prominent members, Sandor Racz and Sandor Bali, spent the 9 and 10 December in the Beloiannis factory under the protection of the workers, who refused to permit the police to enter and arrest their leaders even when the factory was menacingly encircled by Soviet tanks. On the morning of 11 December, Janos Kadar issued a personal invitation to Racz and Bali to meet with him in the parliament for discussions. Racz and Bali accepted Kadar's invitation and presented themselves at the parliament, whereupon they were immediately arrested and imprisoned.

The banning of the Central Workers' Council and the imprisonment of its leaders gave an added impetus to the strike of 11 and 12 December. As work came to a halt both in Budapest and throughout the country, even the Communist Party's own paper *Nepszabadsag* was to describe the strike as one "the like of which has never before been seen in the history of the Hungarian workers' movement". In the course of the two-day protest, demonstrations, disturbances and even armed clashes with the authorities occurred in a number of provincial towns, at Eger, Miskolc, Ozd and Kecskemet.

In reply to the strike, the government declared a state of emergency and banned all meetings and demonstrations called without official permission. At the same time all territorial workers' councils, at district, town and county level, were declared disbanded. On 13 December, the government issued a further decree establishing detention without trial for up to six months, and setting up special courts of summary jurisdiction throughout the country.

These actions, however, only further increased the antagonism of the working class towards the government. Straight on the heels of the forty-eight-hour strike, the workers of the Csepel iron and steel works occupied their factory with a sit-in strike, demanding the release of Sandor Racz and Sandor Bali. Their action was immediately joined by the workers of the Beloiannis factory, and followed by those in at least a dozen more large factories. In counter-action, many of these factories were now occupied by Soviet troops.

The following month saw the last-ditch stand of the workers' councils, operating in semi-legality, to prevent the control of the factories being wrested out of their hands by the Communist Party bureaucracy backed up by the Soviet armed forces. Spasmodic strikes and demonstrations continued to occur throughout the country, and further armed clashes took place between workers and both AVH and Soviet soldiers in the industrial centre of Csepel and in a number of provincial towns. In the face of terror and intimidation, and overwhelming military might, the workers' resistance was courageous but doomed to eventual defeat.

On 5 January a new decree reduced even further the legal competence of the workers' councils, and Kadar's Revolutionary Worker-Peasant Government extended the death penalty to striking or inciting to strike. Faced with daily increasing intimidation, on 8 January the workers' council of the Csepel iron and steel works announced its resignation, declaring:

> "Under the presently prevailing circumstances, we are no longer able to carry out our obligations . . . and for this reason, we are returning our mandate into the hands of the workers."[25]

Many of the remaining workers' councils followed the lead given by Csepel and announced their own disbandment. The government responded to what it considered "the provocative self-dissolutions of the workers' councils" by increasing the scope of the death penalty to almost any act of criticism. In Csepel itself, Soviet troops sent in to disperse demonstrating workers were again involved in heavy fighting.

On 15 January the Central Workers' Council, still functioning in illegality, issued its final appeal to the workers to keep up their resistance:

> "Because of the terror, however, and the death penalty even for distributing leaflets, the Council exhorts the workers to spread all news concerning the underground by word of mouth. Sabotage and passive resistance are the order of the day."[26]

Sabotage and passive resistance, and even the occasional strike and demonstration, continued throughout 1957, but the organised power of the Hungarian workers' councils had now been broken. Finally, on 17 November 1957, a government decree declared the dissolution of all remaining workers' councils.

6 The Hungarian Socialists against the Kadar Régime

> "If we perish, it is all the more important to preserve our ideological line and give a lesson to our continuators. This should never be forgotten, even in hopeless circumstances."
>
> *V. I. Lenin, March 1921*

The second phase of the Hungarian revolution, in which the leading role had been taken by the organised working class, was also reflected at the level of theory, in the ideas of the intellectuals and leaders of the former opposition movement.

In the months preceding the revolution the stubborn loyalty of Imre Nagy, and most of the members of the reformist opposition, to the official procedures of the Communist Party had prevented them from acting independently and establishing any real contact with the working masses. Right up to and even during the revolution the main concern of the opposition had been to achieve political change at the top of the régime, not to assist in the activities and organisation of working people at the base of society. The idea of workers' councils found no mention in Imre Nagy's writings, and had been only rarely considered even by the radical wing of the opposition.

In the days of the revolution, however, the workers had increasingly come to the fore, and after its suppression the workers' councils played the leading role in the attempt to defend the revolution's achievements against the counter-revolutionary drive of Kadar and the Soviets. In the course of these struggles, the actions of the workers served to effect a further revolution in the ideas and theories of the opposition movement. In this process, all the leaders of the opposition came to recognise the potential of the workers' councils, while its more radical members came to regard them as the foundation on which a new structure of socialism could be based.

While some spokesmen of the opposition now made a last attempt to restate and justify their earlier revisionist belief in the democratic reform of the communist state, the more radical members of the opposition set about a critical re-evaluation of their former actions and ideas in the light of the events of the revolution. This exercise in rethinking, though concerned primarily with the strategy of the opposition within a communist state, was also to go on to re-examine both the theories of marxist-leninism and the entire history of the world communist movement.

The last search for a compromise

In the early hours of 4 November as the working people of Budapest awoke once again to the sound of gunfire, as hundreds of Soviet tanks streamed into the capital, and as Imre Nagy and his supporters fled to sanctuary in the Yugoslav Embassy, one man stayed calmly at his post in the Hungarian parliament, patiently typing out a protest to the world against the new Soviet invasion of his country. When the Soviet soldiers came upon the room in which this man was working, he politely informed them that he was a minister of state working on pressing government business, whereupon they respectfully placed a guard outside his door so that "the Minister" might get on with his work without further disturbance.

This man was one of the most respected of Hungarian political thinkers, Professor Istvan Bibo, a left-wing critic who had courageously and consistently stood out against the dictatorships of Horthy, Szalasi and Rakosi, advocating a "third road" policy for Hungary based on a populist programme of social reform and a foreign policy of independence and neutrality. Though not particularly prominent in the previous years of opposition, nor in the first days of the revolution itself, at the beginning of November Bibo had emerged as one of the leading figures of the new Petofi Party and was made a minister of state in Imre Nagy's final coalition cabinet. On the morning of 4 November, when most of his colleagues had already fled into refuge or hiding, he had felt it his duty to stay on at his post to make an official protest in the name of the Hungarian government against the second invasion of his country by the Soviets.[1]

In the statement which he now composed, Bibo sought to reject the charge that what had happened in Hungary was a counter-revolution. Hungary, he asserted, had no intention of pursuing an anti-Soviet policy, and he rejected categorically any suggestion that the revolution had been stained by fascist or anti-semitic actions. On the contrary, he argued, it had been the entire Hungarian people who had risen up — without any "class or religious discrimination" — against "the foreign army of conquest and its local gangs of henchmen". Then he turned to the Hungarian people, calling on them not to recognise the occupying army and the new "puppet government", and to employ all means of passive resistance against them. Finally and dramatically, he appealed to the West, declaring: "The Hungarian people have sacrificed enough blood. . . . Now it is for the world powers to act".[2]

While the final section of this statement, no doubt motivated by the desperation and drama of the occasion, appears to be a direct appeal for Western armed intervention, and as such highly irresponsible and most out of character for an advocate of "third road" policies, it probably gives expression to the bitterness felt by many Hungarians at this moment in time. Indeed, Bibo was to further elaborate on this viewpoint in a *Political Testament* written in hiding some six weeks later, and smuggled out and published in the West only after Bibo had been arrested and thrown into jail in Hungary. In his *Testament,* Bibo described the Hungarian situation as "a scandal for the Western world", alleging that the West had, before October, urged on the peoples of Eastern Europe to revolt, and then left them in the lurch when they actually did so. This behaviour, he declared, had undermined not only the effectiveness of the West's policy, but its honesty as well.

In this same *Testament,* Bibo condemned with equal bitterness the reaction of the communist world for thinking that the suppression of the revolution was necessary to preserve socialism in Hungary. "The further free development of the Hungarian situation," he argued, "would quickly have shown not only that it was not harmful to the cause of socialism, but that, in fact, it could have served as an example for it," and he went on to suggest that "what was destroyed by the Soviet tanks would have been the beginning of one of the most exciting socialist experiments of this century".[3]

Meanwhile, in the days after his first statement of 4 November, Bibo had put his efforts into drafting proposals aimed to rally the forces who had supported Imre Nagy to seek a compromise settlement with the Soviets. These proposals were put together in a "Plan to Solve the Hungarian Question on a Compromise Basis" drawn up on 9 November. In this plan, Bibo argued that it was impossible to restore order in Hungary so long as the Soviet troops remained, but that if they were withdrawn, any such government as the Kadar régime would immediately collapse. To solve this problem, Bibo proposed that the Hungarians should provide the Soviets with guarantees for the maintenance of socialism in Hungary, in return for a phased withdrawal of the Soviet troops.

Bibo then outlined his proposals for a settlement which he believed could provide the guarantees and safeguards required. First, the only government which could command respect was the coalition of 3 November under Imre Nagy. Second, Hungary's independence could be preserved by a pact of friendship with the Soviet Union outside the military structure of the Warsaw Pact. Third, to prevent the persecution of communists, an amnesty should be declared for all political offences. Fourth, the evacuation of the Soviet troops should be carried out in a phased system of withdrawal coterminous with the gradual establishment of the authority of a Hungarian government and national assembly. Fifth, before any elections, a constitution should be drawn up which would guarantee not only political freedoms and parliamentary democracy, but also the maintenance of a socialist social structure based on social ownership. Finally, after the withdrawal of the Soviet troops and the restoration of order, general elections would be held in which only those parties would be allowed which respected the provisions of the constitution, including the maintenance of a socialist society.[4]

In the weeks which followed the suppression of the revolution, Bibo's ideas were to provide the main impetus to the final attempts to realise the programme of the pre-October revisionist opposition — the internal and democratic reform of the communist state. Indeed, Bibo's set of proposals sought for much the same compromise as Imre Nagy had striven to attain during the days of the revolution. Bibo's vision of a new synthesis of socialism and democracy, of the reconciliation of nationalism and communism, was very similar to Nagy's own dream of a reform of the system which would reconcile the Hungarian people with communism, the Hungarian nation with the Soviet Union. At the same time, Bibo's ideas also incorporated the very naivety and weaknesses of Nagy's own conceptions. Just as they replaced the concept of class struggle with that of national unity, so they implicitly denied the existence of any irreconcilable conflicts of interest within the communist state itself, or of any fundamental conflicts between one communist state and another. Consequently, Bibo was destined to follow in the very footsteps of Imre Nagy, down the very same cul-de-sac, in the belief that the communist state could realise democracy by the internal reform of its own institutions, that the Hungarian nation could achieve independence through negotiation and compromise with the Soviet rulers.

What is even more astounding is that, just as Imre Nagy in the days of the revolution, so now Bibo looked to the salvation of the revolution not through the further development of its most original creations — the revolutionary committees and workers' councils —

but by collaboration with the bourgeois political parties of a previous era, of the 1945-48 coalition period. Even at this late hour, the opposition of the élite had still not really become aware of the true significance of the revolution of the mass, that in the very course of the revolution itself new structures had emerged, and that the revolution could not now be saved by any amount of juggling and tinkering with the old political institutions. On the contrary, the revolution would only have been fulfilled when the old political institutions had been completely swept away, and replaced by the new social structures of the mass uprising. Only then would it have been able to resist the counter-revolutionary drive of the Soviet occupying forces and their puppet Hungarian henchmen.

Despite these limitations, however — indeed, perhaps because of them — Bibo's plan was widely circulated in Budapest and received warm support from both the writers and intellectuals and the politicians of the coalition parties, and even, perhaps ironically, apparent sympathy from Prime Minister Janos Kadar himself. The one significant innovation in Bibo's plan was his proposal for a multi-party system limited to those parties which accepted a common platform of socialism, and this idea seems to have appealed to Kadar as a possible means of harnessing some measure of popular support to his narrow and isolated régime.

As early as 14 November, Kadar had publicly told a delegation of the Central Workers' Council that he wanted to see "a multi-party system and free honest elections", and had implied his readiness to bring into the government some of the "honest middle-class politicians" who supported socialism. Even before this, Kadar had held private meetings with Zoltan Tildy and other non-Communist Party leaders with a view to forming some form of coalition, and reports suggest that agreement in principle had been reached, but that the idea was vetoed by stalinist members of the government and the Soviet military commanders. The major stumbling block to any real success in this direction was probably the non-communist leaders' insistence on the participation of Imre Nagy in the government, while the severest blow to any hopes of co-operation must have been delivered by the abduction of Imre Nagy and his colleagues on 22 November.

Nevertheless, even in the atmosphere of bitterness following the abduction of Imre Nagy, Kadar continued to keep the idea of a coalition alive. In a speech on 26 November, he reaffirmed his desire to include in his government non-communist political figures who "recognised the socialist order and were prepared to work for the defence of the socialist achievements and the building of socialism", and in subsequent days he had further meetings with leaders of the non-communist parties, amongst them the Smallholders' leader, Bela Kovacs. Early in December, the non-communist leaders issued a "memorandum" in which they outlined their minimum conditions for participation in any government. In its essentials, this document repeated the promises and demands of Bibo's earlier plan. While the government made no direct reply to this approach, Kadar himself continued to float the idea of a coalition over the next two months, although he now seemed to have in view the incorporation of certain individuals, rather than any genuine coalition of independent political parties.[5]

In the final analysis, however, the combination of wariness and suspicion on the part of the non-communists, together with resistance from the hardline stalinists in Kadar's cabinet and the Soviet authorities, seems to have prevented the idea of a coalition government ever really coming to fruition. Then, in subsequent months, as the Kadar régime succeeded in consolidating itself in power, less and less came to be heard of the need to broaden its base, and with the demise of the idea of coalition died also the last hopes of any compromise settlement.

The last acts of resistance

In the weeks following the suppression of the revolution, the efforts of the writers and intellectuals were aimed not only at the search for a political compromise with the Kadar régime and the Soviet authorities, but also at preserving and defending the achievements of the revolution.

The first initiative in this direction was taken at a meeting convened by the Writers' Association on 12 November which was attended by almost all of the most prominent of Hungary's writers and intellectuals. It was members of the former opposition, led by Miklos Gimes, who spoke out most strongly in condemnation of the Soviet invasion and demanded the complete withdrawal of Soviet troops from Hungary. It was they too who drew the attention of the meeting to the significance of the workers' struggle and the role of the workers' councils.

After a lengthy discussion of the possibilities for action the meeting voted against the continuation of armed resistance, and also declared that the question of maintaining the strike should be left to the workers to decide. Finally, the meeting declared its support for a proclamation drawn up by the writers Gyula Hay, Laszlo Nemeth and Aron Tamasi which called for a Hungary that would be independent, neutral, democratic and socialist. The proclamation went further than previous statements by the writers in contending that it was no longer sufficient to think purely in terms of political parties, and declared:

> "For this reason we throw in our lot with the Hungarian working class, the peasantry and the revolutionary youth, and in the course of further developments we shall work together with their democratically elected organisations."[6]

Close on the heels of this first meeting called by the writers, the Revolutionary Committee of Hungarian Intellectuals was re-formed under the leadership of the university professor Gyorgy Adam, and in the second week of November it issued a declaration of what it considered to be the minimum programme of the revolution. In this and subsequent declarations, the intellectuals took up and expanded upon the ideas of the writers' proclamation, arguing that it was now necessary "to place our total social, economic and political life on a new basis", and that the principle of such a reconstruction should be "social self-management" based on the revolutionary committees and workers' councils.[7]

On 20 November, the Committee was reorganised as the Revolutionary Council of Hungarian Intellectuals with the world famous composer Zoltan Kodaly as its president, and with a presidium whose members included many of the most prominent of Hungary's writers, intellectuals and academics. On the following day, the Council issued an appeal protesting against the continuing arrests and deportations and calling for the creation of a new national government based on the organised forces of the people. Declaring outright opposition to any form of restoration, either capitalist or stalinist, the appeal called for a new social order based on the democratic organisations of the workers, soldiers and peasants, the youth and intellectuals — "the organisations of power, not of party".[8]

On 24 November, in the face of increasing intimidation by both the Kadar régime and the Soviets, the Council issued a Manifesto signed by a hundred and ten leading intellectuals which declared full support for the continuing struggle for freedom, and ended with the dramatic announcement: "We accept all the consequences that our acts or our words may bring upon us: prison, deportation, and, if necessary, death." A few days later, the Council issued a further statement declaring that it was now the Hungarian working class alone which could provide "the strongest mass force capable of defending the achievements of the revolution", and announced its "complete solidarity with the workers' councils". Throughout these days, the Revolutionary Council of Intellectuals worked closely with the Central Workers' Council of Greater Budapest. In fact its final act was to issue a declaration on 7 December in support of the Central Workers' Council's call for the constitution of a National Workers' Council and the establishment of a Workers' Parliament formed from representatives of workers' councils throughout the country.[9]

The most radical wing of the intellectuals was constituted by a group of young writers and students led by Gyula Obersovszky who had produced the paper *Igazsag* ("Truth") during the revolution, and who now brought out a paper called *Elunk* ("We Are Alive"). Calling itself "the paper of the Hungarian revolution", *Elunk* called upon the workers' councils to establish themselves as a political power, and appealed to the writers and intellectuals to recognise the leading role of the Central Workers' Council in the struggle against the Kadar régime. *Elunk* was printed on the duplicating machinery of a Budapest screw factory, where Obersovszky and the students also helped in producing the leaflets and bulletins of the Central Workers' Council.[10]

When the Kadar régime acted to forestall the establishment of a National Workers' Council by banning the Central Workers' Council and arresting many of its leaders at the end of the first week in December, Gyorgy Adam and Gyula Obersovszky and several other prominent activists amongst the intellectuals were also taken into custody. Finally, on 11 December, the Revolutionary Council of Intellectuals was banned by the government.

The organisation which survived longest under the repression, perhaps because it was not itself a creation of the revolution, was the Writers' Association. However, the Writers' Association had been adamant in condemning the Soviet invasion and at the beginning of December had declared its solidarity with the Central Workers' Council, pledging its support for "the struggle of the workers' councils and other workers' organisations for the workers' self-determination". In fact two delegates of the Writers' Association had participated in the meetings of the Central Workers' Council.

Following the banning of the revolutionary organisations of the intellectuals and the workers, the Writers' Association held a special meeting on 28 December, where the writers reaffirmed their support for the October revolution and condemned the Soviet intervention as a "historic mistake". This act was the last open and public protest by the opposition, for Communist Party and government leaders immediately condemned the writers as "counter-revolutionaries whose profession happens to be writing". On 17

January the Writers' Association was temporarily suspended, and three months later it was officially disbanded.[11]

The fate of the opposition

When the Russians launched their second assault on Budapest on 4 November, Imre Nagy and several of his closest colleagues sought refuge in the Yugoslav Embassy. This group included most of the revisionist communists who had made up the moderate wing of the opposition in the years before October. Amongst them were Zoltan Szanto, Georg Lukács, Geza Losonczy, Ferenc Donath, Sandor Haraszti, Szilard Ujhely, Miklos Vasarhelyi, Ferenc Janosi, Jozsef Szilagyi and Gyorgy Fazekas, as well as the Petofi Circle's secretary, Gabor Tancsos, and Mrs Julia Rajk. These were the people who had participated in the new Communist Party, the Hungarian Socialist Workers' Party, which had been re-formed under Janos Kadar during the revolution, and several of them had also been ministers in Imre Nagy's government or members of his personal secretariat.

As the group included five of the seven members of the committee set up on 1 November to organise the new Communist Party, i.e. Nagy, Szanto, Lukacs, Losonczy and Donath, as well as the editor of the party's paper, Sandor Haraszti, they decided to continue to act as the Provisional Executive Committee of the Hungarian Socialist Workers' Party — in whose name the Kadar government was claiming to rule. Under Nagy's leadership this committee now drew up a new political platform in which they re-affirmed the revolution's demands for the withdrawal of the Soviet troops, the restoration of the multi-party system, the withdrawal from the Warsaw Pact and the declaration of neutrality. And at last, and despite their isolation in the embassy, they finally came round to recognising the importance of the workers' councils, declaring: "The central government of the Hungarian People's Republic should first and foremost rely for its support on the workers' councils."[12]

Nagy and his colleagues were also able to maintain contact with those of their supporters who remained at liberty outside the embassy. In this way they were able to let those outside know of the stand they were taking, and also to be kept informed of the opinions of the opposition and the Hungarian public regarding what action should now be taken. They sought advice in particular on the question of what form of organisation would be most appropriate for carrying on the struggle for the revolution's demands. Their colleagues outside informed them that the Hungarian Socialist Workers' Party now enjoyed no respect whatever, and that in the new situation "it was not a party, but a broad mass movement which was now required".

Nagy and his friends within the embassy, however, were able to do little themselves to create such a movement. As Soviet troops and Hungarian state security forces restored order in the city, they were unable to maintain their contacts with those outside the embassy, and their abduction to Rumania on 23 November brought their role in the events to a final end. Nevertheless, those of Nagy's followers who had remained at liberty outside the embassy were, for the most part, the more radical members of the opposition who even before the revolution had favoured the creation of a broader and more independent movement than was possible within the confines of the Communist Party. Hardly a single one of the more radical members of the opposition had sought refuge with Imre Nagy in the Yugoslav Embassy, while first and foremost amongst those who remained at liberty were the young Communist journalists like Miklos Gimes, Peter Kende, Miklos Molnar, Pal Locsei and Sandor Fekete, who had first raised the banner of the opposition in support of Imre Nagy in the autumn of 1954. It was they too who were now to take the lead in the struggle against the Kadar régime and the occupying Soviet forces, publicly whenever possible, clandestinely when not.

These young journalists had previously been the most prominent of those who had argued for the opposition to organise itself on a clear ideological platform, independent of the official Communist Party, and to appeal to the popular masses outside the party. During the revolution, while supporting Imre Nagy, they had sought to maintain their independence both from his government and from the new Communist Party, and they had published the independent socialist journal *Magyar Szabadsag* ("Hungarian Freedom"). It was exactly this policy which they were now to carry forward in organising the "broad mass movement", the necessity for which even Imre Nagy had finally come to recognise. In this effort they were joined by other former communists like Gyorgy Adam and by a number of young activists from the People's Colleges, the Petofi Circle and the universities.

The moving spirit of this group, just as he had been the moving spirit of the radical wing of the opposition before the revolution, was the journalist Miklos Gimes. In the first days after the invasion, Gimes and his friends had met with representatives of the non-communist parties and other revolutionary groupings including the student group around Gyula Obersovszky's papers, *Igazsag* and

Elunk, with a view to creating a united political organisation to continue the struggle for the revolution's demands. Then, on 11 November, Gimes brought out the first issue of a duplicated broadsheet called *October 23*, in which he issued a call for national resistance in support of a programme for "a democratic, independent, neutral Hungary".[13]

It was after receiving the message from their colleagues in the Yugoslav Embassy that, on 13 November, an organisation was formally constituted to give direction and leadership to the resistance movement. Planned at first as a "League of Hungarian Socialists", it was eventually decided to call it the "Hungarian Democratic Independence Movement" in the hope of rallying the widest possible support behind it. On 15 November the Hungarian Democratic Independence Movement issued a political platform, drawn up by Gimes, entitled "The Ten Commandments of the Hungarian Renaissance". Its main demands were for the withdrawal of the Soviet troops, the restoration of the Imre Nagy government, Hungarian neutrality, a new police force, freedom for all democratic parties and organisations, and the recognition of the workers' councils and revolutionary committees as the main basis of the government. A few days later these demands were repeated in an appeal to the workers' councils and other revolutionary organisations to accept the leadership of the Hungarian Democratic Independence Movement in the struggle against the Kadar régime and the Soviet authorities.

October 23 now appeared as the official mouthpiece of the new movement. In its earliest issues it carried the political platform drawn up by the Nagy group in the Yugoslav Embassy, giving uncompromising expression to the original demands of the revolution and guidance on how to maintain the resistance struggle. Edited by Gimes, its strategy was based on his belief that a determined resistance movement could convince the Russians of the impossibility of restoring order through the Kadar régime, and force them to reach a settlement with the representatives of the revolutionary movement. On 6 December, *October 23* published the "Programme of the Hungarian Democratic Independence Movement", summarised in three points as: complete and unconditional independence; political democracy on the basis of the free activities of the workers' councils, revolutionary committees and political parties, and the maintenance of the land reform and the social ownership of the factories, mines and banks. *October 23* saw the greatest achievement of the revolution as the destruction of the system of one-party rule and the creation of workers' councils and revolutionary committees. Indeed, it called upon the workers' councils to establish themselves as an effective political power by setting up an armed workers' militia, organising themselves on an industrial branch basis, and creating a "National Workers' Council which would be the democratically-elected leading organ of the whole working class".[14]

In support of his aim of forcing a settlement on the Russians which would preserve Hungarian independence and democracy, Gimes was also the main instigator in preparing a "Draft Proposal" to be put to the Russians. This was drawn up jointly by the leaders of the Hungarian Democratic Independence Movement in co-operation with the Revolutionary Council of Intellectuals, the Central Workers' Council and the democratic political parties. The proposal embodied detailed suggestions for a new Hungarian constitution and pact with the Soviet Union which would guarantee the establishment of an independent and democratic Hungarian state that would be both neutral and socialist. In a most characteristic act of courage and bravado, Gimes presented himself at a press reception being held in the Grand Hotel by Mr Kumara P. S. Menon, who had been sent to Budapest as a personal representative of Prime Minister Nehru of India. Though Gimes was now a wanted man, the AVH did not dare to seize him in front of the Indian diplomats, and he was able to have a lengthy discussion with Mr Menon and to present him with a copy of the draft proposal. Needless to say, a few hours later Gimes was arrested and imprisoned, but he had succeeded in his objective, and the draft proposal was subsequently put to the Soviet leader Bulganin by Prime Minister Nehru at a meeting in Moscow in early 1957.

With the arrest of Gimes and other leaders of the resistance and the workers' councils and the banning of their organisations early in December, all organised opposition to the Kadar régime was finally brought to an end, though the strike continued for some time and protesting voices continued to be raised, for instance in the Writers' Association. Indeed *October 23* continued to appear, now being edited by Peter Kende and Miklos Molnar, but towards the end of December one of its main distributors was arrested, and the AVH appeared to be on the verge of uncovering those involved in its production. Its last issue appeared on Christmas Eve 1956, and a few weeks later both Peter Kende and Miklos Molnar fled the country.

The final act of the revolution

In the weeks following the revolution, the most radical members of the former reformist opposition had finally drawn the practical conclusions from the ideals and aspirations earlier expressed in the writings of Imre Nagy and the demands of the opposition. These conclusions implied the creation of an independent political movement, freed from the confines of the official Communist Party, appealing beyond the party to the broad masses of the people, and first and foremost to their democratic mass organisations created during the revolution, the revolutionary committees and workers' councils.

The commitment to new forms of action, however, implied in its turn yet further consequences in the field of theory. This revolution in thought, this transformation of ideology, was carried out after the activity of opposition and resistance had finally come to an end, after the revolutionary organisations of both intellectuals and workers had been disbanded, by a group of younger intellectuals, mostly university lecturers, teachers and students. Several of the members of this group were long-standing communists, a few of whom had been active in the underground Communist Party and the resistance movement during the second world war. Others, however, were younger socialists from the student generation which had been brought up and educated under the communist régime, and who had not suffered the same traumas of loyalty and disillusionment which had shaped so many of the older members of the reformist opposition. These were perhaps the first to be able to look clearly and dispassionately at the régime, to analyse it critically from a marxist standpoint and, in so doing, to revise and rejuvenate the marxist theory on the principles of which it had, allegedly, been established.

Several members of this group had earlier been active in the Students' Revolutionary Committee at the University of Budapest, and following the suppression of the revolution had taken leading parts in the production and distribution of leaflets and posters protesting against the Soviet occupation and the Kadar government. As the repressive measures of the Kadar régime were stepped up, they reorganised themselves as an underground group at the home of a young university professor where they continued to hold meetings, collect information and issue leaflets. Increasingly, however, their attention became centred on the preparation of an analysis of the lessons to be drawn from the experience of the October revolution, in a lengthy pamphlet entitled *On a Few Lessons of the Hungarian National-Democratic Revolution.*

The "Hungaricus" pamphlet was initially drawn up by one member of the group, with the intention of discussing it amongst the others, and then duplicating and distributing it to sympathisers throughout Budapest. It was written and issued in two parts: the first, which looked at the history of Soviet communism and marxism-leninism in the light of the Hungarian revolution, appearing at the end of December 1956, and the second, which surveyed the development of communism in Hungary up to and including the revolution, in the middle of February 1957.[15]

Those who were subsequently arrested and imprisoned for the publication and dissemination of this pamphlet were the psychology professor Ferenc Merei, who had headed the Students' Revolutionary Committee during the revolution; Sandor Fekete, a former *Szabad Nep* journalist and one of the younger and more radical members of the opposition; Jeno Szell, the director of Budapest Radio during the revolution; Gyorgy Litvan, a young history teacher, and Andras B. Hegedus,* a former university lecturer in marxism-leninism.[16]

Hungaricus I: the revolution in theory

The basic perspective of the Hungaricus pamphlet is provided in its opening pages, where the author declares: "The Hungarian revolution has revealed the utter degeneration of the lofty ideals of the Russian October that, forty years ago, inspired half of the world". Yet, he contends, the October events have provided the opportunity for a new beginning for socialism: "New roads, different from stalinist terror-communism or the social democratic trends fawning upon capitalism, are opening before the international working-class movement". The Hungarian socialists, he suggests, can play their part towards the ultimate victory of these new roads by looking squarely at the lessons of 1956 and drawing a clear conception of what has happened.†

The pamphlet then jumps straight into its most central concern —an analysis and critique of the former communist or Nagyist opposition movement. The greatest failing of the opposition, Hungaricus contends, arose from its self-imposed restriction to internal party struggles waged according to party rules, to its failure to organise itself as an independent force or to establish contact with

*This is not the same person as the Andras Hegedus who had been Prime Minister in the months immediately preceding the revolution.
†The quotations in this section are all taken from the English translation of the "Hungaricus" pamphlet (1959).

the people, in the first place the working class. Consequently, when the revolution came, "no one was more dumbfounded by its outbreak than they", and throughout its most hectic days, "they remained isolated when they should have commanded large forces".

Following the suppression of the revolution, however, the time was not ripe to create a new organisation. Rather it would first be necessary to "create the theory of Hungarian socialism" by critically revising all previous theories, and to write the history of the revolution and clarify the lessons to be learned from it. Now was the time "to examine the anatomy of the system more closely", so that "the next time we shall be better prepared to act".

This task of analysis and rethinking is the main concern of the Hungaricus pamphlet. From the very start, the writer disregards Western "bourgeois criticisms" of communism, feeling them to be morally unjustifiable in the light of the capitalist world's own aggressive and imperialistic actions, and prefers to consider the critiques of communism which have come from "opponents within the movement". Of these, the Yugoslav communists in the early fifties were the first to put their ideas into practice and create an alternative society to the stalinist one, and Hungaricus quotes with approval Yugoslav criticisms of Soviet society as a caste system of bureaucratic and imperialist rule. However, in Hungaricus's eyes the Yugoslavs' criticism remains superficial, because they failed to account for the origin of the bureaucratic system itself, contenting themselves with the explanation that the Soviet leaders had betrayed the heritage of the October revolution. This explanation implied that new leaders could easily put matters right, and evaded the question as to whether any fundamental change in the structure of the system itself was called for.

Quoting the Italian communist leader Togliatti, Hungaricus argues that it is necesary to re-examine the history of Soviet communism right back to the October revolution. Had it even been right for Lenin and the Bolsheviks to seize power in 1917 in a backward country like Russia? Yes indeed, declares Hungaricus, for a revolutionary must always seize the opportunities offered by history. The Bolsheviks, however, overestimated the likelihood of world revolution and the speed with which Russia could move from the bourgeois-democratic revolution to the building of socialism. Lenin, it is suggested, later recognised these mistakes and realised that while a revolution led by the working class could be victorious in a backward country like Russia, it would have to work slowly and carefully to lay the foundations on which socialism could only later be built. Stalin, however, believed it was possible to immediately build socialism in one country, and he attempted to do so by forced and rapid socialisation.

In Hungaricus's judgement, Stalin was wrong because the Russia of the twenties was not ripe for the realisation of socialism. Consequently the dictatorial and bureaucratic system which developed under Stalin, and which earlier criticisms of the "personality cult" had failed to explain adequately, was the result of Russia's backwardness. Indeed, once Stalin's aims were accepted, the methods he used to accomplish them became inevitable, because "in a country where the overwhelming majority of the population is peasant, the building of a dictatorship of the proletariat, and socialism, in six to eight years must necessarily result in a system of ruthless despotism, first over the peasantry and subsequently over the entire population".

Lacking popular support for his policies, Stalin built socialism with a centralised state machine relying on violence and coercion. Yet each act of violence reduced even more his popular support and necessitated in turn yet more violence, thereby creating a vicious circle of terror and despotism. As for Stalin's falsification of marxism-leninism, far from this being a conscious attempt to justify his urge for power as the Yugoslavs and later Khrushchev too had suggested, it was itself the result, the ideological reflection, of the growth of terror and despotism. In Hungaricus's words, "The reality of Russian socialism imposed by violence shaped Marx's and Engels's theory to its own image", and "Russian development rendered Stalin's various theories necessary".

Finally, Hungaricus argues that with the growth of the centralised state power, the bureaucratic apparatus on which Stalin had come to rely increasingly emerged as a force and power in its own right, indeed as a new ruling class:

> "Due to its place in production, its ways of earning a living, its share in the national revenue and other important factors, the apparatus transformed itself into a new class. . . . Gradually, the apparatus turned into a class, putting the crown on the edifice of Soviet socialism."

Having completed his account of the development of Soviet communism, Hungaricus next takes what he describes as a "brief detour to Marx and his followers", in which he seeks to preserve the values of Marx's and Lenin's ideas while rejecting the system of marxism-leninism which they had been turned into. Marxism-leninism had developed under Stalin by the distortion and vulgarisation of Marx's and Lenin's ideas into a rigid and closed system. In this way it had become an increasingly conservative dogma which was employed as an instrument for maintaining discipline within the Communist Party, and as an ideology for controlling the masses. This had come about, however, not at Stalin's conscious intent, but under the influence of objective social development, of "the entire system that made Stalin into what he was".

In the final pages of this first part of the Hungaricus pamphlet, the author turns his attention to the Soviet Union's relations with its own national minorities and with the other European communist states. He calls attention to Marx's remark that "no people can be free while it oppresses other peoples", to Engels's statement that "the victorious proletariat cannot save a single people by violence without undermining its own victory", and to Lenin's belief that socialism could not be created by force where the conditions for it were not yet ripe, and he contrasts these assertions with the extermination of the national minorities and the oppression of the people's democracies by the Soviet state in the name of the stalinist theory of the leading socialist nation. Yet even these events are seen as the results of objective social processes; the foreign policy of the Soviet Union was inextricably connected with its domestic social system — "a system built on violence could not help following a course of conquest by violence".

In opposition to stalinist practice, Hungaricus argues that socialists must learn to respect national interests and national pride and reject national oppression carried out in the name of the class struggle, because oppression and servitude, even if well-intentioned, can only harm the cause of socialism. Consequently, he rejects the principle of unquestioning loyalty to the Soviet Union as the basic criterion of proletarian internationalism, arguing that only constructive criticism can help the cause of international socialism and assist the real victory of socialism even in Russia itself. Indeed, he argues that within Russia the objective conditions have already matured for the democratisation of the system, while the subjective forces fighting for socialist democracy are also growing stronger. Consequently, he suggests that the criterion of proletarian internationalism should now be how consistently one fights against stalinism and for the democratisation of the Soviet system, and he concludes with the hope that he will live to see "the inner regeneration of the Soviet Union".

Hungaricus II: the lessons of the revolution

While the first part of the Hungaricus pamphlet had concerned itself with a critical survey of the development of Soviet communism and marxist-leninism, the second part, issued in mid-February 1957 and entitled "A New Socialist Direction", turned its attention to the history of communism in Hungary up to and including the October revolution of 1956.*

Rejecting the official view that the Hungarian revolution was the work of foreign subversive forces, Hungaricus points out that it was the Hungarian communist régime itself that had been brought to Hungary by a foreign army. In 1945 the Soviet army had liberated Hungary from the grip of German fascism, while the social revolution which the Soviets initiated certainly realised both timely and popular aims and won the backing of the most progressive elements of the population. From the beginning, however, the Hungarian stalinists had sought to build socialism in Hungary "with foreign force and an apparatus designed along foreign lines". This approach had proved the greatest drawback to the postwar social revolution in Hungary, and had resulted in the Hungarian people retaining their traditional hatred of the Russians and their distrust of the communists. Despite the achievements of the land reform and the defeat of the feudal-capitalist oligarchy that had ruled Hungary between the wars, the communists won less popular support in the postwar elections in Hungary than in any other Soviet-occupied country. And subsequently, instead of seeking to win over the population, the communists "socialised by decree, or as it appeared to the people, sovietised . . . , from the very beginning substituting external forces for the lacking internal forces".

By 1949 the ever more blatant subordination of Hungarian interests to Soviet commands had cut away whatever popular base the communist state might have attained, and in subsequent years this lost confidence of the people was replaced by the enormous growth of the party and state apparatus. By 1955, Hungaricus maintains, the population of some nine million people included a productive labour force of three-and-a-half million, with a bureaucratic apparatus of almost one million employed to watch over it: "this increasingly anti-socialist socialism, this ever more counter-revolutionary revolution, this people's democracy against the people, rested on the basis of the bureaucratically concentrated planned economy".

The bureaucratically planned economy only made matters worse, as intelligent administrators were replaced by mindless careerists and party hacks. Even the Communist Party itself was numbed and stultified under the rule of the bureaucratic caste until it had

*The quotations in this section are my own translations from the clandestine Hungarian manuscript (1957).

become little more than "a machine for producing applause and organising ceremonies". The inevitable result was that by 1953 the standard of living was seventeen per cent lower than four years before, while Rakosi's only solution was yet greater use of force, the turning of "the majority of party functionaries into slave-drivers, the AVH cadres into mass murderers".

Alongside this went the subordination of Hungarian culture to Russian culture, the introduction of Soviet-style uniforms in the army, of Soviet methods of education in the schools, and even the banning of Hungarian national emblems and celebrations. All this further increased the feeling of national humiliation and servitude. Consequently, argues Hungaricus:

> "These happenings led to the fact that the October revolution was before all else a national movement. Before all else the people wanted independence, because they saw the source of all their troubles in the loss of their independence."

For Hungaricus, however, the revolution was not simply a national revolt, because it was just as much the miserable living conditions of the people that drove them to act. On the basis of official statistics, he argues that only fifteen per cent of Hungarian families were above the régime's own estimated "minimum standard of living", with thirty per cent attaining it, and fifty-five per cent living below it. The daily pay of a worker on a state farm would not buy him one kilo of bread, while in fifteen per cent of working-class families not every member had a blanket to sleep under, and twenty per cent of the workers didn't even have a winter coat. Moreover, the conditions in which the majority of working people lived contrasted sharply with the living standards of their communist leaders — "the special cheap shops, the luxury villas, and the 'Kucsera' life style". For the *sans-manteaux* who were to be found in the front lines of the street battles against the Russian tanks in the days of the revolution, there was little doubt but that it was Russian imperialism that was responsible for their having lived in the last few years even worse than under the Horthy régime.

Despite his criticisms, however, Hungaricus has no sympathy for those seeking a return to the former capitalist régime, for the representatives of the ruling class that had been overthrown in 1945. "History hasn't justified *them*," he declares, "they are the phantoms of a Hungary now dead, they have no right to enter the debate of the living." Indeed, despite their many horrors, the twelve years since the war continue to represent, for Hungaricus, a basically progressive development which has served to lay the foundations of socialism, and render the capitalist system a thing of the past.

The alienation of the people by the Rakosi régime, however, had resulted in the fact that when the revolution came, counter-revolutionary forces were able to muster no little popular support. The forces of "reaction *par excellence*" — the landowners, capitalists and church leaders — would have existed in any case, but the policies of the Rakosi régime had ensured that they would receive support from much wider sections of the population. The forcible expropriation of small proprietors, traders and businessmen, as well as of the richer peasants and big capitalists, had turned thousands of potentially loyal and co-operative citizens into embittered opponents of socialism. At the same time, the regimentation and terror applied against the entire population had led to the development of strong anti-socialist feelings even amongst the propertyless working masses. In this situation, explains Hungaricus:

> "When the system from day to day increased the number of its opponents, when both the people and its former rulers suffered and were punished alike, when more people believed the word of the priest than the Party secretary, it was unavoidable that the formerly defeated forces of real reaction should come to find backing and support amongst the masses of people whom the régime had disappointed and alienated."

The situation could only be saved by a great national reconciliation movement which would unite every progressive force in the country in the effort to "conciliate and reunite the senselessly tortured and in part now reactionary masses in a new national unity and a Hungarian, democratic development". Such a reconciliation, he declares, is exactly what the opposition movement had been struggling to achieve, both before and during the revolution. The main achievement of the Rakosi régime had been "to turn the whole people against the régime, and a part of the people against socialism". The endeavour of the opposition, on the other hand, had been "to show a new way forward to the people", a different way from "either of the miserable alternatives of sovietisation or capitalist restoration".

At this point, Hungaricus returns to the central concern of his study, and attempts to provide a brief analysis of the development of the opposition movement. The figure of Imre Nagy is seen as central to the development of the opposition, for "although he was the banner of the opposition rather than its leader, without him, without his political and moral example, the movement would never have developed so successfully". When Imre Nagy first came to power in June 1953, there was no serious opposition in Hungary.

However, his government provided the first impetus to the emergence of the opposition, and while the changes of June 1953 had been solely the work of the Soviet leaders, Nagy's second victory in October 1954 already represented the developing force of the opposition.

While Nagy's New Course advanced only haltingly and in the face of constant resistance, the "fronts" were now much clearer, so that when Imre Nagy was removed from power in March 1955 he was no longer to be seen as merely "the representative of a more sensible Soviet policy", but as "the leader of a new Hungarian direction". Moreover, in sticking firmly to his beliefs and refusing to practise self-criticism or compromise with Rakosi, he won a moral victory which became one of the greatest spurs to the further development of the opposition. By this time, suggests Hungaricus, "the real kernel of the opposition, its strongest camp, had already come together, and Imre Nagy as the example of integrity and socialist respect, became its most important rallying point".

From this time on, Imre Nagy's personal struggle for principles became increasingly joined with the assembling opposition's political battle against the Rakosi régime. And the members of the opposition, far from reacting against the régime by retreating into chauvinism and conservatism, "placed their faith in a modern, rejuvenated Hungarian socialism", and became "the pioneers of a new socialist orientation". This orientation provided the opposition with a clear and precise political programme, "demanding the realisation of the June 1953 governmental programme, widening this out with the slogan of workers' self-government, with the demand for the cleaning out of the bureaucratic party apparatus, and with increased emphasis on independence".

Moreover, in the course of the struggle to realise these demands, "the most conscious members of the opposition even went beyond this programme to the principles of a truly democratic and independent socialism, corresponding to Hungarian circumstances".

Increasingly the opposition won to itself wider support, eventually becoming a force strong enough to bring about Rakosi's downfall in the early summer of 1956. In this process, there formed at its head "a leading socialist vanguard" firmly committed to the maintenance of Hungarian independence.

In June 1956, the opposition's victory over Rakosi made the mass of ordinary people aware for the first time that it was within their power to effect changes in the system. Suddenly, "their lethargy quickly dissipated, they realised that the terror wasn't permanent", and the people who a year before had remained silent while Nagy and the opposition were trounced by Rakosi, now began to move with surprising strength into political participation and action. Over the summer months the Gero régime became increasingly aware of, and even somewhat responsive to, this wave of popular feeling, but its every manoeuvre and attempt at conciliation only served to increase the people's conviction that "a real break with the past could not be achieved except by breaking with this hated and despised gang of criminals who still clung stubbornly to power".

Before long, "the time came when the masses were no longer willing to live in the old way, and the leaders were no longer able to rule in the old way. The explosion had become unavoidable".

Hungaricus's main criticism of the opposition was that, in this situation, they had let themselves be passed over by the people, so that when the revolution came they were no longer at its head and in no position to give it leadership and direction. Indeed, far from the opposition being responsible for the outbreak of the revolt by taking their criticism "into the streets" as the Kadar authorities alleged, "our mistake was not that we went into the streets and turned to the people, but that we did not turn to them earlier and in a more organised way".

The opposition, Hungaricus contends, never seriously sought to unite and organise its forces, let alone to mobilise mass support:

> "For a long time, the opposition merely took the road of internal party debate, and only when they saw the complete senselessness and uselessness of this, somewhere towards the end of 1955, did they begin to turn to the people, and then only through the press. . . .
>
> And they never tackled the most important task — the rousing and organising of the working class, the essential preparation for the sudden changes which would be required in the event of any collapse."

The opposition did, nevertheless, have a more radical wing which had argued as early as the spring of 1955 that the internal party struggle was in itself pointless, because the ruling bureaucratic caste would never give up its privileges and abandon its policies simply in the face of intellectual criticism. Consequently, they had argued that it was necessary to create "a united and organised direction" to lead the movement of opposition. The course of events at first seemed to be proving the radicals right, yet to the very end the opposition never did step beyond the limits of the inner-party struggle, and after the Twentieth Congress "even the radicals held back from such action, seeing that a general legal and lawful struggle would now develop against Rakosi".

The subsequent struggle took place "according to the constitution and the party's rules — the stories of underground organisation are all lies". In Hungaricus's opinion, however, "it's a pity that they're lies", and he ends by reaffirming his belief in the need to have acted earlier and in a more organised fashion:

> "It was necessary to create a united centre, to agitate amongst the workers according to a co-ordinated plan, to unite with all the progressive forces outside the Communist Party, so that when the people's patience finally broke, it would be us and not the forces of reaction they would follow."

The need for such action, in any future struggle against the stalinist state, is obviously the main lesson which the author of the Hungaricus pamphlet seeks to draw from his analysis of the Hungarian revolution. Though the first attempt had failed, it had provided a clear conception of the nature of the task, ensuring that "the next time we shall be better prepared to act".

7 Conclusions

> "The emancipation of the working classes must be conquered by the working classes themselves."
>
> *Karl Marx, 1864*

The ideology of the Kadar régime

When the Soviet tanks returned to Budapest in the early hours of 4 November, it was in answer to the call of the "Revolutionary Worker Peasant Government" established that same morning by Janos Kadar, Imre Nagy's former colleague in his revolutionary government, and the First Secretary of the new Hungarian Socialist Workers' Party. Kadar had defected to the Russians on the evening of 1 November and was subsequently to serve them in crushing the revolution and re-establishing a Soviet-style communist régime in Hungary.

However, it should not be thought for a moment that Janos Kadar was simply a dogmatic sectarian communist, ruthlessly working to subject the Hungarian working class to communist dictatorship, the Hungarian nation to Soviet imperialism. On the contrary, he was a sincere Hungarian communist who had himself been imprisoned and callously tortured under the stalinist régime of the early fifties. During the revolution, he had described his aim as "Hungarian national communism . . . (in which) there will be an opposition and no dictatorship". Then, on the very eve of his defection to the Russians, Kadar had declared to the Soviet ambassador that if the Russians intervened again, he would have no choice but to go into the streets and fight alongside the Hungarian workers against the Soviet tanks — "with my bare hands too, if I have to!"[1]

Even after his government had been imposed on the Hungarian people at the points of Russian bayonets, he was still to publicly declare: "We want a multi-party system and free honest elections." Still later, receiving a delegation from the Central Workers' Council, he appealed to them: "My friends, help me! You must understand that I am alone amongst all these stalinists. . . . Help me!" He is even reported to have made offers of ministerial posts to at least two members of the Central Workers' Council, Sandor Racz and Miklos Sebestyen.[2]

Some commentators, nevertheless, would still prefer to see in Kadar a weak man, an unprincipled opportunist motivated only by political ambition. When the revolution had been in the ascendant, he had bent over backwards in praise of "this glorious uprising . . . (in which) our people have thrown off the Rakosi régime . . . (and) conquered freedom and independence for our country". But when the Russians crushed this "glorious uprising" in blood, and offered him the highest political post, he was prepared to acquiesce in its denunciation as "a Horthyite-Fascist-Hungarian-capitalist-feudal-counter-revolution".[3]

The opinion which sees Kadar as an unprincipled opportunist, however, must be rejected just as firmly as that of him as little more than a sectarian stalinist. Though a committed and seasoned communist, he was undoubtedly sincere in his wish for a communism with greater respect for both national independence and personal freedom. At the same time, while sympathising with the original demands of the uprising, he became increasingly aware of the attempts of counter-revolutionary elements to whip up hysteria, increase disorder, and so profit from the situation.

That he at no time seriously looked at the ability of the working class, and of the workers' councils in particular, to combat any counter-revolutionary trends, appears certain. Yet his real fear of the forces of counter-revolution was probably that their presence would increase the likelihood of further Soviet intervention. When told in advance of the coming Soviet action, he apparently felt that by placing himself at the head of a Soviet-imposed régime, he would be able both to minimise the bloodshed and to save what he could from the achievements of the revolution.

Kadar was soon to find, however, that he had underestimated the bitterness and determination with which the Hungarian workers would turn against his régime. He was also to find that the intervention at the head of which he had allowed himself to be placed, in the hope of controlling its eventual course, was to restrict his freedom of movement to almost nothing. Between the mass strike of the Hungarian working class and the armed might of the Soviet occupying forces, he was to find himself totally deprived of any independent power base.

Evidently the only way that Kadar could secure his rule was to achieve the consolidation of political order and the resumption of production. What hopes he may originally have held of achieving this with the backing of the Hungarian workers, in order to gradually ease the Russians out, were now shattered. The working class was even more adamant than its leaders in the workers' councils in rejecting out of hand any form of collaboration with the régime that had agreed to serve the Soviet intervention. In this situation, Kadar soon found that the only way he could achieve political consolidation and restore production was by relying on the AVH and the Soviet army against the Hungarian working class.

The battle then developed into the struggle which has been described earlier, in which the Communist Party under Kadar's leadership literally wrenched control of the means of production out of the hands of the working class by physically destroying the workers' councils and replacing them with a bureaucratic hierarchy of management installed under the intimidation of the AVH and the fixed bayonets of the Soviet army. In the course of this struggle, every independent organisation of the working class had to be smashed and every striving towards working-class autonomy mercilessly crushed.

In this attack on the workers' organisations the Kadar régime was to employ every slander against the working class that had ever been found in the capitalists' ideological arsenal. A "reign of terror" was said to exist in the factories where, it was alleged, workers' councils were elected in an atmosphere of "overwhelming moral pressures, demagogy and threats". "The workers", it was now explained, "are being terrorised by counter-revolutionary strikers", who were said to be physically preventing workers from entering the factory gates, or driving them out of the factories by force.[4]

In attacking in this way every spontaneous initiative of the workers, the Communist Party was to appropriate to itself the sole right to represent and express the interests of the working class. Any efforts of the working class to act or organise in independence of the Communist Party were from this moment on deemed counter-revolutionary. Thus on 26 February 1957, a resolution of the Hungarian Socialist Workers' Party was to adamantly declare:

> "We have rejected the reactionary demands that the trade unions should be 'independent' from both the party and the workers and peasants' government, and for the right to strike in defiance of the workers' state. . . . In a dictatorship of the proletariat the working class cannot have an organisation independent of the party."[5]

This ethos of centralisation, in which the Communist Party is completely substituted for the working class as the creative force of socialism, came in the end to be expressed equally adamantly by Kadar himself, who even went so far at one point as to assert that "the working class cannot exist without the party". Kadar, however, was at least honest enough to state quite clearly the belief he had now come to hold in the need for a dictatorship of the party over the workers, explaining to the National Assembly in May 1957:

> "In my opinion, the task of the leaders is not to put into effect the wishes and will of the masses. . . . In my opinion, the leaders' task is to realise the interest of the masses. . . .
>
> In the recent past, we have encountered the phenomenon that certain categories of workers acted against their own interests and, in this case, the duty of the leaders is to represent the interest of the masses and not to implement mechanically their incorrect ideas. If the wish of the masses does not coincide with progress, then one must lead the masses in another direction."[6]

With this speech, the final and irrevocable point of divorce between Kadar and the working class had been reached. The Communist Party, he declared, was able to know and express the interests of the workers better even than they themselves. What better example could have been found of what Karl Marx used to refer to as ideological thought — the representation of the consciousness of one particular group in society as that of the whole, the claim to universality of the interest of a particular ruling class? What better illustration could have been offered of the truth revealed by the young Leon Trotsky in prophetically declaring in 1904 that a party organised on leninist lines would eventually come to "substitute itself for the working classes", or for his judgement some thirty years later that "the former Bolshevik Party is now no longer the vanguard of the proletariat, but the political organisation of the bureaucracy"?[7]

The dilemma of the opposition

If the ideology of the Kadar régime is best understood, following Trotsky, as the substitution of its own power-political interests for the direct class interests of the Hungarian workers, then the basic dilemma of the reformist opposition arose from the fact that it represented in many ways a "halfway house" between the substitutionist ideology of the party leadership and the spontaneous self-activity of the masses. Consequently, at each moment of crisis, the more moderate members of the opposition found themselves attracted back into the fold of party orthodoxy, while the more radical members hesitatingly and unsurely moved towards the adoption of a more independent stance.

While the substitutionist ideology had reached its most extreme expression in the ultra-stalinist Rakosi régime and, after the revolution, in the apologetically stalinist Kadar régime, both of which claimed to represent the true interests of the workers better than they could themselves, the reformist opposition itself had never been completely free from such conceptions. As we have already seen, right up to the very climax of the revolution, Imre Nagy remained almost totally a prisoner of such ideas, and the stubborn loyalty to the party of the majority of the opposition's members prevented them from acting independently and establishing any real contact with the working masses.

In this loyalty to leninist conceptions of the revolutionary party and its relationship to the masses can be seen the continuity between the orthodox marxist-leninist ideas of the stalinist party leadership and the revisionist beliefs of Imre Nagy and the reformist opposition, a continuity which was only challenged and eventually broken by the revolution itself. The persistence of these beliefs in the leading role of the party also helps to explain the disorientation of many members of the opposition when faced with the actual outbreak of revolution, and their slowness to recognise the potential of the spontaneously arising revolutionary committees and workers' councils.

The origins of these conceptions are to be found in ideas expressed by Lenin in 1903 in his pamphlet *What Is To Be Done?* where he argued that it was not sufficient for the working class to pursue merely trade-union interests within capitalist society, but that they must be led by a party of professional socialist revolutionaries. In subsequent years Lenin was to build up his Bolshevik Party into just such a disciplined organisation as he had previously advocated, and to lead them in the successful seizure of power in October 1917, and the establishment of the centralised and dictatorial Soviet state. The development of the totalitarian party-state was carried even further by Lenin's successor, Stalin, under whose rule the party was turned into a mere instrument of the stalinist state power.

Stalin's principal opponent, Leon Trotsky, had also been one of the earliest critics of Lenin's views on party organisation, characterising them as the ideas of an "orthodox theocracy" which would inevitably lead to personal dictatorship. In 1917, however, Trotsky had joined with Lenin in establishing the one-party state, and had at times appeared even more substitutionist than Lenin, in advocating state control of trade unions and the militarisation of labour, as well as in suppressing the independent peasant army of Nestor

Makhno and the revolt of the workers and sailors of Kronstadt in 1921. Later too, after being defeated by Stalin and banished from Russia, Trotsky was to remain loyal to the leninist belief in the "vanguard party", and to see the main problem facing the revolutionary movement as "the crisis of the revolutionary leadership".[8]

Consequently, the whole history of the world communist and marxist movements since the Bolshevik revolution and under the inspiration of the ideas and practice of Lenin, Stalin and Trotsky, has been characterised by élitist ideologies stressing the leading role of the revolutionary vanguard and the party state. So entrenched had such ideas become in the ideology of the communist movement that they were never questioned by the moderate wing of the Hungarian reformist opposition in 1956, and only slowly and hesitatingly criticised by the more radical members of that movement.

The revolution in theory had thus not moved as rapidly as the revolution in practice, the revolution which was characterised not by leading parties and revolutionary vanguards but by spontaneously arising revolutionary committees and workers' councils. Had the members of the opposition, however, looked more closely at some of the ideas of the founders of communism, Karl Marx and Friedrich Engels, they might well have found that the events which occurred in the course of the Hungarian uprising had more in common with the ideas of Marx and Engels on the nature of the socialist revolution than with the theories that had dominated the communist movement since 1917.

In the *Communist Manifesto,* Marx and Engels had declared that the communists had no interests separate and apart from the working class as a whole, and that they had no intention of setting up any separate party to shape and mould the workers' movement. For them, the socialist revolution was distinguished from all previous revolutions by the very fact that it was not carried out by a small conscious minority, but was a movement of the entire proletarian class. More specifically, in the *Address to the Communist League* of 1850, Marx and Engels had spelt out their conception of the action to be taken by the workers in the course of revolution. What they advocated, however, was quite definitely not the leadership and control of the revolutionary movement by any political party, but the creation of organs of direct class rule by the workers themselves. Over twenty years later, Marx was to greet the Paris Commune of 1871 as "a working-class government . . . , the political form at last discovered under which to work out the economic emancipation of labour". The direct self-organisation and activity of the working people of Paris was for Marx "a resumption by the people for the people of its own social life".[9]

For Marx and Engels, the society which was to emerge from a socialist revolution would not be a party-state such as Lenin and Stalin were later to establish, but a commune-state created around the workers' own organisations. Thus while there would be the need for a party to lead the workers towards revolution, the revolution itself would lead to the power not of a political party but of a social class, not to the establishment of new political or state institutions ruling over society, but to the creation of organs of direct rule by the working class itself.

Moreover, these ideas can also be seen as less inconsistent with those of Lenin than has often been thought. Lenin too had been arguing about the role of the party in the struggle for revolution, not in the building of a socialist state, and *What Is To Be Done?* in particular had been written in the context of a polemical debate concerning the strategy for revolutionaries working in illegality during the years of reaction and oppression before the first world war. On the eve of the October revolution, Lenin had set out his ideas on the future socialist society in *State and Revolution,* in which he envisaged socialism as a commune-state of mass participatory democracy, in which political representatives would be delegates subject to immediate recall, and in which the people themselves would take over the everyday administration of the state.[10]

The shortcomings of the Hungarian reformist opposition arose from their continuing attachment to earlier leninist conceptions of the revolutionary party, at a time when the stage was being set for the creation of exactly such organs of direct class rule by the workers as Marx and Engels, and even Lenin himself, had seen as the real basis of a socialist society. The dilemma of the opposition arose from their inability to face up to this new reality, and to question their long-held views on the role of the party. To have done so would have been to see their role in the revolution not as one of replacing the former stalinists in the seats of power but as one of overthrowing this party-state itself, and of enabling power to be taken over directly by the spontaneously created organisations of the masses, the revolutionary committees and workers' councils.

Right up to and even during the revolution, however, Imre Nagy and the moderate majority of the opposition had rarely concerned themselves with the autonomous self-activity of the workers, or even with the idea of workers' councils. In fact, it was only when the workers' councils had already established themselves as the only organised force capable of resisting the repression of the Kadar régime and the Soviet occupying forces, that first the more radical members of the opposition, and then the writers, intellectuals and politicians too, came to recognise their potential.

The practical reality of the workers' councils as organs of the direct class rule of the workers thus came into existence before the theoretical awareness that they might play such a role. In this process, the original leninist schema was almost totally reversed. Far from socialist consciousness being brought to the workers from outside by the intellectuals of the revolutionary party, it arose amongst the workers as the result of their own socialist practice, and only then came to be recognised by the intellectuals of the reformist opposition movement.

The political role of the workers' councils

The reformist intellectuals, however, were not the only people who at first resisted suggestions that the workers' councils had an important political role to play. Even some of the leaders of the workers' councils themselves were adamant in asserting that the workers' councils were not, and had no intention of becoming, the political representatives of the workers. The clearest statement of this viewpoint was made by Sandor Bali in a speech to the special conference in the Hungarian parliament on 25 November, in which he declared:

> "We know quite well that the workers' councils cannot be political organisations. . . . We do not want to commit the same error as that of the Communist Party in the past, which regarded itself at the same time as both the ruler of the country and the factories, and the only organisation to represent the interests of the workers.
>
> If we should make the same mistakes, we'll be back just where we started. We want the workers' councils to run the country's economic affairs, and the trade unions to have the right to call strikes and deal with all matters concerning the protection of the workers' interests."[11]

It is clear from these remarks, however, that Sandor Bali's main concern was to avoid the monolithic control of production which had previously prevailed when the Communist Party held all the reins — political, managerial, and trade union — of control over the workers. The party appointed the factory director and other leading managerial staff, the party controlled the organisation of the shop-floor through the party structure within the factory, and the party controlled the workers through the trade unions. The workers, needless to say, controlled nothing.

The basic motivation of the revolution in the factories had been to do away with this situation. The party-appointed managers were given the boot by the workers, the Communist Party organisers were driven out of the factories, and so were those union officials who had never given a damn for the workers' interests. The workers' councils were then set up as organisations through which the workers could themselves control their factories. Their leaders, however, recognised that if they were going to take responsibility for the management of production themselves, separate and independent organisations would be needed to defend the workers' interests. They therefore continued to demand the creation of free and democratically elected trade unions which would have the right to press for improvements in the wages and working conditions of the workers and to call them out on strike, even against a management itself directed by elected workers' representatives.

But if the workers' councils recognised that they had this kind of responsibility, this did not mean that they denied themselves any form of political role. On the contrary, their major conflicts with the Kadar government had arisen from the efforts of the latter to restrict the councils to purely economic functions within their respective factories. In this conflict the councils had been fully aware of their political role, as becomes clear from a statement of the Central Workers' Council issued on 27 November, which declared:

> "We protest against the arguments of the recently constituted 'trade unions' according to which the workers' councils should be organisations having solely economic functions.
>
> We can categorically state that the real interests of the working class in Hungary are represented by the workers' councils, and that in addition there is no stronger political power in existence than theirs.
>
> We shall work with all our might for the strengthening of this workers' power."[12]

This workers' power did not require for its implementation that the workers' councils should take over the direction of the political parties, of the parliament, or of the Council of Ministers. On the contrary, the very long and hard fight that Kadar had to put up against the workers' councils in order to establish the power of his government, when he already had all these political institutions of the *ancien régime* (the parties, the parliament, and the government) firmly under his control, show that the power against which he was struggling was based in very different organisations at a very different level of society. This workers' power was realised in the very existence and activity of the councils which the workers had themselves created, and through which they were directly controlling the means of production. The workers' councils did not seek to seize power from the government, they did not need to, for it was rather the government that was trying to seize *back* power from them.

This is, after all, the very essence of revolutionary change, the conflict between different principles for the structuring of society, based on the conflicting interests of major social groups, and representing different institutional structures making different claims to legitimacy. It is reformist politics which seeks to occupy or take over the positions of power in the already existing structure of society. Revolution, however, seeks to overturn these positions of power, and to recast the structure of society itself in a radically new fashion. In the French revolution of 1789 which saw the ascendancy of the bourgeoisie to political power, the French bourgeois class did not crown its own king and appoint its own representatives to the royal court, but cut off the king's head, banished the aristocracy, and established a new central power, the National Assembly. Similarly, in the Russian revolution of October 1917, no voice was heard for the appointing of a people's tsar, while the Bolsheviks' entry into the Winter Palace was very different from that of Kerensky.

In just the same way, the working class in the Hungarian revolution did not seek to create a new political party, a new parliamentary assembly, or appoint a new proletarian dictator. It was not they who sent delegates milling up the steps and thronging the ante-chambers of parliament. It was not they who sought to reopen the former offices of the defunct bourgeois political parties. Instead, the workers established a power which represented their lives and defended their interests, a power which was realised in rule of the streets and control of the factories.

In asserting their power, however, the Hungarian workers' councils did not set themselves up as a new privileged élite or a new bureaucratic caste, cut off from and raised above the workers. On the contrary, even the executive members of the Central Workers' Council spent the full working day on the factory floor, while the members of the Central Council were neither independent representatives, like Western parliamentarians, nor appointed officials, like Soviet state bureaucrats. Instead, they were delegates of their workers' councils, expected to report back to the workers after every session, and subject to recall and replacement at any time.

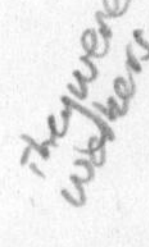

The greatest achievement of the Hungarian revolution should thus be recognised as the creation of this totally new structure of popular power — of a state of workers' councils directly controlled by the workers. The central executive organs of the workers' councils were not, and never sought to be, "responsible" to some "independent" parliamentary assembly. They were directly answerable to the workers' councils themselves. In this way the "workers' power" was really identical with the nationwide structure of workers' councils. And these in turn were directly and immediately responsible to the workers. The assault of the Kadar government and the Communist Party clearly showed that it was *their* aim to take power out of the hands of the workers and secure it in a government body separated from (though formally responsible to) a parliamentary assembly, itself connected by no direct organic relations with the working population, though again theoretically responsible to it.

The workers' councils, however, did not seek to conquer or take over some independent power, abstracted from society and isolated from the people. Neither their social origins nor their political interests implied any conception of ruling over the people, any need of controlling society from above. Indeed, their very essence as revolutionary institutions was that they were organs through which the people would directly rule, through which society could exercise its own self-mastery. The Hungarian workers, in establishing direct control over their factories through the workers' councils, had thus in one blow both smashed the former state power ruled over by the Communist Party, and reopened the road to that society which had been the original aim of marxism and socialism — in which hierarchy would give way to equality, in which political institutions would be replaced by popular organs, in which political rule would be replaced by social power, and where "the government of persons is replaced by the administration of things".

Notes

(Where sources are included in the bibliography, they are referred to by author and date of publication only.)

Introduction (pages 17-18)

1. Bain (1960), p. 97.
2. George Paloczi-Horvath, *Youth Up In Arms,* London, Weidenfeld & Nicolson, 1971, p. 32.
3. Zinner (1962), and Kecskemeti (1961).

Chapter 1 (pages 19-50)

1. Imre Nagy (1957), pp. 45 and 66.
2. Peter Kende, *The History of Szabad Nep,* a memorandum in the archives of the Columbia University Research Project on Hungary (CURPH), p. 5.
3. The CURPH material includes interviews with several of the journalists, as well as the memorandum cited in the previous footnote. In the present section I have drawn heavily on this material.
4. The CURPH material includes a memorandum by Miklos Molnar entitled *The History of Irodalmi Ujsag.*
5. The various examples of literary dissent quoted here are taken from: Miklos Molnar (1971), p. 64 (Csoori); Juhasz (1965), p. 169 (Konya); Aczel and Meray (1960), p. 268 (Benjamin), and Kecskemeti (1961), p. 66. Further examples can be found in Paloczi-Horvath (1957).
6. Aczel and Meray (1960), pp. 345-57.
7. CURPH interview 567, p. 13.
8. Considerable information concerning the Imre Nagy group can be found in the CURPH interviews. The group's composition and organisation is also discussed in Miklos Molnar (1971), and in Molnar and Nagy (1959).
9. CURPH interview 563, pp. 73 and 75.
10. CURPH interview 500, pp. 73-4.
11. The fullest account of the Petofi Circle is provided by Balazs Nagy in *The Petofi Circle,* a manuscript included in the CURPH material.
12. Quoted in Aczel and Meray (1960), pp. 401-2.
13. *Ibid.*, p. 411.
14. Litvan's intervention at this meeting appears to have made a very strong impression throughout Budapest and is reported in several of the CURPH interviews as well as in Aczel and Meray (1960), p. 395.

15. Cited in Zinner (1956), p. 524.
16. CURPH interview 405, p. 11.
17. CURPH interview 444, pp. 23 and 27.
18. CURPH interview 501, p. 12.
19. CURPH interview 500, p. 33.
20. CURPH interview 444, p. 39.
21. CURPH interview 501, pp. 30-32.
22. CURPH interview 455, p. 14.
23. CURPH interview 155, p. 5.
24. CURPH interview 505, p. 3.
25. Imre Nagy (1957), p. 54.
26. These strikes and disturbances are reported in several of the CURPH interviews, and also in a study published in Hungary by Berecz (1969), pp. 64-5.
27. Scarlett (1959), p. 239.
28. Aczel and Meray (1960), p. 428.
29. Gyula Hay's poem is included in Paloczi-Horvath (1957), p. 58.
30. CURPH interview 217, p. 3.
31. CURPH interview 244, p. 4.
32. CURPH interview 226, p. 8.
33. Bela Kiraly (1966), p. 713.
34. Tamas Aczel in a private interview with the author in Amherst, Massachusetts, in November 1968.
35. CURPH interview 444, p. 46.
36. CURPH interview 226, p. 2.
37. The discontent among students and young people is described in Baudy (1957).
38. Balazs Nagy, in an account published in *The Truth about the Nagy Affair* (1959), p. 64.
39. Miklos Molnar (1971), p. 114.
40. CURPH interview 509, p. 13.
41. This episode is related in Peter Kende, "*A Szabad Nep szerkesztosegeben*" ("In the editorial office of *Szabad Nep*"), in Borbandi and Molnar (1966), p. 124.
42. CURPH interview 508, p. 18.
43. Gyorgy Faludy, in a private interview with the author in New York in December 1968.
44. CURPH interview 616, p. 32.

Chapter 2 (pages 51-77)

1. For the autobiographies of two of the best-known of the pre-war émigrés, see Ignotus (1964), and Paloczi-Horvath (1959); and for a discussion of populism and its influence, see Zinner (1962), pp. 10ff. There is an abundance of information about the ex-stalinist intellectuals in the CURPH interviews.
2. Nagy's dissertations are published in English in Imre Nagy (1957).
3. Quoted in Imre Nagy (1957), p. 18.

4. The first quotation is a comment by François Fejto in his preface to the French edition of Nagy's dissertations; the second is a translation of the title of that edition.
5. Miklos Molnar, "The Heritage of Imre Nagy", in Aczel (1966), p. 168.
6. Imre Nagy (1957), pp. 3-4.
7. *Ibid.*, p. 7.
8. *Ibid.*, p. 9.
9. *Ibid.*, p. 157.
10. *Ibid.*, p. 100.
11. *Ibid.*, p. 195.
12. Imre Nagy's speech is reprinted in Juhasz (1965), pp. 156-60.
13. Imre Nagy (1957), p. 86.
14. *Ibid.*, pp. 49-51.
15. *Ibid.*, p. 48.
16. *Ibid.*, p. 65.
17. *Ibid.*, p. 209.
18. *Ibid.*, p. 50.
19. *Ibid.*, pp. 50-51.
20. *Ibid.*, pp. 48-9.
21. *Ibid.*, pp. 243-4.
22. *Ibid.*, p. 63.
23. *Ibid.*, p. 34.
24. *Ibid.*, p. xlii.
25. *Ibid.*, p. 49.
26. Molnar and Nagy (1959), p. 168.
27. *Ibid.*
28. *Ibid.*, p. 184.
29. Quoted in Zinner (1956), pp. 417-18, which reproduces these and other speeches made by Imre Nagy as Prime Minister during the revolution.
30. CURPH interview 563, p. 120.
31. Quoted in Zinner (1956), p. 410.
32. Quoted in Bain (1960), p. 136.
33. Quoted in Zinner (1956), p. 429.
34. *Ibid.*, p. 454.
35. *Ibid.*, pp. 458-9.
36. These and the previously quoted statements are cited in Fryer (1956), p. 71.
37. Wiktor Woroszylski, quoted in Lasky (1957), p. 212.
38. Bela Kiraly (1966), p. 721.
39. Quoted in Zinner (1956), p. 472.
40. Molnar and Nagy (1959), p. 265.
41. Quoted in Berecz (1969), p. 142.
42. Quoted in *Irodalmi Ujsag*, Paris, 1-15 June 1968, p. 1.

Chapter 3 (pages 79-103)

1. Much of the information on Szeged is taken from an interview with Dr and Mrs Lorinc Czigany who were students at Szeged in 1956. Their account is confirmed by similar reports in Baudy (1957), pp. 137-40, and Janos Molnar (1967), pp. 36-7.
2. Quoted in Bain (1960), p. 96.
3. Cited in Lasky (1957), pp. 113-14 and 142.
4. The fullest account of this and other events in Gyor is provided in Arpad Szollosy, "*A forradalom Gyorott*" ("The revolution at Gyor"), in Borbandi and Molnar (1966).
5. The CURPH material contains a number of interviews with people who participated in the events at Gyor, including one with Gyorgy Szabo.
6. Fryer (1956), pp. 18-19.
7. Fejto (1966), pp. 188-9.
8. The Somogyvari incident is reported most fully in Szollosy, *op. cit.*, and in the CURPH interview with Gyorgy Szabo. The details are generally confirmed in official Hungarian accounts, e.g. Janos Molnar (1967), p. 150.
9. Marie and Nagy (1966), pp. 204-5.
10. Woroszylski (1957), pp. 23-4.
11. Free Europe (1956), pp. 15-16. This is a compilation of monitored radio broadcasts from Hungary, and is the source for most of the declarations from Miskolc referred to in this section.
12. Hollos (1967), pp. 135-6.
13. Marie and Nagy (1966), pp. 205-6.
14. Cited in Gyorgy Heltai, "Imre Nagy au Parlement", in Gosztony, *Histoire* (1966), p. 183.
15. This account of the revolution at Pecs is taken largely from J. Pecsi, "Revolution à Pecs", in Gosztony, *Histoire* (1966), pp. 355-76.
16. For the events at Salgotarjan, see Antal Garamvolgyi, "Revolution à Salgotarjan", in Gosztony, *Histoire*, pp. 303-319, and Valeria Boszik, *A Nogradi Kommunistak Harca az Ellenforradalom ellen* ("The struggle of the Communists of Nograd against the Counter-revolution"), Budapest, 1957.

Chapter 4 (pages 105-45)

1. United Nations (1957), pp. 75 and 76. (Note that the English translation on p. 75 is incomplete.)
2. Slightly different versions of this document can be found in United Nations (1957), p. 5, and in Meray (1959), pp. 67-8.
3. These slogans are among those recalled in the CURPH interviews. See also Scarlett (1959), pp. 249-50.
4. Berecz (1969), pp. 86-90.
5. The doctor's remarks are quoted in Hungaricus (1957), p. 21. For details of casualties, see Berecz (1969), p. 89.

6. Almost every study of the Hungarian revolution contains an account of the fighting at the radio building. For the official Hungarian accounts, see Hungarian People's Republic (1957), Vol. II, pp. 17 and 25-8, and Janos Molnar (1967), p. 55.
7. CURPH interview 563, pp. 111-12.
8. CURPH interviews 213, p. 24, and 133, p. 11.
9. The scene is described in Peter Gosztonyi, "Diary: The Kilian Barracks during the Revolution", in *The Review,* No. 6, Brussels, October 1960, p. 72, and in Gosztony, *Volksaufstand* (1966), pp. 233-4.
10. Quoted in Davidson (1957), p. 19.
11. Quoted in Lasky (1957), p. 251.
12. Peter Gosztony, "Armée sovietique en Hongrie 1956", in Gosztony, *Histoire* (1966), p. 234.
13. Stephen Vizinczey, *In Praise of Older Women,* London, Barrie & Rockliff, 1966, p. 130.
14. Bain (1960), p. 115. The incident is also reported in considerable detail in Gosztony, *Volksaufstand* (1966), pp. 222-4.
15. Bain (1960), p. 117.
16. Paul Ignotus, "Eyewitnesses from Hungary", *New Statesman,* 20 April 1957, p. 521.
17. A number of these reports are assembled in Hungarian People's Republic (1957), Vol. I, pp. 4 and 56, Vol. II, p. 137.
18. *Ibid.,* Vol. I, p. 9; Vol. II, pp. 59-62; Vol. III, p. 86.
19. The Hungarian authorities' account of the massacre and those who perpetrated it is given in Hollos (1967), pp. 37-9, 56-62, and 93-109. Recently a more detailed study has been published in Hungary; see Hollos and Lajtai (1974).
20. Quoted in Peter Gosztonyi, "*Az AVH es a forradalom*" ("The AVH and the revolution"), in Borbandi and Molnar (1966), p. 115, note 54 a.
21. Cited in Meray (1959), p. 155.
22. Quoted in Paul Jonas, "Foreigners in the Hungarian Revolution", in *Scope,* New York, Spring-Autumn 1967, p. 45. The earlier cited Hungarian authority is Janos Molnar (1967), p. 167.
23. Woroszylski (1957), p. 13.
24. Fejto (1957), p. 225.
25. Bela Kovacs in *Magyar Nemzet* ("Hungarian Nation"), Budapest, 20 February 1959, quoted in *Hungarian News,* New York, March 1959, pp. 2-3.
26. Ferenc B. Nagy, quoted in Janos Molnar (1967), p. 206.
27. Quoted in Lasky (1957), p. 196.
28. The full text of Mindszenty's speech is now available in Jozsef Mindszenty *Memoirs of Jozsef Cardinal Mindszenty,* London, Weidenfeld & Nicolson, 1975, pp. 331-3.
29. CURPH interview 508, p. 21.
30. Free Europe (1956), p. 14.

31. Marie and Nagy (1966), p. 207. For the role of students in the establishment of the first revolutionary committees, see Laszlo Arato, "La révolution vue par un étudiant", in Gosztony, *Histoire* (1966), pp. 52-3.
32. Quoted in Zoltan Garamvolgyi, "Episode retraçant l'activité du Comité Révolutionnaire des Etudiants", in Gosztony, *Histoire* (1966), p. 71.
33. Free Europe (1956), p. 56.
34. Coutts (1957), p. 11.
35. Woroszylski (1957), p. 9.
36. Erno Kiraly (1961), p. 24.
37. Marie and Nagy (1966), pp. 187-8, and Janos Molnar (1967), pp. 130-33.
38. Marie and Nagy (1966), pp. 203-4.
39. Zinner (1956), p. 449.
40. *Ibid.*, pp. 464-5.
41. Lasky (1957), p. 177.
42. Free Europe (1956), p. 63.
43. Woroszylski (1957), p. 11.
44. Lasky (1957), p. 188.
45. Free Europe (1956), p. 97.

Chapter 5 (pages 147-69)

1. Kecskemeti (1961), p. 115.
2. Marie and Nagy (1966), p. 222.
3. Erno Kiraly (1961), p. 35.
4. Balazs Nagy (1961), p. 9.
5. Marie and Nagy (1966), pp. 223-4.
6. *Ibid.*, p. 224.
7. *Ibid.*, pp. 225-6.
8. Information about the foundation of the Central Workers' Council and its leading members can be found in Balazs Nagy (1961), pp. 41-5 and 54-8, and in Ferenc Toke, "Ce que furent les conseils ouvriers hongrois", in Marie and Nagy (1966), p. 252, and Miklos Sebestyen, "Mes expériences dans le Conseil Central Ouvrier du Grand Budapest", also in Marie and Nagy (1966), p. 300.
9. For Kadar's speech, see Lasky (1957), pp. 262-3.
10. Toke, *op. cit.*, p. 258.
11. Janos Molnar (1969), pp. 63-4, and Sebestyen, *op. cit.*, p. 301.
12. CURPH interview 407, pp. 5-6.
13. Quoted in Toke, *op. cit.*, p. 260.
14. Quoted in Marie and Nagy (1966), p. 286.
15. *Ibid.*, p. 279.
16. Sebestyen, *op. cit.*, p. 303.
17. Marie and Nagy (1966), p. 287.
18. Relations between the workers' councils and the trade unions are

discussed in Erno Kiraly (1961), pp. 41-52.

19. Considerable information relating to the conflicts between the workers' councils and the Party organisations, trade unions and factory directors is provided in Janos Molnar (1969), pp. 73-82.
20. These statements are taken from Janos Molnar (1969), p. 73.
21. Marie and Nagy (1966), pp. 317-8.
22. Details of the Central Council's memorandum, and of its plans for a National Workers' Council and a Workers' Parliament, can be found in Janos Molnar (1969), pp. 118-9 and 129-30.
23. Cited in Toke, *op. cit.*, p. 267.
24. Janos Molnar (1969), p. 132.
25. Marie and Nagy (1966), p. 326.
26. Quoted in Anderson (1964), p. 45.

Chapter 6 (pages 170-92)

1. For Bibo's collected writings, see Istvan Bibo, *Haramadik Ut* ("The Third Way"), London, Magyar Konyves Ceh, 1960.
2. For the text of Bibo's statement, see Lasky (1957), p. 234.
3. For Bibo's *Political Testament*, see *The Truth about the Nagy Affair* (1959), pp. 142-6.
4. For Bibo's *Plan*, see *The Truth about the Nagy Affair* (1959), pp. 139-42.
5. The various moves towards a coalition are discussed in United Nations (1957), pp. 105-6 and 115-17.
6. Janos Molnar (1969), pp. 51-3.
7. Marie and Nagy (1966), pp. 226-9 and 238-42.
8. *Ibid.*, pp. 273-4.
9. Janos Molnar (1969), pp. 126-7.
10. *Ibid.*, p. 33.
11. United Nations (1957), p. 118.
12. Quoted in Hungarian People's Republic (1958), p. 128.
13. *Ibid.*, pp. 131-2.
14. Marie and Nagy (1966), pp. 235-8.
15. The first part of the Hungaricus pamphlet has been published in English as *Hungaricus: On a few lessons of the Hungarian national-democratic revolution*, Brussels, Imre Nagy Institute for Political Research, 1959. The second part, entitled "A New Socialist Direction", has not been translated or published in the West.
16. Their conviction was reported in *Hungarian News*, New York, April 1959, pp. 19-20.

Chapter 7 (pages 193-203)

1. Kadar's outspoken defiance of the Soviet ambassador is related in Gyorgy Heltai, "Imre Nagy au Parlement", in Gosztony, *Histoire* (1966), p. 182, and also in Vincent Savarius, "Janos Kadar: Man and Politician", *East Europe*, New York, October

1966, p. 20.

2. Miklos Sebestyen, "Mes expériences dans le Conseil Central Ouvrier du Grand Budapest", in Marie and Nagy (1966), p. 303.
3. From a resolution of the Hungarian Socialist Workers' Party of 5 December 1956, cited in United Nations (1957), p. 20, paragraph 147.
4. Janos Molnar (1969), pp. 90 and 136.
5. Quoted in Hugo Dewar and Norman Daniel, *Revolution and Counter-Revolution in Hungary,* London, Socialist Union of Central-Eastern Europe (1957), pp. 29-32.
6. *Ibid.*
7. Leon Trotsky, *The Revolution Betrayed,* London, New Park Publications, 1967, p. 138.
8. See, in particular, Leon Trotsky, *The Transitional Program For Socialist Revolution,* New York, Pathfinder Press, 1973.
9. For a much fuller discussion of the ideas of Marx and Engels on the role of the Party, see Monty Johnstone, "Marx and Engels and the Concept of the Party", in R. Miliband and J. Saville (eds.), *The Socialist Register 1967,* London, Merlin Press, 1967, pp. 121-58.
10. For Lenin's views on future socialist society, see Ghita Ionescu, "Lenin, the Commune and the State", *Government & Opposition,* Spring 1970, pp. 131-65. For the change in Lenin's views from *What Is To Be Done?* to *State and Revolution,* see Marcel Liebman, *Leninism under Lenin,* London, Cape, 1975.
11. Marie and Nagy (1966), pp. 286-7.
12. *Ibid.,* p. 284.

Bibliography

Aczel, Tamas (ed.), *Ten Years After,* London, MacGibbon & Kee, 1966. (Contains a very useful bibliography.)

Aczel, Tamas *and* Tibor Meray, *The Revolt of the Mind,* London, Thames & Hudson, 1960.

Anderson, Andy, *Hungary 1956,* London, Solidarity, 1964.

Aptheker, Herbert, *The Truth about Hungary,* New York, Mainstream, 1957.

Bain, Leslie, *The Reluctant Satellites,* New York, Macmillan, 1960.

Baudy, Nicolas, *Jeunesse d'Octobre,* Paris, La Table Ronde, 1957.

Berecz, Janos, *Ellenforradalom: tollal es fegyverrel, 1956* ("Counter-revolution: with the pen and the sword, 1956"), Budapest, Kossuth, 1969.

Borbandi, Gyula *and* Jozsef Molnar (eds.), *Tanulmanyok a Magyar Forradalomrol* ("Studies from the Hungarian Revolution"), Munich, Aurora, 1966.

Coutts, Charlie, *Eye-Witness in Hungary,* London, Daily Worker, 1957.

Davidson, Basil, *What Really Happened in Hungary,* London, Union of Democratic Control, 1957.

Fejto, François, *Behind the Rape of Hungary,* New York, McKay, 1957.

Fejto, François, *Budapest 1956,* Paris, Julliard, 1966.

Fejto, François, *A History of the People's Democracies,* London, Pall Mall, 1971.

Free Europe Committee, *The Revolt in Hungary,* New York, 1956. (A collection of monitored radio broadcasts.)

Fryer, Peter, *Hungarian Tragedy,* London, Dobson, 1956.

Gosztony, Peter (ed.), *Histoire du soulèvement hongrois: 1956,* Paris, Horvath, 1966.

Goszotony, Peter (ed.), *Der Ungarische Volksaufstand in Augenzeugenberichten,* Dusseldorf, Rauch, 1966.

Harman, Chris, *Bureaucracy and Revolution in Eastern Europe,* London, Pluto Press, 1974.

Hollos, Ervin, *Kik voltak, mit akartak?* ("Who were they, what did they want?"), Budapest, Kossuth, 1967.

Hollos, Ervin and Vera Lajtai, *Koztarsasag Ter 1956* ("Republic Square 1956"), Budapest, Kossuth, 1974.

Hungarian People's Republic, *The Counter-Revolutionary Conspiracy of Imre Nagy and his Accomplices,* Budapest, Information Bureau of the Council of Ministers, 1958.

Hungarian People's Republic, *The Counter-Revolutionary Forces in*

the October Events in Hungary, Budapest, Information Bureau of the Council of Ministers, 1957 (4 volumes).
"Hungaricus", *Egy Uj Szocialista Irany* ("A new socialist direction"), Budapest (clandestine manuscript), 1957.
"Hungaricus", *On a few lessons of the Hungarian national-democratic revolution*, Brussels, Imre Nagy Institute for Political Research, 1959.
Ignotus, Paul, *Political Prisoner*, New York, Collier, 1964.
Juhasz, William (ed.), *Hungarian Social Science Reader: 1945-1963*, New York, Aurora, 1965.
Kecskemeti, Paul, *The Unexpected Revolution: Social Forces in the Hungarian Uprising*, Stanford, Calif., Stanford University Press, 1961.
Kiraly, Bela K., "From Death to Revolution", *Dissent*, New York, November-December, 1966.
Kiraly, Erno, *Die Arbeiterselbstverwaltung in Ungarn*, Munich, Oldenbourg, 1961.
Lasky, Melvin J. (ed.), *The Hungarian Revolution: A White Book*, London, Secker & Warburg, 1957.
Magyar Forradalmi Szocialistak Szovetsege, *Az 1956-os Magyar Forradalom* (League of Hungarian Revolutionary Socialists, "The 1956 Hungarian Revolution"), Basle, 1964.
Marie, Jean-Jacques and Balazs Nagy (eds.), *Pologne-Hongrie 1956*, Paris, Etudes et Documentation Internationales, 1966.
Meray, Tibor, *Budapest: 23 Octobre 1956*, Paris, Laffont, 1966.
Meray, Tibor, *Thirteen Days that Shook the Kremlin*, London, Thames & Hudson, 1959.
Meszaros, Istvan, *La rivolta degli intelletualli in Ungheria*, Torino, Einaudi, 1958.
Molnar, Janos, *Ellenforradalom Magyarorszagon 1956-ban* ("Counter-revolution in Hungary in 1956"), Budapest, Akademia, 1967.
Molnar, Janos, *A Nagybudapesti Kozponti Munkastanacs* ("The Central Workers' Council of Greater Budapest"), Budapest, Akademia, 1969.
Molnar, Miklos, *Budapest 1956*, London, Allen & Unwin, 1971.
Molnar, Miklos and Laszlo Nagy, *Imre Nagy: reformateur ou révolutionnaire?*, Geneva, Publications de l'Institut Universitaire de Hautes Etudes Internationales, 1959.
Nagy, Balazs, *La formation du Conseil Central Ouvrier de Budapest en 1956*, Brussels, Imre Nagy Institute for Political Research, 1961.
Nagy, Imre, *On Communism: In Defence of the New Course*, London, Thames & Hudson, 1957.
Paloczi-Horvath, George (ed.), *One Sentence on Tyranny: Hungarian Literary Gazette Anthology*, London, Waverley Press, 1957.
Paloczi-Horvath, George, *The Undefeated*, London, Secker & Warburg, 1959.

The Review (quarterly journal of the Imre Nagy Institute for Political Research), Brussels, 1959-1963.
Sartre, Jean-Paul, *The Spectre of Stalin*, London, Hamish Hamilton, 1969.
Scarlett, Dora, *Window onto Hungary*, Bradford, Broadacre, 1959.
Szasz, Bela, *Volunteers for the Gallows*, London, Chatto & Windus, 1971.
The Truth about the Nagy Affair, London, Secker & Warburg, 1959.
United Nations, *Report of the Special Committee on the Problem of Hungary*, New York, General Assembly Official Records, 1957.
Vali, Ferenc A., *Rift and Revolt in Hungary*, London, Oxford University Press, 1961.
Woroszylski, Wiktor, *Diary of a Revolt: Budapest through Polish Eyes*, London, Segal & Jenkins, 1957.
Zinner, Paul E. (ed.), *National Communism and Popular Revolt in Eastern Europe*, New York, Columbia University Press, 1956.
Zinner, Paul E., *Revolution in Hungary*, New York, Columbia University Press, 1962.

Index

Aczel, Tamas, 27-8, 29, 40
Adam, Gyorgy, 44, 138, 176, 177, 179
Adenauer, Konrad, 135, 136
Ajka, 39
Andropov, Yuri V., 15, 75, 166, 193
Angyalfold, 34, 111, 140, 150, 151, 153
Anti-semitism, 111, 127, 171
Apro, Antal, 161
Armed fighting groups, 116-20
Arms stores, raids on, 114, 116
Army, Hungarian, 43, 85, 114, 116, 118-19
Army, Soviet. *See* Soviet military command; Soviet troops
Arrow Cross Party, 9, 86, 91, 125, 135. *See also* Szalasi, Ferenc
Austria, 65, 82, 128-9
AVH (Allamvedelmi Hatosag), Hungarian state security or "secret" police, 10, 12, 14, 21, 40, 43, 70, 72, 99;
  involved in massacres, 83, 84-5, 94, 113-14, 122;
  violence against, 84, 85, 94, 123-8;
  after revolution, 162-3, 165, 167

Babay, Istvan, 153-5
Bain, Leslie, 17
Balazs, Arpad, 153, 156
Balazs, Jozsef, 153
Balazs, Sandor, 153
Bali, Sandor, 16, 152-5, 157, 162, 164, 168, 169, 200
Balinka, 85, 88
Baranya, county of, 99
Baross Square, armed group, 116, 117, 125-6
Batthany, Lajos, 45
Bandung Conference, 65
BBC (British Broadcasting Corporation), 123
Beloiannis factory, 16, 140, 150, 152-4, 168, 169
Bem, General Jozef, 47
Bem Square, 47, 110
Benjamin, Laszlo, 27, 29, 36
Berlin, East, workers' rising, 19, 38
Betlen, Oszkar, 21, 25
Bibo, Istvan, 74, 133, 171-5
Bolsheviks, 184, 196-7, 202
Bonapartism, 61-3
Boraros Square, armed group, 116
Borsod, district of, 92, 149; workers' council of, 96
Brodovics, Ferenc, 124
Bulganin, Nikolai A., 12, 25, 166, 181

Catholic People's Party, 135
Cease-fire, 14, 72, 86, 89, 119, 123
Central Committee, of Hungarian Communist Party, 11-13, 21, 23-5, 28, 30, 34, 43, 45, 58, 69, 70, 142
Central Workers' Council of Greater Budapest, 15-16, 151-69, 174, 177, 181, 193, 201-2
"Chicago", 118
Christian Democratic Party, 135-6
Christian Front, 135-6
Christian People's Party, 135
CIA (Central Intelligence Agency), 128
Coalition, proposals for (after 4 Nov), 173-5, 181
Collas, Baron Tibor, 129
Collectivisation, 10, 11, 58, 60
Cominform, 25
Comintern, 53
Communist Party, Hungarian, 9-16, 19-26, 28, 33, 40, 41, 43, 51, 73, 125-7, 129, 142-5, 187-9, 195. *See also* Central Committee; Politburo; Hungarian

Socialist Workers' Party; Opposition, communist
Communist Party, Soviet, 12, 32. *See also* Twentieth Congress
Corvin Alley, armed group, 72, 117, 118-19, 127, 149
Counter-government, demands for, 82, 87-90
Counter-revolution, dangers of, 74, 86-92, 132, 135-7, 139, 189, 194
Criminals, 94, 117-18, 124, 126-7
Csepel, district of, 15, 19, 37-9, 44, 114, 138, 140, 149-50, 153, 157, 161, 168-9;
  central workers' council of, 140, 142, 150, 157, 160-61, 169;
  iron and steel works. *See* Rakosi iron and steel works
Csikor, Kalman, 99
Csoori, Sandor, 26, 36
CURPH (Columbia University Research Project on Hungary), 23-4 fn.
Czechoslovakia, 38, 83, 100

Daily Express, 123
Daily Telegraph, 123
Danubian Federation, 65, 93, 95
Democratic People's Party, 134
Demonstrations, in Budapest, 13, 14, 16, 30, 45, 48, 109-10, 161, 166;
  in Szeged, 81;
  in Gyor, 83;
  in Miskolc, 93;
  in Salgotarjan, 100, 102, 167
Dery, Tibor, 12, 13, 29, 33-4, 109
Deutscher, Isaac, 2, 82
Devenyi, Jozsef, 153, 155, 156
Dilinko, Gabor ("Jewel"), 118
Dimavag iron and steel works, 92-3, 97
Diosgyor, 19, 92, 97, 149
District workers' councils, 140, 142, 150, 152
DISZ (Communist Youth League), 32, 80-81, 106-8, 109
Donath, Ferenc, 11, 29, 31, 70, 142, 143, 178
Dudas, Jozsef, 91, 129-32, 133
Dunapentele, 148-9

Education, Minister of, 46, 80
Eger, 168
Egyesult Izzo. *See* United Lamp Factory
Egyetemi Ifjusag ("University Youth"), 138
Ekren, Kemal, 117
Elites, 17-18, 19, 35, 47, 67, 174, 198, 202
Elunk ("We Are Alive"), 177, 180
Enczi, Endre, 28
Engels, Friedrich, 186. *See also* Marx, Karl, and Friedrich Engels
Engels
Eorsi, Istvan, 30, 36
Erdei, Ferenc, 73, 142
Esti Budapest ("Evening Budapest"), 23, 41

Farkas, Ferenc, 74
Farkas, Mihaly, 11, 21, 42
Fascists, 91, 126, 127, 128-9, 135. *See also* Arrow Cross Party; Fraternal Society of Hungarian Fighters
Fazekas, Gyorgy, 29, 30, 50, 178
Fejto, François, 130
Fekete, Sandor, 21, 29, 30, 144, 179, 183
Ferencvaros, 111
Fischer, Jozsef, 74
Foldes, Gabor, 83-7
Foldvari, Rudolf, 23, 93-4, 97
Football rioting, 38
Foreign Affairs Ministry, "siege" of, 131
Fraternal Society of Hungarian Fighters, 129. *See also* Fascists; Zako, Andras
Fraternisation, 14, 120-22
French Revolution, 202

Galambos, Iraneous, 87-8
Ganz shipyards, 38
Ganz works, 109, 140, 150
Gati, Gyula, 94
Gehlen, General Reinhard, 128
Gero, Erno, 11-14, 34-5, 40, 44, 49, 56, 69, 71, 93, 106, 113, 115, 120, 142, 191
Gimes, Miklos, 12, 16, 21, 25-6, 29, 30, 42, 48, 50, 71, 115, 144, 175, 179-81

Gomulka, Wladislaw, 13, 46, 111
Grebennik, Major-General K.S., 150, 158
Gyenes, Antal, 33
Gyor, 14, 30, 82-92, 129, 151, 157, 159

Hamos, Gyorgy, 27, 28
Haraszti, Sandor, 21, 27-8, 29, 36, 48, 143, 178
Hay, Gyula, 28, 29, 41, 44, 83, 138, 175
Hegedus, Andras, 12, 25
Hegedus, Andras B., 183
Heltai, Gyorgy, 29
Hetfoi Hirlap ("Monday News"), 41-2
Horthy, Admiral Miklos, 9, 129
Horthyites, 82, 91, 99, 129, 135, 194
Horthy régime, 9, 51, 124, 135, 139, 188
Horvath, Marton, 20, 23
Horvath, Zoltan, 29
Hungarian Christian Party, 135
Hungarian Democratic Independence Movement, 180-81
Hungarian Freedom Party, 135
Hungarian Independence Party, 134
Hungarian News Agency (MTI), 24
Hungarian Radical Party, 134
Hungarian Socialist Workers' Party, 15, 143-5, 178, 193, 195. *See also* Communist Party, Hungarian
Hungarian Soviet Republic, 9, 53
Hungaricus, 51, 182-92

Igazsag ("Truth"), 177, 179
Ignotus, Paul, 40
Illyes, Gyula, 134
Information Bulletin of Central Workers' Council of Greater Budapest, 155, 163
Intellectuals, 26, 32, 137, 175-7. *See also* Revolutionary Committee of Intellectuals; Revolutionary Council of Intellectuals; Writers
Irodalmi Ujsag ("Literary Gazette"), 26-8, 41

Janosi, Ferenc, 29, 48, 178
Journalists, 11, 20-26, 29, 30, 40-41, 48, 50, 143-4, 179-81
Jovo Mernoke ("Engineer of the Future"), 109
June Resolutions, 11, 58-9. *See also* New Course

Kadar, Janos, 11-16, 23, 71, 73, 75, 101, 142-3, 145, 148, 155-6, 161, 162-8, 174-5, 178, 193-6, 201
Kadar régime, in Budapest, 147, 152, 155-7, 164-9, 193-6, 197, 201, 203;
in provinces, 92, 97, 100-103
Kallai, Gyula, 11
Kalocsai, Gyorgy, 153, 155, 162
Kardos, Laszlo, 33
Karoly, Mihaly, 9
Karsai, Sandor, 153-5
Kecskemet, 168
Kecskemeti, Paul, 17
Kelemen, Gyula, 74
Kellenfold, 150, 151, 153
Kende, Peter, 21, 24, 144, 179, 181
Kerensky, Alexander, 202
Kethly, Anna, 74, 133, 134
Khrushchev, Nikita S., 12, 19, 25, 32, 35, 55, 65, 105, 185
Kilian barracks, 14, 118-19, 129, 149
Kiraly, Bela, 43, 75, 124, 131
Kispest, 150
Kiss, Jozsef, 96
Kiss, Sandor, 134
Kobanya, 149, 153-4
Kodaly, Zoltan, 31, 176
Kodolanyi, Lajos, 134
Komlo, 98, 159
Konya, Lajos, 26
Kopacsi, Sandor, 97, 138-9, 143
Kossuth, Lajos, 23, 65
Kovacs, Bela, 14, 72, 73-4, 132-3, 175
Kovacs, Istvan, 23, 43
Kovago, Jozsef, 133-4
Krasso, Miklos, 151
Kronstadt revolt, 198
Kucsera, unpopular comrade, 41, 188
Kuczka, Peter, 27
Kun, Bela, 9, 12, 51

Labour camps, 11, 60, 117, 130
Land reform, 10, 187
League of Hungarian Socialists, 180. *See also* Hungarian Democratic Independence Movement
Left Opposition, 53
Lenin, Vladimir Illich, 51, 54, 55, 59, 115, 147, 170, 184, 186, 197-8, 199;
  State and Revolution, 199;
  What Is To Be Done? 197, 199
Leninism, 196, 197-8, 199, 200
Litvan, Gyorgy, 34, 183
Locsei, Pal, 21, 29, 30, 115, 144, 179
Losonczy, Geza, 11, 12, 16, 20-1, 27, 29, 31, 34, 40, 42, 44, 48-9, 70, 73-4, 113, 131, 142, 143, 178
Lowenstein, Prince Hubertus, 129, 136
Lukács, Georg, 139, 143, 144, 178
Lukacsy, Sandor, 39
Lumpenproletariat, 125, 132
Luxemburg, Rosa, 79

Magyar Fuggetlenseg ("Hungarian Independence"), 127, 130-31
Magyar Jovo ("Hungarian Future"), 138
Magyar Nemzet ("Hungarian Nation"), 22, 25, 40, 49
Magyar Szabadsag ("Hungarian Freedom"), 132, 144, 179
Makhno, Nestor, 197-8
Malenkov, Georgi M., 105
Maleter, Pal, 14-16, 73, 119-20, 124, 129, 131, 133
Mariassy, Judit, 41
Marosan, Gyorgy, 161-2
Martial Law, 14, 70
Marx, Karl, 52, 115, 185, 186, 193, 196, 198-9
Marx, Karl, and Friedrich Engels, 54, 185, 198, 199;
  Address to the Communist League, 198;
  Communist Manifesto, 198.
  See also Marx, Karl; Engels, Friedrich
Marxism-Leninism, Imre Nagy on, 54-6, 66-7;
  Hungaricus on, 185-6
Masses, discontent and unrest amongst, 17-18, 19, 22, 35-9, 41-2, 47-8, 61, 67-8, 72, 174;
  Kadar on, 196;
  Marx and Engels on, 198-9
Mavag works, 109, 140
Mecsek hills, 97-9
MEFESZ (independent student organisation), in Szeged, 13, 46, 80-81;
  in Miskolc, 93;
  in Pecs, 98;
  in Budapest, 106-7
Memorandum of the writers, 27-8
Menon, Kumara P. S., 181
Meray, Tibor, 21, 25, 29, 40
Merei, Ferenc, 138, 183
Mesz, Janos ("Peg-leg Janko"), 118, 124, 126
Metalworkers' Union (pre-war), 152-3
Metropolitan National Committee, 134
Mezo, Imre, 43, 125-6
Mikoyan, Anastas I., 31, 34
Mills, C. Wright, 19
Mindszenty, Cardinal Jozsef, 10, 14, 15, 133, 135-7
Miskolc, 14, 23, 92-7, 149, 151, 168
Mlinarik, Istvan, 100-101
Molnar, Miklos, 21, 26, 47, 53, 69, 75, 143, 144, 179, 181
Moricz Zsigmond Square, 116, 149
Mosonmagyarovar, 84-5
Mrazik, Janos, 101
Multiparty system, 15, 63, 71, 73, 144, 174-5, 178, 193. *See also* Parties, non-communist; Coalition
Munkasujsag ("Workers' News"), 163
Munnich, Ferenc, 15, 75

Nagy, Balazs, 33
Nagy, Imre, 10-16, 19-31, 34, 35, 38, 41, 48-9;
  ideology of, 52-67;
  during revolution, 68-77, 110, 124, 131, 132, 143, 147, 161, 170, 174, 178-9, 189-90, 197, 199
Nagy, Laszlo, 69, 75
Nagybatony, 99, 102

Nagyists, 28-32, 40-41, 42-3, 48-50, 68-70, 142-3, 144, 170, 178-9, 179-81. *See also* Opposition, communist
National Assembly, 31
National Communism, 32, 143, 193. *See also* Native Communists; Titoists
National Councils: Gyor, 84-6;
Miskolc, 96;
Salgotarjan, 101-2
National Guard, in Miskolc, 95;
in Pecs, 99;
in Salgotarjan, 101;
in Budapest, 14, 75, 117, 127, 131, 139
National Peasant Party, 10, 73, 84, 132, 134. *See also* Petofi Party
National Revolutionary Council, 91, 130-31. *See also* Dudas, Jozsef
National Workers' Council, 15, 16, 154, 159-60, 167, 177, 181
Native Communists, 10, 11, 23. *See also* National communism; Titoists
Nehru, Pandit, 181
NEKOSZ. *See* People's Colleges
Nemeth, Laszlo, 134, 175
Nepszabadsag ("People's Freedom"), 132, 143, 163, 168
Nepszava ("Voice of the People"), 24
Neutralism, 65
Neutrality, declaration of, 14, 66, 73, 96, 144, 178
New Class, 185
New Course, 11, 12, 19, 21-5, 28, 53, 58-64, 67-8, 71, 190
New Economic Policy (NEP), 59
Nickelsburg, Laszlo, 117
Nograd, county, 99
county workers' council, 102
Novobaczky, Sandor, 21, 41

Obersovszky, Gyula, 177, 179
Obuda, 140, 150
October Revolution (Russia), 183, 184, 197, 202
October 23, 180-81
Opposition, communist, 19-50, 137-8, 142-5, 170, 178-84, 189-92, 196-200;
ideology of, 51-68.
See also Nagyists; Petofi Circle
Ozd, 19, 92, 97, 148-9, 159, 168

Paloczi-Horvath, George, 17, 40
Paris Commune, 198
Parliament Square, 14, 49, 50, 110, 122-3
Parties, non-communist, 63, 73-4, 132-6, 174-5, 179, 181, 202. *See also* Multiparty system
Party of the Hungarian Revolutionaries, 135
Peasants, 19, 27, 37, 58
Peasant Alliance, 134
Pecs, 97-9, 149, 159
"Peg-leg Janko". *See* Mesz, Janos
People's Colleges, 32-3, 51, 110, 179
People's Democracy, 55-6, 61, 64
People's Patriotic Front, 22, 23, 29, 60, 62-3
Peter, Gabor, 21
Petofi, Sandor, 32, 109
Petofi Brigade, 118
Petofi Circle, 12, 13, 32-4, 36, 39, 43-4, 47, 51, 81, 83, 109, 111, 138, 179
Petofi Military Academy, 109, 117
Petofi Party, 74, 134, 171. *See also* National Peasant Party
Petofi statue, 47, 109
Pilfering, 38
Poetry of revolt, 26-7, 40
Poland, 13, 39, 46, 69, 109-10
Police, 38-9, 42, 75-6, 138-9
Politburo, of Hungarian Communist Party, 12, 13, 20, 22-5, 34, 47, 49, 70, 73
Pongracz, Gergely, 118, 127
Pongracz, Kalman, 29
Populism, 51, 171. *See also* Third Road programme
Poznan riots, 13, 39
Prater Street School, 118, 124
Pravda, 21, 143
Prisoners, political, 11, 12, 21, 27, 38, 40, 60. *See also* Criminals; Rehabilitations
Provinces, 79-103
Purges, stalinist, 12, 20-22, 25, 33, 44

Racz, Sandor, 16, 154-7, 168-9, 193
Radio, Budapest, 24;
Gyor, 86, 88;
Miskolc, 94, 95-6
Radio building, fighting at, 13, 49, 112-14
Radio Free Europe, 86, 87, 91, 128-9
Radio Liberty, 129
Radio Rajk, 144-5, 148
Rajk, Julia, 12, 33, 44, 178
Rajk, Laszlo, 10-13, 20, 25, 32, 33, 44-5, 77
Rakosi, Matyas, 11-13, 19-29, 32, 34-5, 39, 41, 42, 44, 51, 56, 58, 81, 110, 115, 188, 190, 192
Rakosi iron and steel works, 19, 37, 39, 140, 153, 160, 168-9
Rakosi régime, 187-9, 190, 197
Refugees, 15, 128
Rehabilitations, 12, 20, 21-2, 25, 27, 32, 43, 44. *See also* Prisoners, political
Republic Square, massacre at, 14, 124-7, 139
Reuters, 124
Revai, Jozsef, 20-21, 115
Revisionism, 54-6, 66, 170, 173, 197
Revolutionary Committees (district), 138
Revolutionary Committee of Hungarian Intellectuals, 138, 176
Revolutionary Council of Hungarian Intellectuals, 16, 161, 176-7, 181
Revolutionary Youth Party, 139
Revolutionary Worker Peasant Committee (Salgotarjan), 101-2
Revolutionary Worker Peasant Government, 101, 148, 169, 193
Rumania, 15, 76, 179

Salgotarjan, 99-103, 149 ,159, 167
Scarlett, Dora, 40
School students, 35, 46, 111, 117
Sebestyen, Miklos, 153-5, 162, 163, 193
Secret police. *See* AVH
Serov, General Ivan A., 158
Seton-Watson, Hugh, 135
Sinkovits, Imre, 109
Sixteen points, students' demands, 46, 107-8, 112
Smallholders' Party, 10, 11, 72, 73-4, 129, 132-4, 175
Social Democratic Party, 10, 11, 73-4, 132, 134, 152-3
Somogyvari, Lajos, 89-90
Soviet ambassador. *See* Andropov, Yuri V.
Soviet Communist Party. *See* Communist Party, Soviet; Twentieth Congress
Soviet military command, 155, 158, 166
Soviet troops, intervention in Hungary, 14, 15, 49, 70-73, 75, 96, 147-9, 169;
in Budapest, 116, 119, 120-23;
in Gyor, 86;
demands for withdrawal of, 13, 14, 45, 72-3, 81, 83, 85, 88, 90, 94-5, 101, 106-8, 110, 140, 150, 152, 173, 175, 178
Squatters, 38-9
Stalin, Iosif V., 11, 12, 19, 25, 32, 36, 38, 51, 53, 81, 115, 184-6, 197-9
Stalin statue, 13, 106, 110, 111-12, 115
State security police. *See* AVH
Strikes, before revolution, 13, 19, 22, 38, 39;
during revolution, 14, 84-5, 88, 91, 94-6, 98, 101-2, 140, 142;
after second Soviet intervention, 15, 16, 102, 147, 149, 155-8, 160, 168-9, 175
Students, 13, 30, 36-7, 38, 43, 45-6, 48, 80-82, 93, 98, 106-11, 133, 137-9, 177, 182
Students' Revoluntionary Committee, 138, 182
Szabad Ifjusag ("Free Youth"), 30, 46
Szabad Nep ("Free People"), 11, 20-26, 28, 30, 44-5, 48, 115, 130, 132, 143. *See also* Journalists
Szabo, Bela, 43
Szabo, Ervin, 102
Szabo, Gyorgy, 84, 86-90, 92
Szabo, Istvan B., 74, 133

Szabo, Janos ("Uncle Szabo"), 117
Szalai, Sandor, 29
Szalasi, Ferenc, 9. *See also* Arrow Cross Party
Szanto, Zoltan, 22, 29, 113, 143, 178
Szechenyi, Countess Beatrix, 129
Szeged, 13, 46, 80-82
Szeifert, Tibor, 131
Szell, Jeno, 183
Szena Square, armed group, 116-17, 149
Szigethy, Attila, 30, 84, 86-92
Szilagyi, Jozsef, 16, 29, 44, 178

Tamasi, Aron, 175
Tancsos, Gabor, 33, 138, 178
Tardos, Tibor, 21, 34
Tatabanya, 85, 149, 159
Technological University, 13, 46, 106-9, 155
Third Road Programme, 51, 171. *See also* Population; Bibo, Istvan
Tildy, Zoltan, 14, 73, 174
Tito, Josip B., 12, 13, 25, 35-6, 44-5, 55, 65
Titoists, 10, 25. *See also* National Communism; National Communists: Native Communists
Togliatti, Palmiro, 184
Toke, Ferenc, 153-5, 167
Toth, Ferenc, 124
Trade Unions, 31, 68, 164-5, 168, 195, 197, 200-201
Tramways, Municipal Company of, 153, 154, 156
Transdanubian National Council, 14, 84, 88, 90-91. *See also* Gyor
Trotsky, Leon D., 196, 197-8
Twentieth Congress of Communist Party of Soviet Union, 12, 30, 32-4, 42, 128, 191

Ujhely, Szilard, 29, 31, 178
Ujpest, 15, 114, 138, 139, 140, 149, 150, 153
Ujpest Revolutionary Committee, 142
Ujpest Revolutionary Workers' Council, 15, 136, 151
Underworld, 117-18. *See also* "Chicago"; Lumpenproletariat
United Lamp Factory (Egyesult Izzo), 15, 139-40, 151, 153
United Nations, 14, 15, 65-6, 131
Universities: Budapest, 13, 24, 36, 45-6, 106, 179;
  Miskolc, 92;
  Szeged, 13, 46, 80-81.
  See also Students; Technological University

Varga, Lajos, 155
Vas, Zoltan, 142
Vasarhelyi, Miklos, 21, 22, 27-8, 29, 31, 48, 113, 178
Veres, Peter, 47, 134
Veszprem, 159

Warsaw Pact, 12, 14, 66, 73, 95, 173, 178
Wazyk, Adam, 36
Western agents, 128-9
White Books (of Kadar régime), 124, 128
Workers, 13, 18, 37-9, 44, 48, 112, 135, 137-8, 139-42, 147-69, 170, 188, 191, 194-6, 200-203
Workers' councils, in Budapest, 14-16, 139-42, 147-69, 170;
  in Gyor, 85, 90;
  in Miskolc, 93, 96;
  in Pecs, 98;
  in Salgotarjan, 101-2;
  Kadar régime and, 194-5 201;
  opposition and, 175-7, 178-81, 197, 199-200;
  political role of, 200-203
Workers' control, 140-41
Workers' News. *See* Munkasujsag
Woroszylski, Wiktor, 74, 82, 91, 130, 132, 144
Writers, 26-8, 29, 35, 41, 47-9, 61, 137, 175-6
Writers' Association, 12-13, 26-8, 39, 41, 47, 49, 87, 109, 137, 175-6, 177-8, 181

Youth, 35-6, 43, 111, 138-9
Young Writers' Group, 36
Yugoslav Embassy, 15, 45, 75, 147, 161, 178-80
Yugoslavia, 12, 25, 44, 113, 184. *See also* Tito, Josip B.

Zako, General Andras, 91, 129. *See also* Fascists; Fraternal Society of Hungarian Fighters
Zelk, Zoltan, 28, 29
Zinner, Paul E., 17
Zuglo, 150, 153, 155

Some other titles in the MOTIVE series

Michel Raptis
Revolution and Counter-Revolution in Chile

Henri Lefebvre
The Survival of Capitalism

Frank Jakubowski
Ideology and Superstructure in Historical Materialism

Jiri Pelikan
Socialist Opposition in Eastern Europe

Agnes Heller
The Theory of Need in Marx

Mihaly Vajda
Fascism as a Mass Movement

Hilda Scott
Women and Socialism — Experiences from Eastern Europe

Andras Hegedus
Socialism and Bureaucracy

Andras Hegedus, Agnes Heller, Maria Markus, Mihaly Vajda
The Humanisation of Socialism

Herni Laborit
Decoding the Human Message